D1257949

Nietzsche's Critiques

Nietzsche's Critiques

The Kantian Foundations of his Thought

R. Kevin Hill

CLARENDON PRESS · OXFORD

OXFORD

UNIVERSITY PRESS

Great Clarendon Street, Oxford OX2 6DP

Oxford University Press is a department of the University of Oxford.
It furthers the University's objective of excellence in research, scholarship,
and education by publishing worldwide in

Oxford New York

Auckland Bangkok Buenos Aires Cape Town Chennai
Dar es Salaam Delhi Hong Kong Istanbul Karachi Kolkata
Kuala Lumpur Madrid Melbourne Mexico City Mumbai Nairobi
São Paulo Shanghai Taipei Tokyo Toronto

Oxford is a registered trade mark of Oxford University Press
in the UK and in certain other countries

Published in the United States
by Oxford University Press Inc., New York

British Library Cataloguing in Publication Data
Data available

Library of Congress Cataloging in Publication Data
Data available

ISBN 0–19–925583–0

1 3 5 7 9 10 8 6 4 2

Typeset by Hope Services (Abingdon) Ltd.
Printed in Great Britain
on acid-free paper by
T.J. International Ltd.,
Padstow, Cornwall

♯ ♭ 1964820

To Arthur Melnick and Richard Schacht

ἄλλα γὰρ πολλὰ οὕτω ταύτης τῆς τέχνης κρίνεται· τὸ γὰρ ξενοπρεπὲς
οὔπω συνιέντες, εἰ χρηστόν, μᾶλλον ἐπαινέουσιν ἢ τὸ σύνηθες, ὃ ἤδη
οἴδασιν ὅτι χρηστόν, καὶ τὸ ἀλλόκοτον ἢ τὸ εὔδηλον.

Hippocrates, *On Fractures*

Acknowledgements

My deepest debts are to Arthur Melnick and Richard Schacht, whose inspiration, support, and encouragement have been invaluable. Keith Ansell-Pearson, Victoria Berdon, James Bradford, Thomas Brobjer, Malcolm Brown, Howard Caygill, Hugh Chandler, Paul and Patricia Churchland, Maudemarie Clark, Christoph Cox, Derrick Darby, Lester Hunt, Philip and Patricia Kitcher, Sven Kuehne, Laurence Lampert, David Levin, Tom McCarthy, John McCumber, Richard Mohr, Ted Morris, Kurt Mosser, Robert Pippin, John Richardson, William Schroeder, Emmett Silverman, Robert Solomon, Iain Thomson, Steven Wagner, Wayne Waxman, and Allen Wood all helped in too many ways to mention. I have enjoyed fruitful discussions on the topics of this book with many of my students, especially Will Dudley, Rich Foley, Ruple Shah, and Adrian Slobin. I am also indebted to Northwestern University for creating an environment in which things could gel. The various people who have written on Kant or Nietzsche who have influenced me through their work are cited throughout, though all errors remain mine. My family and friends have been a source of strength during the various trials that attended composition. Finally, I wish to remember Cecile Dore, my late great-aunt, from whom I inherited a copy of Thomas Common's translation of *Zarathustra* when I was but a teenager. *Amor fati* requires me to acknowledge everything and everyone not here acknowledged. Duly noted.

Contents

Contents

Conclusion: The Ruins of Reason? *230*

Abbreviations

All works are by Nietzsche unless otherwise stated. References to the *Kritische Gesamtausgabe* of Nietzsche's works and letters are to the volume and page numbers. References to individual works by Nietzsche are to the part and section numbers.

A	*The Antichrist*
Ak.	Kant, *Werke*
BGE	*Beyond Good and Evil*
BT	*The Birth of Tragedy*
CJ	Kant, *Critique of Judgement*
CPrR	Kant, *Critique of Practical Reason*
CPR	Kant, *Critique of Pure Reason*
D	*Daybreak*
EH	*Ecce Homo*
Fischer	Fischer, *Geschichte der neuern Philosophie*
GM	*On the Genealogy of Morals*
GS	*The Gay Science*
HA	*Human, All-too-human*
KGB	*Kritische Gesamtausgabe (Briefe)*
KGW	*Kritische Gesamtausgabe (Werke)*
Lange	Lange, *Geschichte des Materialismus*
NCW	*Nietzsche contra Wagner*
PTG	*Philosophy in the Tragic Age of the Greeks*
SW	Schopenhauer, *Sämtliche Werke*
TI	*Twilight of the Idols*
TL	*On Truth and Lie in an Extramoral Sense*
UM	*Untimely Meditations*
W	*The Case of Wagner*
WP	*The Will to Power*
WWR	Schopenhauer, *The World as Will and Representation*
Z	*Thus Spoke Zarathustra*

A Note on Textual Methodology

Any proposal to interpret Nietzsche's texts encounters a methodological difficulty that has been much discussed: which texts to interpret and how much weight to give texts of various types. The reasons for this difficulty are various. First, there is the sheer difficulty of the texts themselves. For the most part they consist of brief paragraphs, each of which contain a fragmentary but usually not explicitly qualified discussion of a particular topic. If these paragraphs are collated by topic, often two different paragraphs appear to contradict each other. One plausible response to this sort of problem is to find criteria for assigning greater weight to one paragraph over another. The texts' vague yet emphatic style only makes matters worse.

Second, Nietzsche, especially in his later works, often writes of masks and disguises. This has led some interpreters to believe that he often presents views which are not his own for pragmatic or heuristic purposes. Heidegger, for example, believed that the unpublished notebooks are more reliable on the assumption that these purposes do not play a role in the construction of texts that Nietzsche did not intend to see read. Others, like Kaufmann, regarded the very fact that Nietzsche did not intend the notebooks to be read as grounds for assigning them less weight.

Third, some of the most politically provocative statements can be found only in his unpublished notebooks. Commentators sympathetic to the National Socialists used some of these remarks to bolster the view that such political tendencies could gain aid and comfort from Nietzsche's texts.

Finally, Bernd Magnus, who follows Kaufmann's methodological principles, has suggested that the Nietzsche of the notebooks is a far more traditional philosopher, working through technical problems in metaphysics, epistemology, and ethics. By contrast, the work Nietzsche published is the work of a deconstructivist who has transcended traditional philosophy.[1] Thus, to preserve Nietzsche's most radical insights, one must follow what he chose to publish, rather than the incomplete and insufficiently radical reflections of the notes.

---

[1] Bernd Magnus, 'The Use and Abuse of the *Will to Power*', in Robert Solomon and Kathleen M. Higgins (eds.), *Reading Nietzsche* (Oxford: Oxford University Press, 1988), 218–35.

A Note on Textual Methodology

The issue of what weight one should assign to published as opposed to unpublished texts has generated a concern which is quite disproportionate to the actual problem. If our concern is with making sense of Nietzsche's thought, then naturally all of the texts are relevant. The assumption that there is a *real* Nietzsche who is primarily represented by one set of texts or another strikes me as an especially perverse appeal to authorial intention. It is as much out of place in analytic circles, where the substance of an argument matters more than to whom it is attributed, as it is in circles given to speaking of 'the death of the author'. If the content of the published as opposed to unpublished texts were radically divergent, a special methodology might be appropriate. But if an interpretation that maximizes agreement among the texts is possible, then no special methodology should be called for. It is true that there are tensions and paradoxes in Nietzsche's thought, but this is far less often the case than is commonly thought. While it is true that he does sometimes adopt 'masks' in his writing, it is generally not too difficult to detect which positions he endorses and which positions he attacks. Also, Nietzsche sometimes experiments with a position to see where it will lead (in his notebooks) and upon seeing where it leads, comes to reject it (in his published works). Finally, we must accept that he does on occasion contradict himself and that he is therefore at least sometimes *wrong*. *That* sort of problem should not be interpreted away by a special textual methodology that licenses the elimination of inconvenient evidence. My interpretation attempts to exercise textual charity—within reasonable limits. This is how we interpret most philosophical texts. Nothing about Nietzsche's texts suggests they need to be interpreted any differently.[2]

The textual foundations of this interpretation are editions of Nietzsche's books published in his lifetime and the posthumous manuscripts stored at the Goethe–Schiller Archiv in Weimar. Several scholarly editions have appeared, but few have employed a rigorous historical-critical methodology which makes them reliable sources for the posthumous material. One of them is the now standard *Kritische Gesamtausgabe (Werke und Briefe)* edited by G. Colli and M. Montinari. Whenever possible, I have relied on this edition, which is substantially complete as to the letters, and contains almost all of the work from 1869 to 1889. Though it remains incomplete as to the juvenilia (*Nachlaß* material dated before 1869), I only consider *Nachlaß* material dated after Nietzsche's discovery of Schopenhauer in 1865 but before the Basle period in 1869 as

---

[2] For a detailed discussion of the proper methodology for interpreting texts in the history of philosophy, see Michael Rosen, 'The Interpretation of Philosophy', in *Hegel's Dialectic and its Criticism* (Cambridge: Cambridge University Press, 1982), 1–22. Much of my own approach to Nietzsche is inspired by Rosen's analogous approach to Hegel.

significant for adequately interpreting his metaphysics. This material, however, is available in the *Kritische Gesamtausgabe*.

Inevitably, mention must be made of the so-called *Grossoktavausgabe*. In this 1911 edition, a second attempt was made to produce an anthology of the *Nachlaß* of the 1880s, arranged topically, named by the editors *Der Wille zur Macht*. As with the books Nietzsche himself published or prepared for publication, the sections of this text are numbered to ease reference. This text, one of several constructed texts appearing under this title, is the most widely read, and references to it are common. Walter Kaufmann has provided a translation of this text preserving almost entirely the numbering of the 1911 text of the second edition of the *Grossoktavausgabe*. For readers using this text, I have provided a dual reference system, first to the text as it appears in *KGW* and then the *WP* section number. My quotations from this material, however, follow the Colli–Montinari texts; patchwork texts, altered sentence order, incorrect manuscript dating, and other artefacts of the editors' activity have been eliminated.

All quotes appear in English. As the English translation of the Colli–Montinari edition (the so-called Stanford Edition) is incomplete, I have been guided by Kaufmann's translations of *Birth of Tragedy*, *Gay Science*, *Beyond Good and Evil*, *Genealogy of Morals*, *Case of Wagner*, *Twilight of the Idols*, *Antichrist*, *Ecce Homo*, *Nietzsche contra Wagner*, and *Will to Power*.[3] I have been guided by R. J. Hollingdale's translations of *Untimely Meditations, Human, All-too-human*, *Daybreak*, and *Zarathustra*. I have also generally followed Daniel Breazeale's translation of *Truth and Lie*. Translations have always been checked against original texts and, occasionally, modified. All other translations are mine.

In deference to longstanding precedent, all citations of the first *Critique* are by page numbers to both the first and second editions, referred to as 'A' and 'B' respectively. I follow Werner Pluhar's excellent new translations of this and the third *Critique*; I also follow Lewis White Beck's translation of the second *Critique*. I follow E. F. J. Payne's translation of Schopenhauer's *The World as Will and Representation*, and Ernest Chester Thomas's translation of Lange's *The History of Materialism and Criticism of its Present Importance* (3rd edn., trans. from 2nd German edn., London: Kegan Paul, Trench, Trubner & Co., 1925).

---

[3] Many English-speaking readers have relied upon Kaufmann's text of *The Will to Power* for access to the unpublished Nietzsche of the 1880s. However, the texts on which this translation is based are inadequate in the light of Colli and Montinari's editorial work on the *KGW*. It may be several years before the Stanford Edition is completed. As an English anthology of the 1880s *Nachlaß* is desirable meanwhile, it would be worthwhile to translate those *KGW* texts from which *The Will to Power* was constructed.

A Note on Textual Methodology

I have generally relied upon this translation, though the second German edition upon which it is based is much larger than the first edition with which Nietzsche was acquainted. I have only attributed to Nietzsche the reading of passages which correspond to passages in the German first edition. I have generally relied upon John Mahaffy's 1866 translation of volume 4 of Fischer's *History of Modern Philosophy: A Commentary on Kant's Critick of Pure Reason* (repr. New York: Garland, 1976).

Nietzsche's Flesh, Kant's Skeleton   1

It is said that the spirits of the night are alarmed when they catch sight of the executioner's sword: how then must they be alarmed when they are confronted by Kant's *Critique of Pure Reason*! This book is the sword with which deism was put to death in Germany. Frankly, in comparison with us Germans, you French are tame and moderate. You have at most been able to kill a king . . . Immanuel Kant has stormed . . . heaven, he has put the whole crew to the sword, the Supreme Lord of the world swims unproven in his own blood.

Heine

From Kant to Nietzsche

Nietzsche interpretation has become a central enterprise in making sense of the often referred to but little understood phenomenon of postmodernism. There is a widespread belief that we have entered a phase, not only in the history of philosophy, but in many cultural spheres, which leaves the characteristic commitments, values, and dilemmas of modernity behind. Restricting our compass to philosophy, it is noteworthy that many contemporary figures identify Nietzsche with the turning point away from modernity. This claim about Nietzsche's historical importance appears to originate, in the first instance, with Nietzsche himself. 'We [i.e. Nietzsche and his readers?] have found the exit out of the labyrinth of thousands of years. Who else has found it? Modern man perhaps? I have got lost; I am everything that has got lost, sighs modern man' (*A* 1).

Here Nietzsche implicitly claims not only to have transcended modernity, but to have transcended the premodern, a feat 'modern man' attempted without success.

Nietzsche is not alone in claiming a unique historical status for himself; such claims come hard on the heels of historicism itself.[1] Hegel's encyclopaedic system completes the efforts of the history of philosophy to achieve a perfect representation of reality (including itself as a part of it). Marx ushers in a period in which philosophers will no longer seek to understand the world, but to change it; the last in a series of historical changes is here—after that, philosophers will have little to do. Heidegger, not to be outdone, claims that Nietzsche was mistaken in regarding himself as the first post-metaphysical philosopher free of the nihilistic burdens of the old tradition. In a spirit of healthy competition, he reserves that distinction for himself; generously, Nietzsche is at least allowed to be the last metaphysician.

To be fair, Heidegger did more than perhaps any one else to establish Nietzsche's reputation as a philosopher of the first rank, and not a mere literary dilettante.[2] And despite Heidegger's one-upmanship, his insistence on Nietzsche's historical singularity directed attention to Nietzsche's own claims, which are frequently endorsed in Continental philosophy. Subsequently, Nietzsche has become associated with scepticism about or outright rejection of just about anything familiar and of putative value; invocation of his name, especially in literary-critical circles, has become one with the elevation of philosophical avante-gardism to a principle. Nietzsche heralds, not just the death of God, but the death of Man; Nietzsche is against truth, dishonesty, science, Romanticism, democracy, capitalism, socialism, morality, and decadence.

To be sure, there have been dissenters to this view all along. Walter Kaufmann, in a concerted effort to cleanse Nietzsche's reputation of its association with a half century of German imperialism, produced the decisive American interpretation: Nietzsche, like Emerson, challenges us to rise out of our existential complacency; Nietzsche's is a critique of religion much as many liberals proffer.[3] This attempt to sanitize Nietzsche rested on the claim that he

---

[1] Such claims are not unique to Continental philosophy. After the seeming debacle of British idealism, Russell and Moore presented their new sobriety and detail-work as revolutionary; similar claims can be found in the Vienna Circle, in Wittgenstein early and late, and in the Oxford language philosophers. The moment the history of philosophy is thematized, everyone wants to wake up from it as if from a nightmare.

[2] Martin Heidegger, *Nietzsche*, trans. David Farrell Krell (New York: Harper and Row, 1979).

[3] Walter Kaufmann, *Nietzsche: Philosopher, Psychologist, Antichrist* (Princeton: Princeton University Press, 1950).

2

is strongly committed to epistemic and moral views of his own. These commitments serve as the foundation upon which he builds his own radical critiques of other positions, especially Christianity.

Both interpretations lose something of the bite of Nietzsche's thought, but they do capture important aspects of it. Yet their seeming exclusivity stalemates attempts to do justice to the texts. How can the reader make sense of the seeming cohabitation of drastic scepticism ('*Ultimate Scepsis*— What are man's truths ultimately? Merely his *irrefutable* errors' (*GS* 265)) with dogmatic *pronunciamentos* ('This world is will to power—and nothing else besides!' (*KGW* vii.3. 339 (1885)/ *WP* 1067)), the uncomfortable proximity of an almost Wildean freedom from morality with extreme ethical demands and condemnation? How to make sense of such seeming paradoxes in Nietzsche?

To answer these questions, I will attempt to reconstruct what I take to be the skeletal structure of Nietzsche's thought, stripped of its literary and rhetorical surface. It would be a mistake to dismiss such a project on the grounds that Nietzsche's (or anyone else's) thought cannot be cleanly distinguished from the literary structures within which it is found. The same is true of skeletons more generally. A skeleton is not the *essence* of an animal body, nor can it function without complex relations of interdependence upon viscera, muscles, skin, blood, etc. One might also argue in Nietzschean fashion that our ability to distinguish between where a skeleton begins and where the softer flesh ends depends upon various processes of reification, the imposition of imaginary boundaries upon experiences that are essentially fluid and chaotic, and so on. Still, it seems that anatomists do manage, in a rough-and-ready way, to find such distinctions, whatever their ontological status. My interpretation is offered in that spirit: I find it useful to regard certain central claims Nietzsche makes as the relatively fixed carriage upon which Nietzsche hangs and carries about his more changeable observations about specific topics. In the post-Quinian era, it may no longer be possible to make sharp distinctions between metaphysics and science, between framework and fact. But one can speak, if necessary, of those parts of the web of someone's beliefs that are closer to an entrenched centre.

My further claim, as I hope will be borne out by the interpretation given below, is that this skeletal structure is broadly Kantian. Only in this way can one reconcile two competing strands of Nietzsche interpretation that dominate scholarship and discussion today. On the one hand, there are those who emphasize the ontological side of Nietzsche, seeing him as answering traditional philosophical problems within the context of an interpretation of reality as will to power. Among these interpreters, most noteworthy are Heidegger,

Schacht, Deleuze, and, more recently, Richardson.[4] On the other hand, there are those who emphasize the epistemological side of Nietzsche, seeing him rejecting the possibility of philosophical knowledge in particular, and perhaps knowledge more generally. The term of art here is 'perspectivism'. Those who stress this side of Nietzsche see him as some sort of sceptic, empiricist, pragmatist, relativist, deconstructionist, or epistemological pluralist. These interpreters include Jaspers, Schacht again, Nehamas, Derrida, and more recently, Clark and Poellner.[5] As my lists of interpreters should make clear, these two approaches cut across not only national boundaries, but also across the notorious Analytic–Continental divide. To put it in Heideggerian language: to what extent is Nietzsche a metaphysical or anti-metaphysical thinker? The contest between these interpretations has thus far been stalemated by the wealth of texts available to support either view, once one brings into play the extensive posthumously published notes. There is, however, precedent for such an ambiguity in a philosopher. It is an ambiguity with which many readers are far more familiar and far more equipped to deal. That philosopher is Kant.

Kant's project has often been read as a merely analytical or epistemological one. Certain types of problematic, allegedly synthetic *a priori* claims, are isolated (those of geometry, pure physics, metaphysics, and ethics), their meaning analysed, and their epistemological status interrogated. Once their validity is determined, one should know both the scope and limits of their application. Epistemological assessment (via transcendental argument) thus goes hand in hand with the critique of dogmatic metaphysics.[6] However, there is another side to Kant, far less favourably received at least until very recently: the transcendental idealist, psychologist, and metaphysician. This more extravagant Kant does not merely claim that there are limits to what we know; he seems to claim that there is an unknowable reality beyond experience—the reality of things-in-themselves or noumena. Furthermore, this Kant seeks to explain the

---

[4] Heidegger, *Nietzsche*; Richard Schacht, *Nietzsche* (London: Routledge and Kegan Paul, 1983); Gilles Deleuze, *Nietzsche and Philosophy*, trans. Hugh Tomlinson (New York: Columbia University Press, 1983); John Richardson, *Nietzsche's System* (Oxford: Oxford University Press, 1996).

[5] Karl Jaspers, *Nietzsche: An Introduction to the Understanding of his Philosophical Activity*, trans. Charles F. Wallraff and Frederick J. Schmitz (Chicago: Regnery, 1965); Schacht, *Nietzsche*; Alexander Nehamas, *Nietzsche: Life as Literature* (Cambridge MA: Harvard University Press, 1985); Jacques Derrida, *Spurs: Nietzsche's Styles*, trans. Barbara Harlow (Chicago: University of Chicago Press, 1979); Maudemarie Clark, *Nietzsche on Truth and Philosophy* (Cambridge: Cambridge University Press, 1990); Peter Poellner, *Nietzsche and Metaphysics* (Oxford: Oxford University Press, 1995).

[6] Despite their substantial differences, representative figures here include Peter Strawson, *The Bounds of Sense* (London: Routledge, 1966); Paul Guyer, *Kant and the Claims of Knowledge* (Cambridge: Cambridge University Press, 1987); and Henry Allison, *Kant's Transcendental Idealism* (New Haven: Yale University Press, 1983).

restricted validity of the problematic claims in question by appealing to Vico's Maxim: 'we can have complete insight only into what we can ourselves make' (*CJ*, Ak. v. 384). Since the world of experience is the only world where our cognitive capacities gain a foothold, this world must be our construction. As Kant details the mechanics of this construction, he finds himself speculating about the structure that the mind must possess to construct successfully. It has been popular in the past to separate the 'good' epistemological Kant from the 'bad' psychologist and metaphysician. Such a separation cannot do justice to the texts, their immediate influence, or their philosophical fruitfulness: critique and idealism go hand in hand.[7] Nietzsche's own dual project, at once deconstructive and systematic, inherits this duality from Kant.

Nietzsche and Kant? Two thinkers could not be more different! Kant's apriorism and ahistoricism, his insistence upon the inviolate character of the rules that constitute objective phenomena, his unknowable noumena, his dogged moralism, his disinterested conception of aesthetic reception—none of this could be more alien to the perspectivist, immoralist, Dionysian Nietzsche. Nietzsche uses no one else, except Plato, to better effect as a foil for his own views.[8] At times he even presents his own views as the natural critical alternatives to Kant's. At the end of his career, he began work on a magnum opus, *The Revaluation of All Values*, to appear in four parts, of which only the first part was completed (*The Antichrist*). He subtitled each of the first three parts 'a critique', in self-conscious competition with Kant's own three *Critiques*. Furthermore, the second and third parts correspond closely in topic though not in proposed treatment with Kant's first and second *Critiques*. The 'critique of philosophy', variously titled 'The Free Spirit' or 'The Affirmer (*Ja-Sager*)', is Nietzsche's own critique of pure reason; the 'critique of morality' or 'The Immoralist' is Nietzsche's own critique of practical reason. Not only that: there is a great deal of evidence to suggest that much of this latter text was to concern Kant's own second *Critique*. However, Nietzsche did not plan to write a counterpart to the

---

[7] For this way of approaching Kant, I am deeply indebted to Patricia Kitcher, *Kant's Transcendental Psychology* (Oxford: Oxford University Press, 1990); Wayne Waxman, *Kant's Model of the Mind: A New Interpretation of Transcendental Idealism* (Oxford: Oxford University Press, 1991); and Beatrice Longuenesse, *Kant and the Power of Judgment: Sensibility and Discursivity in the Transcendental Analytic of the Critique of Pure Reason*, trans. Charles T. Wolfe (Princeton: Princeton University Press, 2001).

[8] According to the index to the *Kritische Studienausgabe*, a subset of *KGW*, Nietzsche's references to other philosophers appear in the following order of descending frequency: Schopenhauer, Plato, the Presocratics (if taken together), Kant, Socrates, Epicurus, Aristotle, Comte, Hegel, Pascal, von Hartmann, Rousseau, Spinoza, Dühring, and Spencer. After Spencer, the number of references to other philosophers drops off dramatically.

third *Critique*. Significantly, Nietzsche planned to offer a fourth part in which his own positive, post-critical claims were to be presented.[9]

If this were all, this alone would justify extended discussion. To what degree does the contrast with Kant effectively bring out the fundamentals of Nietzsche's thought? To what degree does Nietzsche succeed in undermining Kant's critical project? More: to what degree is Nietzsche's project generated out of a negation of Kant's?

Nietzsche's criticism of Kant is not only fundamental for articulating Nietzsche's own position; it also masks Nietzsche's deep debt to Kant. This debt is sometimes obvious ('critique of metaphysics'), at other times complex and problematic ('autonomy'), and finally, until now scarcely explored ('the sublime').[10] This suggestion, however, raises other objections.

First, how could Nietzsche *not* be influenced by Kant? Who was not? In the sense that thinkers with as widely diverging agendas and methodologies as Hegel, Kierkegaard, Heidegger, and Carnap are 'post-Kantian' thinkers, the appellation borders on the meaningless. But this is not the sense of influence that I wish to make out. Rather, I want to suggest that Nietzsche's relationship to Kant should be modelled on Hegel's. For Nietzsche, as for Hegel, Kant is *the* philosopher with whom one must come to terms. One must either become a Kantian, or, starting from a Kantian foundation, think one's way out of Kantianism. Near the beginning of his career, in a letter dated November 1866, Nietzsche wrote to Herman Mushacke: 'The most meaningful philosophical work which has appeared in the past ten years is undoubtedly Lange's *History of Materialism*, about which I could write a ream of panegyrics. Kant,

---

[9] Four different drafts of the plan appear, at *KGW* viii.3. 347, 397, 402, 423 (1888). In three of the four drafts, three of the four proposed works is subtitled a 'critique of' the topic in question. One plan (p. 402) substitutes the phrase 'deliverance from' the topic. The following draft is representative:

Revaluation of All Values
The Antichrist. Attempt at a critique of Christianity.
The Immoralist. Critique of the most fatal kind of ignorance, morality.
The Affirmer. Critique of philosophy as a nihilistic movement.
Dionysus. The philosophy of the eternal recurrence. (*KGW* viii.3. 397 (1888))

[10] Concern with Kant's Analytic of the Sublime has been on the rise in recent years in French circles formerly interested in Nietzsche. Representative of this trend is Jean-François Lyotard's *Lessons on the Analytic of the Sublime*, trans. Elizabeth Rottenberg (Palo Alto: Stanford University Press, 1994). However, Lyotard's 'Nietzschean' interpretation (which I believe is problematic in many respects) does not address the question of Nietzsche's own reading of the Analytic of the Sublime. Julian Young has briefly alluded to the relationship between Kant's concept of the dynamical sublime and Schopenhauer's theory of music and tragedy, but does not discuss in detail Nietzsche's reading of *CJ* and its likely effect on *BT*. See Julian Young, *Nietzsche's Philosophy of Art* (Cambridge and New York: Cambridge University Press, 1992).

Schopenhauer, and this book of Lange's—I don't need anything else' (*KGB* i.2. 184). These, then, were his three philosophical inspirations at the most formative stage (1865–72) of his development: Kant, Schopenhauer, and Friedrich Lange (the early Neo-Kantian[11] mentor of Herman Cohen). One might distinguish, then, between Kantian with a capital 'K' (i.e. influenced by and preoccupied with Kant's texts) and kantian with a lowercase 'k' (e.g. interest in broadly constructivist themes in metaphysics and ethics). My claim is that Nietzsche's thought is broadly Kantian in the former, and not merely the latter, sense.

Second, though this may be granted, the further objection suggests itself. Isn't what I am calling Kantian really just Schopenhauerian? It is true that Nietzsche was preoccupied with Schopenhauer, and that his reading of Kant is a partially Schopenhauerian reading. But Schopenhauer was not the sole source for Nietzsche's understanding of Kant; nor does he identify Kant with Schopenhauer. Not only did Nietzsche read Lange; he was a very close reader of Kuno Fischer's reading of Kant, which, though in part inspired by, in many respects deviates from Schopenhauer's.[12] Anyway, as we shall see, Nietzsche's own metaphysical commitments had already deviated from Schopenhauer's as early as 1867–8. Despite Schopenhauer's commitment to the transcendental ideality of space and time, and the phenomenal/noumenal contrast, Schopenhauer's account of mental activity is far more empiricist than Kantian. Nietzsche, however, learned much from the first *Critique*: under its influence, he developed an account of mental activity that was not only broadly Kantian, but in many respects represented a remarkable synthesis and unification of Kant's transcendental psychology.

[11] I use the expression 'early Neo-Kantian' to designate Schopenhauer, Lange, and Fischer. Nietzsche read all three, as did most of the first Neo-Kantians proper (e.g. Cohen, Paulsen) in the 1860s. This expression should also be extended to Liebmann, Helmholz, and others, but I will restrict my discussion to Schopenhauer, Lange, and Fischer.

Lange's influence on Nietzsche at this formative moment is what links him to Neo-Kantianism. Lewis White Beck, in a backhanded compliment, has said: 'No great neo-Kantian book (with the possible exception of Lange's *History of Materialism*) . . . give(s) narrative structure to the rise and spread of neo-Kantianism' (Forward to Köhnke, p. ix, cited below). Friedrich Paulsen, Paul Natorp, and Hans Vaihinger, all describe their reading of Lange as a conversion experience initiating them into philosophy. All shared opposition to the spirit of Bismarck's Germany, 'in which respect they were to some extent even in harmony with the youthful Nietzsche' (Köhnke, p. 213, cited below). For a fuller discussion, see Klaus Christian Köhnke, *The Rise of Neo-Kantianism: German Academic Philosophy between Idealism and Positivism*, trans. R. J. Hollingdale (Cambridge: Cambridge University Press, 1991), 211–13.

[12] Kuno Fischer's interpretation can be found in his *Immanuel Kant und seine Lehre* (Geschichte der neuern Philosophie, iv–v), 4th rev. edn. (Heidelberg: C. Winter, 1898); Nietzsche cites both volumes in 'On Teleology' (*KGW* i.4. 549–78 (1868)). For a fuller discussion of Nietzsche's reading of Fischer and Lange, see 'Nietzsche's secondary sources concerning Kant' below.

I shall discuss two further cases in detail. The first is Kant's substitution of theoretical with practical justification for metaphysics in the second *Critique*, a notion utterly absent from Schopenhauer's thought. This notion of practical justification then inspired Kant's theory of reflective judgement in the third *Critique*. Early Nietzsche, in his own idiosyncratic way, endorsed this notion. The appearance of metaphysical claims coupled with radical scepticism in *BT* and in *TL* can only be understood by reference to the notion of reflective judgement; later he rejected the legitimacy of practically justified, and reflective, judgements, and used their unacceptability as a tool in his critique of Kant. Of all this, there is no inkling in Schopenhauer.

The second example is Nietzsche's critical account of the idea of the substantial soul. Nietzsche's discussion here is indebted to Kant's difficult notion of the transcendental unity of apperception. This doctrine enables Kant to claim that the empirical self is as much a product of synthesis as empirical objects are. In the Paralogism chapter of the first *Critique* Kant then argues against the transcendental temptation to inflate this necessary unity into a substantial one. This line of argument echoes repeatedly in Nietzsche. Again, there is no inkling of any of this in Schopenhauer.

Thus far, such observations are suggestive only. I hope to support them by producing an interpretation of Nietzsche's thought, one which is admittedly speculative in many respects. Taking the entire Critical system, we will see how one can arrive at distinctively Nietzschean positions by making plausible, intelligible moves in response to Kantian problems. The result will be a picture of Nietzsche that is much more firmly rooted in the philosophical tradition.[13]

One final worry: by historicizing Nietzsche in this way, doesn't one run the risk of trivializing him as well? Doesn't Nietzsche become a minor Neo-Kantian, a footnote in the history of the nineteenth century rather than a living force in the twentieth and beyond? In a sense, the answer to this question depends upon our assessment of Kant. If we regard Kant as modernity's most articulate spokesperson,[14] then Nietzsche's emergence from Kant is an emergence from the centre of the agenda of modernity; Nietzsche's critique of Kant cuts to the heart of that agenda.

[13] To my knowledge, there is no previous book-length study of this sort. Jules de Gaultier's *From Kant to Nietzsche*, trans. Gerald M. Spring (New York: Philosophical Library, 1961) is inadequate. If there is any previous work that is similar in spirit, it would be Olivier Reboul's excellent *Nietzsche, critique de Kant* (Paris: Presses universitaires de France, 1974). Reboul restricts his focus, understandably, to the late Nietzsche, and thus he does not discuss the relationship between the *Critique of Judgement* and the *Birth of Tragedy*.

[14] For this conception of Kant, I am indebted to Robert B. Pippin, *Idealism and Modernism: Hegelian Variations* (Cambridge: Cambridge University Press, 1997).

If there is an ideological difference between the medieval and the modern, it is the difference between theocentric and anthropocentric conceptions of the world. Since Nietzsche shares the anthropocentrism of Kant and other Enlightenment thinkers, in what sense is he postmodern? The key is the *mode* of anthropocentrism. For modernity, there are two projects around which human activity organizes itself. First, the scientific project: nature must be demystified by scientific methods, such understanding being both an end, and a means to the technological mastery of nature. These methods are allegedly self-validating, that is, they do not depend upon any textual or institutional authority, and are in principle available to all. Second, the egalitarian project: society (and the state) must be regulated by egalitarian principles of morality, to be justified by secular means. Though Lockeans, Rousseauists, and utilitarians differ about what is the best articulation and defence of the egalitarian principle, they are in fundamental agreement as to the goal. Nietzsche rejects both projects. Yet Nietzsche declines the Romantic temptation to return to a premodern, theocentric perspective.

Whether this suffices to warrant calling Nietzsche 'postmodern' will return to haunt us at the end of the book. For his debt to Kant and the early Neo-Kantians was far more extensive than is usually thought. In that Nietzsche's confrontation with and appropriation of Kant was central, he was far more characteristic of his time than of ours. To the extent that Nietzsche is now central to our philosophical concerns, those concerns prove to have an ancestry reaching far back into the nineteenth century. To see that, it will help to have a clearer sense of what the character and motives of early Neo-Kantianism were. What social, political, and philosophical pressures promoted its ascendancy? In what sense was Nietzsche subject to those same pressures?

Germany in the later nineteenth century

Nietzsche's interest in Kant was not an isolated phenomenon, nor can it be explained simply by reference to Kant's status as a German classic. His concern with Kant, starting in the mid-1860s, was of a piece with a larger revival of Kant studies that was very much in the spirit of the times. Herman Cohen, the founder of the Marburg school of Neo-Kantianism, was only two years Nietzsche's senior. Cohen's mentor Lange was a central formative figure in Nietzsche's development, and a key secondary source that Nietzsche consulted while forming his early impressions of the Kantian system.

Nietzsche's Flesh, Kant's Skeleton

One begins to see why Nietzsche turned to Kant by looking at why so many figures in the 1860s were doing so. Though Nietzsche is obviously quite different in tone and temper from the early Neo-Kantians, they initially shared many common concerns. It is not my intention to reduce Nietzsche's thought to a function of the *Zeitgeist*, but it is illuminating to see how that *Zeitgeist* brought Kant to Nietzsche's attention.

The period in Germany from 1832 (Hegel's death) to 1865 (the beginnings of Nietzsche's philosophical thinking) is often regarded as something of a philosophical desert, interrupted only by Marx. In consequence, this period has become alien to us today. Furthermore, our twentieth-century eyes show us a nineteenth-century Germany of unrepresentative figures who proved to be most fruitful (for us) subsequently.[15] Again, Marx serves as a useful example. Marx's early philosophical writings only became a focus of attention when they were published in the twentieth century (1927–32). Lotze, by contrast, is almost completely forgotten today.

If one turns instead to those figures who garnered attention in their own day, a very different picture emerges. These figures grappled with (and avoided) issues in response to the political, economic, social, and ideological forces that surrounded them. Though it would be unfair to reduce Nietzsche's own thought to such a response, much of his work was conditioned by sources from whom he borrowed liberally, who were in turn far more engaged in the times than he. This is especially the case with his reading of Kant, and the way this reading was shaped by the early Neo-Kantians he read simultaneously.

There were three factors that profoundly affected the circumstances in which Nietzsche and the early Neo-Kantians found themselves. The first was an ambivalent relationship to the legacy of German classicism and German idealism. German intellectuals could look back proudly to the period before the deaths of Goethe and Hegel. Yet this pride was qualified by painful nostalgia for a sensibility rapidly disappearing under the pressures of modernization. The memory of German idealism also evoked embarrassment over the backwardness, naivety, and scientific (more specifically, *naturphilosophische*) errors of the period. Silk and Stern have discussed this issue in terms of Nietzsche's relationship to professional philology,[16] but the phenomenon was a much broader one; Nietzsche was not the only figure who felt its sting. Nietzsche

---

[15] Karl Löwith's *From Hegel to Nietzsche: The Revolution in Nineteenth Century Thought*, trans. David Green (New York: Holt, Rinehart and Winston, 1964), represents such a reconstruction of the nineteenth century from the vantage point of characteristically twentieth-century 'Continental' interests.

[16] M. S. Silk and J. P. Stern, *Nietzsche and Tragedy* (Cambridge: Cambridge University Press, 1981), 4–24.

sought through philology to return to the Goethean notion of being formed by an encounter with antiquity, only to discover that philology had become academic research. The values of objectivity had supplanted those of *Bildung*.[17] However, the impression that the legacy of classicism and idealism was impossible to abandon and impossible to resuscitate was a common one.

In philosophy, this ambivalence found expression in the competing claims of idealism and materialism.[18] Idealism, of course, represented the distinctive product of German thought during its moment of greatest achievement. However, frustration with Hegel's system began to grow almost immediately after his death. The conviction that his panlogicism was too abstract, impersonal, alienated, and necessitarian appeared first among the Young Hegelians (especially Feuerbach, Stirner, and the early Marx). It soon became an article of faith to German intellectuals of all persuasions. Philosophy of nature came in for special ridicule, given its alleged apriorism and its ever growing distance from mainstream scientific research. Philosophy of right became seen as special pleading for conservative Prussian interests. Even Hegel's groundbreaking studies of the history of art, religion, and philosophy came to be criticized for lacking historical *Verstehen*, so eager was he to subordinate the facts to a general narrative unity. Matters were made even worse when, ironically, Prussian authorities came to associate Hegel with his own Young (Left) Hegelian critics. Young Hegelians were too closely tied to the revolutions of 1848; even Right Hegelianism came to represent at least a precursor to those thoughts which had, apparently, unleashed social chaos.

Materialism seemed a natural alternative to idealism, given the second factor shaping the later nineteenth century: industrialization. The economies of many German states underwent significant economic and technological development in the decades after 1848, though intensive industrialization only became apparent by the 1870s. The tough-mindedness (and a certain *anomie*) found in late nineteenth-century German thought is often attributed to the collapse of bourgeois hopes after the revolutions of 1848. However, it seems as plausible to attribute them to the effects of industrialization itself. A sense of the impotence of culture and politics in the face of the might of technology and economics was one way Marx distinguished himself from the utopian socialists. Perhaps the greatest beneficiary of these developments was natural science. Science was now

---

[17] Nietzsche's unhappiness with this state of affairs is manifested in *BT*, where he offers an alternative example of how to approach the Greeks. In *UM* II, he takes on the putative value of historical objectivity directly.

[18] Köhnke, *Neo-Kantianism*. Also see Herbert Schnädelbach, *Philosophy in Germany 1831–1933* (Cambridge: Cambridge University Press, 1984).

pursued not as a private hobby, but as a domain of organized, collective research, under the management and support of universities, foundations, and business. As the economic benefits of such research became apparent, resources were funnelled into it, producing an ever-accelerating process of investment, scientific research, and technological development. In such an atmosphere, the ideologues of science, self-proclaimed materialists,[19] came to have a credibility that far outweighed the claims of the old classical idealists and their pupils. Increasingly, academic philosophers felt obliged to do justice to natural science and its accomplishments while avoiding the crudities of the materialist popularizers. Furthermore, wholehearted commitment to nihilistic materialism only intensified anxiety in the face of eroding cultural and political ideals. Vindicating the cognitivity of philosophy without impinging on natural science acquired an urgency that it had never had in the age of the systems of Fichte, Schelling, and Hegel. It was not merely that *Naturphilosophie* had got so much wrong, a problem that began with Goethe's critique of Newton's optics and only got worse. It was that philosophy seemed otiose.

In this setting, Kant's distinction between phenomena and noumena seemed again to hold real promise of doing justice, in as hard-headed a fashion as one might like, to the claims of natural science to reveal the empirical world, while leaving an open space where transcendent metaphysics had once been, an open space for cultural and political ideals. In this way, the prestige of science could be respected while the *anomie* it was associated with could be addressed. The very dualism that had been the source of anti-Kantian polemics in Hegel's day now seemed to reflect in an uncanny way the split in the German mind of the late nineteenth century. Thus, from about 1860 onward, a surprising diversity of voices began to demand a return to Kant.

For the most part, in academia, this was a matter of returning to Kant's epistemology. Emphasizing epistemology suggests timidity in the face of larger questions of metaphysics, religion, ethics, and politics. Such discussions might very well aggravate the authorities of the post-1848 era.[20] During the centennials of Fichte's and Schiller's births, events that aroused much liberal-nationalist sentiment, Kant's authority as their mentor was also cited in ethical, political, and cultural contexts. Ironically, the cosmopolitan Kant was now being resurrected as the spiritual grandfather of German nationalism!

That said, the use of Kant as a political icon was not completely opportunistic: classical liberals and, increasingly, non-Marxist social democrats also used

---

[19] e.g. Ludwig Büchner, Jacob Moleschott, Karl Vogt, and Heinrich Czolbe.
[20] Köhnke, *Neo-Kantianism*, 77–96.

Kant's ethical and political thought as a rallying point throughout the late nineteenth century. Before the founding of the Second Reich, liberals saw the formation of a unified German nation and the securing of individual rights as complementary tasks. The immediate political climate after 1848 was quite chilly for liberals. But by 1858, with the dismissal of the conservative Prussian minister Otto von Manteuffel and the appointment of a partly liberal cabinet, there were grounds for optimism. It was only after Bismarck unified Germany without satisfying the other demands of liberalism that nationalism and liberalism began to drift apart. By the 1870s and after, neo-Kantian liberalism had gone into quiet opposition, and began to experience a tension between Prussian triumphalism and the claims of a cosmopolitan, liberal culture. Nietzsche's anti-political stance has its own origin here; his own polemical writings in the early 1870s, the *Untimely Meditations*, share to a remarkable degree the concerns and sensibility of contemporary disaffected neo-Kantian liberals.[21]

Interest in Kant was also on the rise outside academia. Schopenhauer, a self-professed Kantian of sorts, was tremendously popular from the mid-1850s on. The popular emphasis was more on restoring moral and cultural ideals one associated with an earlier time than with epistemological problems. Schopenhauer's own hardheadedness about the character of the thing-in-itself lent his own revival of Kant greater credibility in a more cynical age. His 'night watchman' state politics and valorization of art, religion, and philosophy as vehicles of personal salvation expressed the era's sharper distinction between public and private life.

Nietzsche's secondary sources concerning Kant

Apart from Schopenhauer, the two figures who arguably did the most to restore interest in Kant during the later nineteenth century were Kuno Fischer and Friedrich Lange. Born in 1824, one generation Nietzsche's senior, Kuno

---

[21] The meditation on Strauss attacks the easy assumption that a scientific materialist sensibility can coexist with true cultivation. It opens with a warning shot across the bow of Bismarckian triumphalism. The meditation on history is primarily an attack on Hegelianism. The meditation on Schopenhauer is clearly preoccupied with the preconditions of individual *Bildung*, as it criticizes the influence of the state on the universities. The meditation on Wagner represents special problems. There is little in common between the concerns of Neo-Kantians and Wagnerians. Nietzsche's views at the time (1875) as disclosed by his notebooks are significantly at variance with his expressed views in the meditation. He broke with Wagner shortly after that.

Fischer studied from 1844 to 1848, first at Leipzig and later at Halle, where he completed his doctoral dissertation on Plato's *Parmenides*. In 1850 he was appointed to a position at Heidelberg, where he began work on his multi-volume *History of Modern Philosophy*, the first volume of which appeared in 1852. In this work, one could detect a residual Hegelianism according to which the history of philosophy possessed a narrative unity as the progressive growth of the human spirit. By 1853, however, he was dismissed from his position there when he came under suspicion of irreligion for his sympathetic lectures on Spinoza. During the following two years, he continued his research and writing without support; finally, through the intercession of Alexander von Humboldt, he secured an appointment at Jena, which began in 1856. It was at Jena, in 1857, that Fischer began to lecture on Kant; by 1860–1, the fourth and fifth volumes of his *History* appeared, offering a detailed exegesis and defence of the Critical system, emphasizing Kant's idealist metaphysics of the transcendental subject. Though the accuracy of his interpretation of Kant is questionable, the impact of this work on academic philosophy was profound, and may be the true beginning of early Neo-Kantianism.[22] Fischer's subsequent career was productive and well received. In 1872 he took a chair at Heidelberg, a chair he held until 1903. From this position, he played a formative role in the development of later Heidelberg Neo-Kantianism as exemplified by Wilhelm Windelband and Heinrich Rickert. He officially retired in 1906 and died in 1907.

Friedrich Lange, though at times a philosophy professor, had his greatest impact by way of his popular writing and political activism, a striking contrast to Fischer's essentially academic life. Born in 1828, Lange spent much of his childhood in Switzerland until he began his studies at the University of Bonn in 1848. Fischer remained aloof from the events of 1848; Lange seems to have felt an enthusiasm for the revolution, though his attention was drawn more by its liberal than its nationalist aspect. He completed his studies in 1851, and after a brief interval of military service and *gymnasium* (pre-college) teaching, took up an appointment at Bonn that extended from 1852 to 1858. In 1857, he began planning a series of lectures on the history of materialism that would serve as the seed for his later book. From 1858 to 1862, he returned to *gymnasium* teaching and immersed himself in Kant, natural science, and the history of philosophy. Lange's interest in Kant was due to the critique of rationalist metaphysics; in this, Lange saw Kant struggling alongside empiricism and

---

[22] Fischer seems to have imported claims about the nature of the will and the thing-in-itself derived from Fichte and Schopenhauer into Kant's text.

positivism against superstition rather than as a source of a new idealist metaphysics. After a conflict with government authorities over his public political speaking, he resigned from the *gymnasium* in 1862. After that he pursued politics and journalism full time, while completing his *History of Materialism*. A lifelong social democrat, Lange was deeply concerned with the future of agricultural and industrial labour; however, he grounded these commitments in a Kant-inspired ethical individualism while opposing materialist, Marxist, and revolutionary variants of socialism. In 1865 these views were expressed in his book *The Worker Question*; a year later, the first edition of the *History of Materialism* was published. Lange's *History* presented a rich account of the history of the sciences. Woven into the history is a polemic against the natural tendency to see science as lending support to a materialist metaphysics. Materialism can and should be resisted in favour of a Kant-inspired critical empiricism without metaphysical commitments. Though less successful as Kant exegesis than Fischer's work, the book greatly affected a generation of scholars. Many of its first readers turned away from an initial interest in natural science (and a background commitment to materialism) and towards Kantian philosophy of science; representative figures in this development, as mentioned above, were Cohen, Natorp, Paulsen, and Vaihinger. Lange left politics and returned to academia in 1872 when he received an appointment at Marburg that he held until his death in 1875. His teaching and writing there, and those of his student Herman Cohen, led to the 'Marburg school' of Neo-Kantianism.

Below, I will discuss the three interpretations of Kant that Nietzsche knew best: Schopenhauer's, Kuno Fischer's, and Friedrich Lange's. Nietzsche was probably also influenced, though to a far lesser degree, by the Kant interpretations of Eugen Karl Dühring and Afrikan Spir. The importance of Nietzsche's reading of Dühring for our purposes lies primarily in his discussion of Kant's Antinomies, which I discuss below with the eternal recurrence. Spir's importance rests on his arguments against the Kantian doctrine of the transcendental ideality of time in *Thought and Reality*. Nietzsche checked this book out of the University of Basle library several times in the early 1870s. He not only accepted these arguments, but they decisively shaped his reception of Kant's theoretical *and* practical philosophy. Nietzsche's personal library contained works discussing Kant by the following figures: Julius Bahnsen, Alfonz Bilharz, Paul Deussen, Maximillian Drossbach, Leon Dumont, Harald Høffding, Rudolf Lehmann, Otto Liebmann, O. Plümacher, Paul Rée, W. H. Rolph, Heinrich Romundt, Paul H. Widemann, and Johann C. F. Zöllner. However, none of these figures had the impact on Nietzsche's development that Schopenhauer,

Lange, and Fischer did.[23] By briefly examining their respective interpretations, further light can be shed on what Nietzsche took to be Kant's thought. It is often said that Nietzsche's sense of Kant was superficial because Schopenhauer's was as well (and, arguably, this is a fair assessment of Schopenhauer). However, Nietzsche could have constructed a much richer understanding of Kant by combining elements from these three interpretations.

In some respects the three interpretations reinforced each other; in other respects their disagreements would have aided Nietzsche in developing a sense of the richness and ambiguity of Kant's texts. As for their agreements, Schopenhauer, Fischer, and Lange all agree that Kant is committed to the mind-dependence of the empirical world, glossing this mind-dependence in terms of psychological processes. In this respect, their Kant is a 'subjectivist' quite unlike the Kant to be found lately in Strawson, Bennett, Guyer, or Allison. However, each conceives of the mind that constructs the empirical world in different terms. Each differs from the others on the crucial question of what to make of the world in so far as it is not mind-dependent, the so-called things-in-themselves.

Regarding mind-dependence, all three accept Kant's claim that the space and time with which we are in perceptual contact are products of our sensibility. All three further agree that the *a priori* status of geometry confirms this claim. Fischer is more strongly committed to the details of Kant's account of intuition, and of the role space and time play as forms of intuition. Schopenhauer and Lange are both unclear about how it is that the mind imposes geometrical and temporal form on experience. Lange in particular takes issue with the whole intuition-as-matter within space-and-time-as-forms model. Yet all agree that Kant's epistemology of geometry is essentially correct. Space and time are mind-dependent. Therefore, the empirical world does not exist apart from our perception of it.

Beyond this consensus about the Transcendental Aesthetic, their respective accounts of Kant's thought begin to diverge. While all three consider Kant's theory of causality as the most significant element in the Transcendental Analytic, their attitudes toward Kant's goals, methods, and results there differ. Fischer means much of the first volume of his text to be a faithful yet charitable account of the first *Critique*. He appears to accept the project of a metaphysics of experience, rooted in a transcendental psychology, whose results will be *a priori*. Fischer also appears to accept the Metaphysical and Transcendental

---

[23] Though the catalogue of Nietzsche's library has been published, I am indebted to Thomas Brobjer, *Nietzsche's Ethic of Character* (Cambridge: Cambridge University Press, forthcoming), for identifying which of these texts contain extensive discussions of Kant.

Deductions as he understands them. He even finds the latter especially profound. The Transcendental Deduction revealed the transcendental unity of apperception and thus paved the way for a Fichtean metaphysics of the subject, with which he is in considerable sympathy. Furthermore, he finds the notion of rule-governed synthesis, and the role the categories play in guiding it and thus producing the empirical world, important and illuminating. For Fischer, the Transcendental Deduction furthers the project of a metaphysics of experience while deepening our grasp of transcendental psychology. By contrast, Lange and Schopenhauer regard almost everything about the Deductions a disaster. For both of them, the table of categories is an artefact of Kant's obsession with architectonic. The Transcendental Deduction itself is not only hopelessly obscure, but responsible for the metaphysical excesses and opacity of later idealists.

Both Schopenhauer and Lange find the project of a transcendental psychology uninteresting. This affects both their own psychological commitments and their accounts of Kant's theory of causality. For them, Kant is correct in holding that the mind introduces causal order into experience. However, neither of them accepts Kant's arguments in the Analogies of Experience, and neither of them provides as detailed a psychological account of how the mind introduces this order. Lange simply attributes the introduction of causal order to our 'psycho-physical organization' and leaves it at that; Schopenhauer borrows Kant's term 'the understanding'. Absent any theory of synthesis or any other categories, Schopenhauer's understanding simply becomes identified with the faculty of the mind that introduces causal order into experience. Because of this, both end up supplanting Kant's psychology with something altogether different. Schopenhauer replaces the Kantian account of the subject with a Lockean one.[24] Lange thinks the very job of providing psychological theories should be taken away from the philosopher and handed over to the experimental psychologist and neuroscientist; for Lange, the discovery that a species of knowledge is *a priori* is the empirical discovery that the relevant psychological process associated with it is contingently universal. Thus Lange suggests that Fechner's Law may be another synthetic *a priori* claim, to be arrayed next to the propositions of Euclidean geometry!

---

[24] I exclude here Schopenhauer's account of the 'principle of sufficient reason' in *The Fourfold Root*, which shows considerable originality. But if we ask how conceptual representation of appearances is possible given the data of sense, Kant sees a daunting problem requiring a daunting theory (the Subjective Deduction). Schopenhauer assumes that a Lockean notion of abstraction will readily suffice. Much of Schopenhauer's disdain for the difficulties of the Transcendental Analytic seems rooted in a failure to see the very problems Kant intended to solve.

The most interesting difference among the three figures lies in their responses to Kant's distinction between phenomena and noumena. This distinction plays a crucial role for Kant in safeguarding the possibility of free will, immortality, and God. Schopenhauer is here clearly the most heretical of the three. His doctrine of the noumenal unity of the will entails the rejection of any notion of personal free will or personal immortality. Nonetheless, he saw himself as developing further Kant's phenomena/noumena contrast, which he interpreted as a contrast between appearances and a real substrate upon which they depend. Schopenhauer agrees with Kant that the methods of scholastic or rationalist metaphysics are unable to discover this substrate's character. However, he takes such a discovery to be attainable by other means. For Schopenhauer the discovery that the mind imposes space, time, and causality on experience *entails* that the noumenon is non-spatial, atemporal, and without causal structure. However, in a surprising move we shall have occasion to discuss at length below, Schopenhauer does not identify the mind upon which appearances depend with a noumenal subject. Instead, he argues for the identification of transcendental subjectivity with the empirically disclosed brain. Fischer, who has sympathy for Schopenhauer's account of noumenon as will, also infers that if something is characteristic of phenomena, then it is absent in the noumenal realm. However, he vehemently rejects Schopenhauer's attempt to 'naturalize' the Kantian subject, reaffirming its noumenal nature. Instead, he associates it with that transcendental spontaneity underlying the mind's generation of experience that cannot be understood as part of the natural world.

Lange, by contrast, reads the phenomena/noumena contrast in purely epistemological terms: phenomena are the objects of our methods of investigation, and these are all empirical. Even transcendental reflection must give way to empirical methods, for like Schopenhauer, Lange identifies the mind that constructs appearances with the brain. Noumena, then, are those conceivable objects that our methods cannot reach, and therefore we can say nothing about them.[25] Since we can make the contrast, however, we need not be materialists, which would be to identify things-in-themselves with the objects of empirical investigation. Thus liberated from the confines of materialism, we may imagine things-in-themselves in terms of orientating aesthetic, moral, and political

---

[25] This applies with equal force to what Lange regards as illegitimate attempts to know the transcendental subject, conceived as outside experience, by way of transcendental reflection. If such reflection does yield important results about the subject, then this subject must be the empirical subject. Otherwise, the strict boundary between appearances and things-in-themselves would have been breached.

ideals. Kant of course differs from Lange in thinking that these ideals themselves have a necessary structure, given to them by reason; Lange regards them as free creations of the human mind.

To repeat, all three agree that psychologism is the interpretative key to Kant. All infer Berkeleian idealism from Kant's doctrine of the transcendental ideality of space and time. Schopenhauer has a dogmatic picture of things-in-themselves, an empiricist account of cognition, and therefore little appreciation either of the criticist approach to regulative Ideas and noumena, or of the constructivist account of perception and cognition. By contrast, Fischer has a lively appreciation of the constructivist account of perception and cognition, but also lacks appreciation for the criticist side and therefore, like Schopenhauer, seeks the metaphysical lessons of the *Critique*, finding them not only in dogmatic claims about things-in-themselves, but also in the discovery of a Fichtean subjectivity; Fischer seems to want to identify the two. Lange is far more receptive to the empirical realism and epistemic modesty in Kant and refuses to spin tales of either noumena or of transcendental subjectivity. Instead he leaves us with an idealism grounded in empirical facts about perception, and a limit-concept of the non-phenomenal, which is linked to his freer conception of the regulative Ideas.

Fischer's Fichtean Kant and Lange's empirical realist Kant taken together get Kant essentially right, not in detail,[26] but in broad themes and spirit. I believe that these two are more important for Nietzsche's reading of Kant than Schopenhauer. Such an interpretation will go some way towards addressing the concern that Nietzsche's grasp of Kant, being based in a reading of Schopenhauer alone, was superficial, thus rendering both his debt and his criticisms of Kant unworthy of further consideration. Such a worry should be reduced even more, since it can be shown that Nietzsche read Kant himself.

Table 1. *References to Kant in Nietzsche's works*

1865–9	1870–4	1875–9	1880–4	1885–9
36	78	14	89	164

[26] Fischer is routinely attacked by Kant scholars for his erroneous interpretations of specific arguments and for his psychologism. We must be cautious, however, in assuming that the former failings necessarily impugn the later claim. However deficient his accounts of specific arguments may be, a psychologistic approach of *some* sort is, I am convinced, essential to a correct reading of Kant.

Nietzsche's reading of Kant

Nietzsche's knowledge of Kant was not confined to secondary sources; his reading of Kant can be shown to have been far more extensive than usually thought. There are 381 instances of the expressions 'Kant' and related terms (e.g. 'Kantian') in the Colli–Montinari edition; Nietzsche also refers to Kant in twenty-six letters. He refers to Kant more than any other modern philosopher, excepting Schopenhauer; of philosophers more generally, he refers only to Plato and Schopenhauer more often. Most of these references to Kant cluster around two distinct periods: from mid- to late 1860s to the early 1870s, and from the mid-1880s onward. Table 1 illustrates this pattern. I will call them the first reading and the second reading respectively. Fortunately for us, Nietzsche's concerns during the first reading were primarily with aesthetics and teleology, and their relationship to metaphysics and epistemology. His primary documented source was the *Critique of Judgement*, which Nietzsche read closely in the late 1860s and again in the late 1880s.[27] During Nietzsche's later preoccupation with Kant, his interest was primarily with metaphysics, epistemology, and morality; Nietzsche's close reading of the *Critique of Practical Reason* can be documented.[28] There is some evidence suggesting a direct acquaintance with the first *Critique* in 1872–3[29] and 1886[30] as well, which would have supplemented his earlier reading of Kuno Fischer's close commentary.[31]

Nietzsche's image of Kant

In Nietzsche's early published remarks about Kant's metaphysics and epistemology, Nietzsche emphasizes the appearance–reality contrast that Kant

[27] 'On teleology' (*KGW* i.4. 549–78 (1868)) contains many page references to the third *Critique*, suggesting a close reading. Also see Nietzsche's quotations from *CJ*, Ak. v. 309, 323, 330 (*KGW* viii.1. 275 (1886–7)).

[28] See Nietzsche's quotations from *CPrR*, Ak. v. 97, 161–2 (*KGW* viii.1. 277–8 (1886–7)).

[29] Nietzsche quotes from *CPR*, footnote on A 37, in *PTG* 15 (*KGW* ii.2. 351 (1873)). One can also find there an inexact patchwork quote from Kant's *Universal Natural History*, Ak. i. 225–6, 229–31 (*KGW* iii.2. 361 (1873)), suggesting Nietzsche may have been quoting from memory. Nietzsche quotes from *CPR* B xxx (*KGW* iii.4. 14–15 (1872–3)). *CPR* B xxx is quoted again in *D* 197.

[30] Nietzsche quotes *CPR* A 319/B 376 in the preface to the second, 1886 edition of *D*.

[31] Besides the works discussed above, there are brief quotations in Nietzsche from the following works of Kant's: *Conflict of the Faculties*, Ak. vii. 81, 88, 91, and *Religion within the Bounds of Reason Alone*, Ak. vi. 186 (*KGW* viii.1. 274–8 (1886–7)); *Anthropology*, Ak. vii. 232 (*KGW* vii.1. 322/ *WP* 698 (1883)); *Prolegomena*, Ak. iv. 261 (*KGW* i.4. 420 (1868) and *BGE* 11) and 320 (*HA* I. 19).

seems to make with his distinction between phenomena and noumena. He suggests that Kant's epistemology leads to a 'gnawing and disintegrating scepticism and relativism' (*UM* III. 3). Simultaneously it leads to the death of rational theology. This sets the Schopenhauerian agenda by underscoring the need for another means of relating ourselves to (noumenal) reality, thus paving the way for tragic wisdom (*BT* 18, 19).

[Kant points] out the limits and the relativity of knowledge generally, and thus [denies] decisively the claim of science to universal validity and universal aims. And [his] demonstration diagnosed for the first time the illusory notion which pretends to be able to fathom the innermost essence of things with the aid of causality. . . . While this optimism . . . had believed that all the riddles of the universe could be known and fathomed, and had treated space, time, and causality as entirely unconditional laws of the most universal validity, Kant showed that these really served only to elevate the mere phenomenon . . . to the position of the sole and highest reality, as if it were the innermost and true essence of things, thus making impossible any knowledge of this essence . . . (*BT* 18)

However, in the 1880s, he objects to his own attempt to express in Schopenhauerian and Kantian formulae evaluations that were at odds with their spirit and taste (*BT*, 'Attempt at a self-criticism': 6).

Nietzsche compares Kant to the Eleatics (*UM* IV. 4); a glance at a contemporary posthumous remark on the Presocratics (Nietzsche calls them the pre-Platonics) suggests that neither Parmenides nor Kant regarded time as altogether real.

In the middle works, Nietzsche's references to Kant's metaphysics and epistemology stress the sceptical motif at the expense of any positive claims about the thing-in-itself. Apparently alluding to the Antinomies, he claims that our sensations of space and time are false. Tested consistently they lead to logical contradictions. Kant's doctrine that the mind imposes structure on experience is correct if by this he would have meant that scientists endorse certain fictions or errors in constructing our concept of nature, prominent among them being the belief that reality has mathematical properties (*HA* I. 19).

More negatively, Nietzsche begins in the middle works to stress that Kant's scepticism has served obscurantist ends, which in turn support religious beliefs that ought not to stand up to rational scrutiny; here Nietzsche recurrently objects to Kant's claim to have limited knowledge to make room for faith (*HA* II: Maxims 27; *D* 142, 197).

And, in a remark that could be applied with equal aptness to Kant's metaphysics of experience, his moral theory, or his philosophy of religion, Nietzsche criticizes the descriptive, rational reconstructive side of Kant's

21

thought. 'Kant wanted to prove, in a way that would dumbfound the common man, that the common man was right: that was the secret joke of his soul. He wrote against the scholars in support of popular prejudice, but for scholars and not for the people' (*GS* 193).

In the mature works, Nietzsche praises Kant for his theory of causality (*GS* v. 357), while rejecting Kant's claim that transcendental faculty psychology can serve to legitimize allegedly synthetic *a priori* claims (*BGE* 11; also see rough drafts at *KGW* vii.3. 68, 165, 204 (1884–5)).[32] Note also that Nietzsche correctly identifies the understanding as the faculty that serves this role. He correctly identifies the faculty of the understanding with the table of categories. He also supports Kant's rejection of rational psychology in the Paralogisms chapter of the first *Critique*, and his alternative account of the unity of the self in the Transcendental Deduction in saying that:

formerly, one believed in 'the soul' as one believed in grammar and the grammatical subject: one said 'I' is the condition, 'think' is the predicate, and the conditioned—thinking is an activity to which thought must supply a subject as cause. [Kant, however, correctly understood that] 'think' [is] the condition, 'I' the conditioned; 'I' in that case [is] only a synthesis which is made by thinking. (*BGE* 54).

Nietzsche then goes beyond Kant in claiming that the real self may not only be inaccessible. It may not exist. Though this was not Kant's official view, 'the possibility of a merely apparent existence of the subject, the soul in other words, may not always have remained strange to him' (*BGE* 54). This 'belief in grammar' (subject–predicate form) is not merely responsible for the synthesis of the subject, but also the synthesis of the object. Nietzsche is quick to point out, as Hegel had before him, that Kant's notion that our organizing of experience (and only experience) makes there be objects or 'things' in the first place, renders all talk of 'such a changeling, as is the Kantian "thing-in-itself"' unintelligible (*GM* I. 13).

Despite Nietzsche's appropriation and modification of these Kantian themes, the note sounded in the mature works, picking up on the 'obscurantism' theme of the middle works, is increasingly negative.

Kant's very idea of a critique of reason, a self-examination of our cognitive faculties, is a form of intellectual masochism, '[an] unnatural [science]—which is what I call the self-critique of knowledge [which] has at present the object of

---

[32] The manuscript for *KGW* vii.3. 68 (1884–5) has not yet been transcribed in *KGW* ix. The manuscript for *KGW* vii.3. 165 (1885) is transcribed at *KGW* ix.1. 143–4. Nietzsche has crossed out this passage. The manuscript for *KGW* vii.3. 204 (1885) is transcribed at *KGW* ix.1. 65–6. Nietzsche has not crossed out this passage.

dissuading humanity from its former respect for itself, as if this had been nothing but a piece of bizarre conceit' (*GM* III. 12, 25), an incoherent enterprise anyway, since it is 'somewhat peculiar to demand of an instrument that it should criticize its own usefulness and suitability. . . [or that it] should "know" its own value, its own capacity, its own limitations'. Again, critique proves to be motivated by the desire to make room for moral and religious commitments, since 'to create room for his "moral realm" he saw himself obliged to posit an undemonstrable world, a logical "beyond"—it was for precisely that that he had need of his critique of pure reason!' (*D* Preface (1886)).

In the end, all of this, the humility and masochism, the attraction to an incoherent project, the moral-religious tail's wagging of the metaphysical and epistemological dog, is 'a suggestion of decadence, a symptom of the decline of life' (*TI* 'Reason' 6). Its popularity reveals a lack of intellectual integrity among his followers (*TI* 'Skirmishes' 16).

Nietzsche is silent concerning Kant's ethics in the early works. He is almost entirely critical of Kant's ethics after that. He criticizes the universalizability test, for '(demanding) of the individual actions which one desired of all' without giving any criterion for what should be desired of all (*HA* I. 25).[33] What is worse, to generate and follow such rules, such tests demand the ability to classify actions as of the same kind. The resources of folk psychology are not fine-grained enough for this purpose; this suggests that it is not practical reason that provides us with morality, but intuition, which is to say, prejudice (*GS* 335). Kant's advocacy of the moral has harmed our understanding of moral phenomena (*HA* II: Wanderer 216). Like Hegel, Nietzsche objects to Kant's rigorism, which shows an excessive fondness for obedience (*D* 207; *BGE* 187; *TI* 'Skirmishes' 29), self-fragmentation (*TI* 'Skirmishes' 49), and sado-masochism (*D* 339; *GM* II. 6)—one would be better off if obligations (if any) were a pleasure to discharge rather than a burden. However, he does occasionally take the reverse side, when the pleasure involved is the pleasure associated with compassion (*D* 132). This claim links with the claim concerning the coarseness of our moral classifications. Nietzsche complains that to submit rigorously to a rule not tailored to the specific circumstances an agent finds herself in can be tremendously destructive for that individual (*A* 11). Kantian ethics

---

[33] Nietzsche here seems to have misinterpreted Kant's view. For Kant, apart from the formal feature of universalizability, and the fact that an act satisfies some agent's preferences, there *is* no further normative dimension to human action. I should desire of all that which would enable me to satisfy *my* preferences; which preferences I, or anyone else should have, apart from questions of universalizability, is a question that cannot be raised for Kant. All else being equal, the fact that something is preferred is a reason for acting to satisfy that preference. To think otherwise would be to introduce an element of heteronomy into Kantian ethics and compromise its commitment to human freedom.

23

presupposes a metaphysical falsehood, that we have free will (*TI* 'Errors' 8; 'Skirmishes' 1). In the end, Nietzsche regards Kant's ethics as not only indefensible on normative and theoretical grounds; it also itself reveals and expresses an absence of intellectual integrity—'Kant tried . . . to give this . . . scientific status with his notion of practical reason: he invented a special kind of reason for cases in which one need not bother about reason' (*A* 12).

Given that the *Critique of Judgement* is the one text that we know beyond doubt that Nietzsche read closely and early, it is surprising to find that he refers to Kant's aesthetics in the published works only once, and late. At *GM* III. 6, Nietzsche correctly observes that 'Kant thought he was honouring art when among the predicates of beauty he emphasized and gave prominence to those which establish the honor of knowledge: impersonality and universality', and goes on to criticize Kant for focusing excessively on the phenomenology of the spectator to the exclusion of that of the artist, and of getting that phenomenology wrong. For the spectator is said to appreciate the art work 'without interest', a claim that Nietzsche seems to interpret incorrectly to mean 'without pleasure', but by which Kant seems to mean 'without motivating to actions'.

Nietzsche's early miscellaneous remarks concerning Kant typically display great respect for Kant as a thinker and even as a stylist (*UM* I. 11), or disrespect for those who show him disrespect (*UM* 4, 6) while expressing reservations about his personality, in particular, his cloistered, scholarly life (*UM* III. 3, 7, 8). Nietzsche also shows awareness of the nascent Neo-Kantian movement, as when he says that: 'lately (philosophers) have been content to assert that they are really no more than the frontier guards and spies of the sciences; to which end they are especially served by the teachings of Kant, out of which they are intent upon fashioning an idle scepticism that will soon be of no interest to anybody' (*UM* III. 8). The middle works confirm this view of Kant as excessively scholarly and impersonal (*HA* II: Wanderer 481), but now Kant is criticized as a stylist for a 'garrulousness due to a superabundant supply of conceptual formulations' (*GS* 97), an objection that intensified as Nietzsche's doubts about Kant's integrity as a moral philosopher grew. By the late works he is now at best a 'philosophical labourer' whose task is description and rational reconstruction, falling short of the 'genuine philosophers (who) are commanders and legislators' (*BGE* 211). Nietzsche's 'concept of a philosopher is worlds removed from any concept that would include even a Kant' (*EH*: UM 3). One can become a 'great philosopher' even of this sort, as Nietzsche so characterizes Kant, Heraclitus, Plato, Descartes, Spinoza, Leibniz, and Schopenhauer (*GM* III. 7). At worst, '(Kant) is that most deformed concept-cripple of all time' (*TI* 'German' 7). And though Kant is accorded greater stature than Hume (*BGE*

252), the final judgement on him is quite negative, not just for what he is, but for his influence. According to Nietzsche, Kant, mistakenly regarded as 'deep' by scholars (*EH*: CW 3), delayed the Enlightenment's extension of its domain to include moral phenomena (*EH*: CW 2), while strengthening a Christian ethic that had almost perished during the Renaissance (*A* 61).

Nietzsche's early unpublished remarks concerning Kant's metaphysics and epistemology follow, for the most part, the published remarks in representing Kant as the great critic of transcendent metaphysics (*KGW* iii.4. 13, 105 (1872–3)), a historic shift in European philosophy and culture leading either to despair over the collapse of religious hopes, as in Kleist (*KGW* iii.4. 348 (1873–4)), a sense of the tragic futility of the high evaluation we place on truthfulness (*KGW* iii.4. 41–2 (1872–3)), or a possible resurgence of a tragic culture based on art (*KGW* iii.4. 14–15, 27 (1872–3)), occupying much the same place in early Nietzsche's thought that rational religion did in Kant's. That Nietzsche reads transcendental idealism in the early notes as a species of scepticism[34] is clear from his remark that 'if the sciences are right, then we are not supported by Kant's foundation; if Kant is right, then the sciences are wrong' (*KGW* iii.4. 47 (1872–3)). In this passage he expresses support for the famous 'neglected alternative'—that things-in-themselves might be just the same as appearances, and empirical science completely adequate to them. While these remarks all display a certain measure of dependence upon Schopenhauer, Nietzsche shows greater fidelity to Kant in his remark that 'we far too readily confuse Kant's "thing-in-itself" with the Buddhists' [read: Schopenhauer's] "true essence of things." On the one hand actuality exhibits nothing but illusion; on the other, it exhibits an appearance which is totally adequate to the truth' (*KGW* iii.4. 54 (1872–3)). Here we see Nietzsche repudiating Schopenhauer's tendency to transform the thing-in-itself into an explanatory posit whose character helps us to make sense of the character of phenomena much in the same way that imperceptible atoms are posited to help explain the properties of macroscopic objects. He also defends Kantian agnosticism about things-in-themselves from Schopenhauer's claim to have discovered a method of knowing them in the fragment 'On Schopenhauer', which we will discuss in Chapter 3, as well as in *Philosophy in the Tragic Age of the Greeks* (*KGW* iii.2. 313 (1873)/*PTG* 4). However, Nietzsche's most radical break from both Kant and Schopenhauer occurs in those notes where he discusses and rejects the transcendental ideality of space and especially time (*KGW* i.4. 418–30 (1868);

---

[34] Nietzsche elides the careful distinctions Kant makes between transcendental and empirical realism, on the one hand, and transcendental and empirical idealism on the other.

KGW iii.2. 351 (1873)/*PTG* 4; *KGW* iii.3. 115 (1870–1); *KGW* iii.4. 55 (1872–3)). One consequence of this early, basic commitment is that transcendental subjectivity must be located within empirical time; it follows that the structure of the former probably evolved over time (*KGW* iii.4. 55 (1872–3)).

Much of Nietzsche's discussion of Kant's metaphysics in his late notes returns to the questionable distinction between phenomena and noumena in a way that highlights the affinity between this doctrine and religious conceptions of the unreality of the world, while exposing the incoherence involved in the very idea of the thing-in-itself (*KGW* vii.2. 116, 271 (1884); *KGW* viii.1. 189–90 (1886–7)/*KGW* ix.3. 187).

Nietzsche continues to accept the 'neglected alternative' approach to the transcendental ideality of space and time in the late notes: 'By my showing the subjective genesis, e.g., of space etc. the thing itself is neither refuted nor proven. Against Kant—Duration belongs to sensation: time is "factual-time," is causal' (*KGW* vii.2. 292 (1884)). Since time is transcendentally real, the categories must have evolved over time (*KGW* vii.3. 164 (1885)).[35] Nietzsche rejects Kant's account of the phenomenality of causality. If real causal connections involve influx of force, and the relata of a causal connection are mere appearances, the notion of force here makes no sense; what Kant describes as the synthesis of data under a rule is better understood in terms of Humean habit and conditioning (*KGW* viii.1. 133 (1885–6); *KGW* viii.3. 68 (1888)). In a long and detailed discussion, Nietzsche criticizes Kant's very conception of synthetic *a priori* judgement (*KGW* viii.1. 272–4 (1886–7)); as we shall see in Chapter 5, Nietzsche's rejection of the synthetic *a priori* is a consequence of his rejection of the transcendental ideality of space and time. Finally, despite Kant's trenchant critique of rational psychology, he is still caught up in the idea of a subject in which experiences inhere (*KGW* vii.3. 343 (1885)), though his conception of synthetic unity opens the door to the possibility that there is no subject (*KGW* vii.3. 368 (1885)).

Nietzsche does not refer to Kant's ethics in his early published works. The remarks in the unpublished notes and papers are quite sparse. The early Nietzsche gave comparatively little thought to this side of Kant's work.

In *The Future of Our Educational Institutions*, a series of lectures delivered at Basle, Nietzsche plays with the Kantian notion of an 'intelligible character' to illustrate the contrast between a person's true nature, and the superficial effects of modern education, which can affect one's 'empirical character' at most

---

[35] The manuscript for *KGW* vii.3. 164 (1885) is transcribed at *KGW* ix.1. 146. Nietzsche has crossed out this passage.

(*KGW* iii.2. 157 (1872)). Nietzsche here is clearly thinking of this true nature in terms of how cultivated it is regarding aesthetic sensitivity and productivity. One's moral intentions are scarcely in view here. Later in the lectures, Nietzsche celebrates the Wars of Liberation for their educative effect on German youth; it is only after serving on the battlefield that the German youth could be said to have 'grasped the significance of Kant's categorical imperative'! Despite the silliness of this remark, associations between Kantian duty and military experience became increasingly common in late nineteenth-century Germany, especially after the Schiller and Fichte centennials.[36]

Nietzsche's early notes touching on Kant's ethics appear in five manuscripts. In PI15a, however, he seems to reject the 'ethic of duty' while appealing to Kant's alleged intuitionism to support his own ethico-cultural ideals. He says: 'What for the individual generates itself as the concept of duty, is only incidentally, however, a thing of the will. "Idealism of ethics," to the pure, this means an idealism of intuition (Kant)' (*KGW* iii.3. 84 (1869–70)). In PI20b, after quoting from the first *Critique*, 'The dogmatism of metaphysics, that is, the preconception that it is possible to make headway in metaphysics without a previous criticism of reason, is the source of all that unbelief, always very dogmatic, which wars against morality' (*CPR*, B xxx), Nietzsche remarks:

Very significant! Kant was impelled by a cultural need! What a curious opposition, 'knowledge and faith'! What would the Greeks have thought of this? Kant was acquainted with no other opposition, but what about us! A cultural need impels Kant: he wishes to preserve a domain from knowledge: that is where the roots of all that is highest and deepest lie, of art and ethics . . . The mastery of the knowledge drive: Does it work to the advantage of a religion? Or to the advantage of an artistic culture? The answer should now become evident; I favour the latter alternative.   (*KGW* iii.4. 14–15 (1872–3))

Here the early Nietzsche endorses Kant's manoeuvre of limiting knowledge to make room for something concerning values; but he substitutes art for faith.

Another surprising affinity between the early Nietzsche and Kant appears in UII2: 'To say the truth without eudaemonological purpose, purely out of duty . . . Kant's discourse about duty. A great person is worth more than an empire, because he is better for all posterity' (*KGW* iii.4. 229 (1873), ellipsis mine). Not only does Nietzsche align his advocacy for telling dangerous truths with the Kantian duty not to lie; he also appropriates the Kantian notion of the infinite worth of an individual, without, of course, appropriating Kant's egalitarian claim that all individuals possess this worth. Elsewhere in this manuscript, Nietzsche comments that Eduard von Hartmann and Heinrich Heine were

---

[36] Köhnke, *Neo-Kantianism*, 115–24.

unconscious ironists, but notes that this is incompatible with Kant's view that self-deception is impossible (*KGW* iii.4. 267 (1873)).

In the middle period, Nietzsche begins to criticize Kant in three manuscripts, UIII1, MpXIV1b, and NII7. His objections depend upon a prior commitment to a consequentialist or teleological ethic: '(there has been a) step backward of the past century in ethics—(from) Helvétius.[37] From there downward: Rousseau, Kant, Schopenhauer, Hegel' (*KGW* iv.3. 414 (1878)). He takes Kant to task for promoting an ethic of selflessness, 'the belief that the unegoistic is the hallmark of the ethical', in which, ironically, one's own moral stature is pettily placed above a concern with humanity's further development. 'This sentence of Kant's ("do what you would want done to you") amounts to a petty-bourgeois private worthiness ethic (*Privat-Achtbarkeit der Sitte*) and stands opposed to ecumenical purposes the existence of which he has no concept' (*KGW* iv.2. 556 (1876–7)). Such an ethic is largely irrelevant to the more important needs of human life.

Pity and love have their centre of gravity in the representation of the other being; revenge and envy seek the preservation of one's own self. Certain presumptuous teachings admittedly seek an isolated subjectivism and, in particular, an abstract unity of the affections. [But] Spinoza is not entitled to speak that way. Against this, Kant displays a basic presupposition concerning this: separation of that morality which concerns itself with mere expediency according to the point of view of human needs, and that morality which focuses on interpersonal considerations. The first genus he despised as mere technology of life, but that is just his one-sidedness. (*KGW* iv.1. 218 (1875)).

In the late notes, Nietzsche's tone is almost uniformly hostile, and the sheer quantity of remarks defies any easy summary. However, the following remarks are representative. Nietzsche reserves his greatest ire for Kant's attempts in the second *Critique* to argue from the content of morality to 'practical postulates' with metaphysical content.

'Duty' means: a goal willed not as a means to another willing, but rather something willed only for its own sake: therefore an absolute goal. . . . *On that* Kant grounded a metaphysics: if there is to be a goal without condition, then this can only be the complete or unlimited good: if there was something else still more complete, or a higher good, it wouldn't be a goal without condition. Therefore: a metaphysical assumption is to be made—how typical of Kant! (*KGW* v.1. 560 (1880), ellipsis mine)

---

[37] Helvétius defends a hedonistic utilitarianism that anticipates Bentham's (Helvétius, Claude Adrien, *A Treatise on Man: His Intellectual Faculties and his Education*, trans. W. Hooper (New York: B. Franklin, 1969)).

Such reasoning is not only wishful thinking, it presupposes that our grasp of the content of morality is assured, that there even are objectively binding moral norms at all. 'It all comes from the belief that morality itself exists, at least as a conscious rule (as with Kant) whereby we know what good and evil are' (*KGW* vii.1. 253 (1883)). Nietzsche also objects to the specific content of Kant's ethics, in particular, its rigorism.

Out of habituation to unconditional authority, finally a deep need for unconditional authorities originates: (this need is) so strong, that (even) in a critical age such as Kant's, the need for criticism proves itself superior only in a certain sense, the entire work of critical understanding makes itself known as subservient and merely for (social) utility. (*KGW* viii.1. 267 (1886–7); cf. *KGW* viii.2. 126 (1887))

But his greatest worry is that the very adoption of the moral stance in the first place expresses asceticism and ultimately commits one to nihilism. 'Granted that the moral norm, even as Kant understood it, has never been completely fulfilled and remains suspended over actuality as a kind of beyond without ever falling down into it, then morality would contain a judgement concerning the whole, which, however, still permits the question: whence does it derive the right to this judgement?' (*KGW* viii.1. 325 (1886–7)).

One remark suggests that Nietzsche, however much he defined his own ethical stance by opposing Kant, was indebted to Kant at a deeper level for his own 'genealogical' method. 'Kant is right that because there are different maxims of differing ethical value, the value of an action always leads back in the end to the question of the values which furnish the reason for the maxim' (*KGW* vii.2. 169 (1884)). Here, Nietzsche takes Kant's rejection of consequentialism and transforms it. Whereas, for Kant, the consequences are to be replaced by the intention that produces the action, here Nietzsche speaks of 'the *values* which furnish the reason for the maxim'. In Kant an act in conformity with the law lacks worth if it is not done out of respect for the law; in Nietzsche, an act, despite its external appearance, loses worth if it expresses decadent values. It will then be the task of genealogy to unearth these values and thus discredit the moral systems built upon them.

Nietzsche's unpublished remarks on the third *Critique* are most extensive during his early phase. Besides the long fragment 'On Teleology', discussed in Chapter 3, Nietzsche refers to Kant's views on reproduction in two notes. Taken together, they link Nietzsche's reading of the third *Critique* to the writing of the *Birth of Tragedy*.

Kant said once that the natural adaptation of attaching all reproduction to the duplication of sex always stands out as astonishing and as an abyss of thought for human reason. (*KGW* iii.3. 157 (1870–1))

Nietzsche's Flesh, Kant's Skeleton

That nature has attached the formation of tragedy to the two basic drives of the Apollinian and the Dionysian we may regard as just as much an abyss of reason as the contrivance of the very same nature of attaching propagation to the duplication of the sexes: this latter always appeared to the great Kant astonishing.   (*KGW* iii.3. 187 (1870–1))

There is no discussion of Kant's views on aesthetics or teleology in the middle period; however, in the late period, Nietzsche rejects Kant's conception of beauty as disinterested pleasure (*KGW* vii.1. 251, 301, 528 (1883); *KGW* vii.2. 31 (1884)). The only other unpublished indication of Nietzsche's late interest in the third *Critique* is a brief discussion of Kant's theory of genius. Kant contrasts Homer and Newton, claiming that genius is not needed to produce scientific knowledge. Nietzsche brands this claim 'Psychological idiotism!' (*KGW* viii.1. 275 (1886–7)).

Nietzsche's miscellaneous unpublished remarks add little to what we have seen so far; as in the published remarks, the image of Kant in the early Nietzsche's notes is of a great intellect, worthy of respect, but whose person was merely scholarly. The late remarks echo the extremely hostile tone of Nietzsche's rejection of Kant's moral philosophy; one passage in particular summarizes the image of Kant in Nietzsche's final assessment:

Kant: makes the epistemological scepticism of the English possible for Germans: 1. by enlisting for it the sympathy of the moral and religious needs of the Germans; just as the later philosophers of the Academy used scepticism for the same reason, as a preparation for Platonism (*vide* Augustine); and as Pascal used even moralistic scepticism in order to excite the need for faith ('to justify it'); 2. by scholastically involuting it and curlicuing it and thus making it acceptable for the German taste regarding scientific form (for Locke and Hume in themselves were too bright, too clear, i.e., judged according to German value instincts, 'too superficial'—) Kant: inferior in his psychology and knowledge of human nature; way off when it comes to great historical values (French Revolution); a moral fanatic *à la* Rousseau; a subterranean Christianity in his values; a dogmatist through and through, but ponderously sick of this inclination, to such an extent that he wished to tyrannize it, but also weary right away of scepticism; not yet touched by the slightest breath of cosmopolitan taste and the beauty of antiquity—a delayer and a mediator, nothing original.   (*KGW* viii.2. 4 (1887))

Nietzsche refers to Kant in his letters far less often than in his notes, and the references are not in themselves terribly illuminating. Again, the references cluster into two periods. From 1866 to 1872, when Nietzsche was developing the ideas that would culminate in the *Birth of Tragedy*, he discusses Kant in sixteen of the twenty-five letters. Between 1872 and 1881, there is only one reference to Kant in a letter. The remaining eight letters all appear between 1881 and 1888 (one in 1881, one in 1885, five in 1887, and one in 1888).

In two of the letters from 1866, Kant is an object of reverence associated with Schopenhauer.[38] In a third, Lange is called a Kantian[39] and, in a fourth, Lange is now part of a trinity: Kant, Schopenhauer, and Lange.[40] In 1868, Kant is again linked with Schopenhauer in a letter discussing Otto Kohl's Kant dissertation.[41] Later that year, very likely after the reading of the third *Critique*, we see Kant referred to in isolation for the first time, as the source of Nietzsche's

solid conviction over the scope of our cognitive faculty. . . . Whoever but takes into account the course of the pertinent investigations, especially the physiological, since Kant, could not have any doubt about it, that these borders have been determined so certainly and unerringly, that besides the theologians, some philosophy professors and the vulgar, nobody creates for themselves conceits here anymore.   (*KGB* i.2. 269 (1868))

Also in this letter, Nietzsche mentions his proposed dissertation on Kant and teleology. Then we have three letters in 1868 commenting on Wenkel's enthusiasm for Kant and Schopenhauer.[42] In 1869, Nietzsche mentions that one of his students, Julius Cornu, is translating the *Prolegomena* into French.[43] In 1870, Nietzsche compares his relationship to Schopenhauer with Schiller's relationship to Kant.[44] Two more letters from 1870 mention Kant with Schopenhauer.[45] In the application to Wilhelm Vischer at Basle for Gustav Teichmüller's chair in philosophy, dated January 1871, after discussing his philological credentials for teaching ancient philosophy, Nietzsche says: 'Of modern philosophers I have studied with special preference Kant and Schopenhauer' (*KGB* ii.1. 177 (1871)). This passage is significant in that Nietzsche would presumably have expected to teach what he claimed competence in; his mention of Kant thus bespeaks a greater degree of confidence in his knowledge of Kant than other references to 'Kant and Schopenhauer'. We have two letters from 1871 and 1872 referring to his friend Heinrich Romundt's manuscript 'Kant and Empedocles'.[46] After this, references to Kant fall off substantially until the second reading. Only the remark to Paul Deussen, in mid-January 1875, 'How fortunate your previous employment with Kant and Schopenhauer now seems!' (*KGB* ii.5. 11 (1875)) appears; Nietzsche would again have occasion to comment on Deussen's fruitful debt to Kant.

Nietzsche's interest in Kant appears to have returned after reading a manuscript on Kant by Romundt, 'Kant's Doctrine concerning God, Soul and Immortality Re-established', which Nietzsche refers to in a letter in 1881.[47]

---

[38] *KGB* i.2. 142, 152 (1866).   [39] *KGB* i.2. 159 (1866).   [40] *KGB* i.2. 184 (1866).
[41] *KGB* i.2. 265 (1868).   [42] *KGB* i.2. 285, 288, 322 (1868).   [43] *KGB* ii.1. 84 (1869).
[44] *KGB* ii.1. 98 (1870).   [45] *KGB* ii.1. 100, 162 (1870).   [46] *KGB* ii.3. 16, 20 (1871–3).
[47] *KGB* iii.1. 116, 119 (1881).

Whereas most of Nietzsche's previous remarks concerning Kant were favourable, this title seems to represent a turning point. After he becomes aware of Romundt's work, Nietzsche asks Franz Overbeck for a copy of Otto Liebmann's *Kant and the Epigones*. This work is most frequently cited as the first Neo-Kantian text, largely for its recurrent refrain, 'We must go back to Kant!' However, Nietzsche mentions the apparent lack of contemporary enthusiasm for Kant and Schopenhauer in a letter to his sister and her husband, dated 1885.[48]

In a letter of 1887, Nietzsche facetiously compares Kant's ethics with Prussian militarism.[49] In two other letters, Nietzsche praises Deussen's research on Indian philosophy. He compares the latter to Kant's thought, suggesting that Deussen's enthusiasm for Kant and Schopenhauer enabled him to appreciate the Vedanta 'from the inside' (*KGB* iii.5. 144, 158 (1887)). Deussen's work, which Nietzsche returned to in 1887, may have influenced Nietzsche's linking Kant with asceticism in *Genealogy of Morals*, Essay III. The remaining two letters to mention Kant are deeply negative. To Heinrich Köselitz (24 November 1887), Nietzsche condemns Kant for being of Rousseau's 'family' of first adherents. Nietzsche's extraordinary hostility to Rousseau in all but the earliest works (*UM* III) is well known.[50] Finally, in 1888, Kant's metaphysics and epistemology are contrasted unfavourably with empiricism; in a remark echoing the anti-German tirade in *Ecce Homo*, Kant is among the 'great *malheurs* (misfortunes) of culture' along with the Reformation, the 'Wars of Liberation', and the Second Reich.[51]

Reading Kant

Since I will clarify Nietzsche by reading him in the light shed by Kant, Kant interpretation will play a significant role. Though most philosophers of the first rank have garnered multiple, conflicting interpretations, Kant is a special case. The literature on Kant is immense, and there is no consensus about the nature of his projects (especially in the first *Critique*). Beyond this interpretative difficulty, Kant scholars also divide over what is living and dead in Kant; unsurprisingly, intuitions about what is of value in Kant have influenced what interpreters find in Kant. Thus one might complain that I am attempting to reconstruct Nietzsche on a shifting foundation. Justifying my interpretation of

---

[48] *KGB* iii.3. 71 (1885).   [49] *KGB* iii.5. 94 (1887).   [50] *KGB* iii.5. 203 (1887).
[51] *KGB* iii.5. 453 (1888); cf. *EH* xiii.2.

Kant to the satisfaction of the specialist would compel me severely to circumscribe the scope of my interpretation of both Kant and Nietzsche.

Consider three recent, representative interpretations. Peter Strawson claims that Kant's transcendental idealist metaphors should be disposed of. If we reinterpret the structure the mind imposes on experience with the structure of our conceptual scheme or language, then we can salvage an 'analytic core' of argument. First, we abandon the distinction between appearance and reality (as later idealists did!) and any talk of mind-imposition. We substitute 'analytic' for 'synthetic *a priori*' and the verification principle for Kant's talk of limiting us to experience. What remains are the various transcendental arguments showing that certain principles must be true if we are to have experience. Such an interpretation saves Kant from himself while making him vulnerable to post-positivist critiques (e.g. Quine).

Henry Allison has argued instead for a dual aspect interpretation of transcendental idealism. Rather than saying that there are two sets of objects, a phenomenon and a noumenon, we say that there is only the object under two different descriptions: the 'phenomenal' description is the description of the object as the referent in our theory, subject to the epistemological constraints on theory-building that transcendental argument reveals. The thing-in-itself is the same object, but not under that description. However, any description we can understand will be of the first sort. Hence the emptiness of an account of an object under a description other than the one we could produce. Such an interpretation must suppress not only the rich psychological analyses of perception Kant offers in the first *Critique*. It also makes it very difficult to understand the use of the idea of noumena in the second and third *Critiques*. Paul Guyer, who also strives to reduce the first *Critique* to epistemology, allows that Kant gave a more 'realist' gloss to his conception of things-in-themselves, but that he ought not to have.

Patricia Kitcher, inspired by cognitive science, tries to resuscitate Kant's mind-imposition thesis. If we set aside the transcendental ideality of time thesis, we can read it as a straightforward psychological claim. Since naive realism in philosophy of perception is false, we must, if not construct, at least reconstruct the empirical world inside our heads, using the resources of our cognitive architecture and the cues available in the data. Transcendental arguments show us what elements the mind must contribute to perceptual and cognitive tasks. After all, we can do these tasks and the data are too thin to explain this ability. On the interpretation that follows, I read Kant very much in Kitcher's spirit.

My historical purposes will be equally served if I use an interpretation of Kant that squares with Nietzsche's reading; the question of the adequacy of

Nietzsche's reading can be set aside for now. However, matters are better than that. First, Nietzsche's reading of Kant is in all essentials what one might call the standard or 'textbook' interpretation. Thus, even if Nietzsche's reading should prove significantly in error, it would probably not be an unwarranted reading. Anyway, it is of a piece with the reading that proved historically decisive for later Idealism, Neo-Kantianism, early analytic philosophy, and phenomenology. All these philosophical developments took as their point of departure a concern with the serious shortcomings of Kant's thought as they understood them. The proliferation of Kant interpretations subsequently has done little to alter the perception of what counts as a shortcoming; rather, interpreters after Heidegger and Strawson have read Kant charitably, exonerating him of the errors of which the textbook Kant stands convicted. Many attempts to read Kant charitably have foisted views on him less credible than the views he maintained. There is life yet in the textbook Kant.

One standard objection post-Kantians made to the first *Critique* concerned Kant's psychologism. Kant had apparently confused conceptual with psychological issues, spinning out psychological fantasies that neither advance Kant's real argument nor the science of psychology. This appearance was reinforced by the belief (shared with Kant) that philosophical claims must be *a priori* and that psychological claims could not be. Opposition to psychologism was a founding dogma of both analytic and phenomenological philosophy, and Kant was the exemplar of psychologism. Thus we have, for example, Strawson's attempt to brush away the Kant of transcendental psychology to reveal the analyst of concepts buried underneath.

The attempt to clean up Kant in this fashion has been far less successful than originally expected. Very few defensible Kantian arguments have emerged from such reconstructions. More important, the motives for the reconstruction ought to look quite different in the light of post-Quinian critiques of *a priori* knowledge. If the epistemological status Kant wanted transcendental philosophy to possess proves to be unobtainable, the justification for eliminating the psychological content from Kant's thought begins to look less compelling. While the historical accuracy of my Kant is not necessary for my Nietzsche (I need only reconstruct *Nietzsche's* Kant), I do recommend it for the reader's consideration.[52]

---

[52] Again, I am deeply indebted to Patricia Kitcher, Wayne Waxman, and Beatrice Longuenesse for this approach to Kant.

The interpretation

Though Nietzsche is quite critical of Kant, it is not uncommon for him to attack those to whom he is most indebted. To be sure, many of his criticisms will prove to be altogether fair and worthy of serious attention. To see the extent of Nietzsche's debt to Kant, one must look beyond the explicit references to and quotes from Kant, and using all Nietzsche's writings, reconstruct, as best as possible, the very movement of Nietzsche's reading of Kant.

This reconstruction will fall into two parts. The first part, 'Judgement', will deal with the first reading (1865–74), discussing the influence of the third *Critique* on the early works, especially *Birth of Tragedy* and *Truth and Lie*. The second part, 'Reason', will deal with the second reading (1880–9), discussing the influence of the first and second *Critiques* on Nietzsche's metaphysics, epistemology, and genealogy of morality. Though such an arrangement is awkward from a Kantian perspective (one would ideally take the *Critiques* in order), it captures the development of Nietzsche's thought.

In the first part, I will argue that Nietzsche's claims about metaphysics and epistemology in *Birth of Tragedy* and *Truth and Lie* can only be made sense of within the context of his appropriation of Kant's third *Critique*. In order to make this case, we will need a new interpretation of this baffling Kantian text. In Chapter 2, I will defend Kant's claim that aesthetic and teleological judgements are both differing types of what he calls reflective judgements. In Chapter 3, I will document Nietzsche's reading of the third *Critique*. In addition to textual support, I will show that the standard interpretation of early Nietzsche's development and debt to Schopenhauer generates difficulties that a more Kantian reading avoids.

The second part will explore the second reading (1880–9), and will focus, first, on the influence of the ideas of the first *Critique* on Nietzsche's metaphysics and epistemology, and then on the influence of the second *Critique*, and related works by and about Kantian ethics, on Nietzsche's critique of morality.

In Chapter 4, I will show that Nietzsche's 'naturalism' is best understood as a rejection of the transcendental ideality of space and time, as Kant argues for it in the 'Transcendental Aesthetic'. However, this generates a puzzle about how to understand the relationship between appearances and reality, given Nietzsche's continuing adherence to the Kantian thesis that the mind imposes order on its experiences, on the one hand, and his abandonment of things-in-themselves, on the other. I also discuss Nietzsche's use of 'cosmological' argument in connection with the doctrine of the eternal recurrence.

In Chapters 5 and 6, I trace the debt Nietzsche's critique of metaphysics owes to Kant. Chapter 5 offers a new account of Kant's notion of the transcendental unity of apperception and the role it plays in generating the illusion of mental substance. Chapter 6 then builds on the foundations laid in Chapters 4 and 5 to show how Nietzsche's critique of metaphysics comes from his reading of the Transcendental Deduction and the Paralogisms in the first *Critique*. Nietzsche's difficulties with the concept of truth are traced to his reliance on the Deduction's model of how the mind constructs both judgements and the facts to which they correspond. Though Kant's conception of empirical objects (and the empirical self) as products of synthesis survives Nietzsche's naturalization of temporality, the Kantian project of vindicating synthetic *a priori* knowledge collapses. The concept of the 'will to power' then serves to unify and generalize Nietzsche's account of experience as synthesized by the subject into a post-Kantian metaphysics.

In Chapter 7, I will turn to Nietzsche's *Genealogy of Morals*. Each essay is seen to derive from an encounter with a different aspect of Kant's moral philosophy: rational reconstruction of moral intuitions, the analysis of agency, and the practical postulates. I will show that Nietzsche's 'immoralism' is best understood as a rejection of the agent-neutral dimension of Kant's analysis of rule-governed action. However, we shall see that Nietzsche's relationship to Kant is ambivalent: Nietzsche is attracted to Kantian notions of freedom and autonomy, and attempts (in *Genealogy* II) an alternative account that is compatible with his rejection of noumenal agency and a morality of universalizable rules.

PART ONE

The First Reading:
Judgement
(1868–1874)

The *Critique of Judgement*   2

The place of the *Critique of Judgement* in Kant's thought

Nietzsche's reading of the *Critique of Judgement* was a crucial influence on *Birth of Tragedy*. It has long been known that Nietzsche read the *Critique of Judgement* in 1868. Because Nietzsche read it so early and seldom discussed it later has not been sufficiently appreciated,[1] Nietzsche scholars have devoted little attention to it. To remedy this deficiency, this chapter provides a brief account of the *Critique of Judgement*, hewing more closely to Kant's intentions in the third *Critique* than is often the case in Kant scholarship.

It has often been claimed that Kant significantly distorted his thought by his penchant for 'architectonic', a tendency towards arranging his material in artificially systematic fashion. This tendency is linked to his psychologism. Given the close relationship between an analysis of the various faculties of the human mind and transcendental philosophy, it is natural that Kant, who finds a high degree of systematicity in the former, should also find the same in the latter. Unfortunately, the natural thrust of Kant's argument seems distorted as he casts about for discussions and arguments that will fill in 'missing' parts of a preconceived scheme. An oft-cited example of this tendency is his treatment of the categories and the principles of the understanding in the first *Critique*. After producing a neat table of twelve logico-syntactic forms in the 'Metaphysical Deduction' Kant then feels himself committed to producing corresponding principles in the 'Analytic of Principles'. Unfortunately, Kant is primarily interested in principles concerning substance, causality, and reciprocity, the so-called 'Analogies of Experience'. Thus Kant feels compelled to embed the

---

[1] The Colli–Montinari edition classifies the notes associated with this reading as 'juvenilia' because of the 1869 cut-off date for the commencement of the 'works' proper. But 1869 marks the beginning of Nietzsche's philological biography, not any break or turn in his intellectual development.

discussion of the analogies in a larger discussion, and must cast about for other principles to discuss, without much success. Examples such as these have led many 'analytic' Kant scholars to heavily discount architectonic in an analysis of Kantian texts, seeking the underlying argument instead.

The *Critique of Judgement*, like all of Kant's works, displays this architectonic penchant. Given the peculiarity of the content of the work, it is understandable that the structure of the work is often ignored. This is especially the case given the uneven assessment of the two halves of the work, the first dealing with aesthetics, the second dealing with philosophy of biology. The second half is of far less interest to most readers. Since Kant's discussion there *seems* to commit him to a theology rendered obsolete by Darwin, it is tempting to focus on the aesthetics as the portion most likely to bear contemporary fruit. This, for example, is the approach of Paul Guyer.[2] It is far from clear how Kant meant the two halves of the third *Critique* to fit together.

On my reading, however, the unity of the *Critique of Judgement* is crucial to grasping its meaning and place within the Critical system as a whole. I do not doubt that the contemporary reader might cannibalize elements of it. If our concern is with understanding what Kant had in mind, we had best attend to the architectonic or risk missing his meaning. More important for my purposes, however, is my suspicion that Nietzsche's reception of the work was conditioned by a sense of its unity. As we shall see in the following chapter, Nietzsche came to the third *Critique* out of an attempt to resolve difficulties in the metaphysics and epistemology of biology. But I believe that he left the reading with a new aesthetics closely linked to that metaphysics and epistemology. To see how that could have happened, we must see how Kant linked these topics himself.

The *Critique of Judgement* is the last of three *Critiques*. Unlike the first and second *Critiques*, it contains two 'sub-critiques', each of which mirrors the pattern of critique laid down in the first and second *Critiques*. The first and second *Critiques* both contain a main part concerned with the 'Elements' of the topic (further divided into an 'Analytic' and a 'Dialectic'), and a second part containing a discussion of its 'Methodology'.[3] The *Critique of Judgement* appears to be *two* separate *Critiques*: a 'Critique of Aesthetic Judgement' and a 'Critique of

---

[2] Paul Guyer, *Kant and the Claims of Taste*, 2nd edn. (Cambridge: Cambridge University Press, 1997).

[3] I am passing over the difference between the first and second *Critiques*. The former further divides the Doctrine of Elements into a Transcendental Aesthetic and a Transcendental Logic, with only the Logic being then divided into an Analytic and a Dialectic. In the second *Critique*, the Elements are directly divided into Analytic and Dialectic, with no part corresponding to the Aesthetic.

Teleological Judgement', each with its own division into Analytic and Dialectic. This immediately poses the question of the *unity* of the work.

There is no indication in any preceding work that there is any *need* for a third *Critique*. Kant intended the *Critique of Pure Reason* to lay the foundation for a systematic philosophy, consisting of two main branches: a metaphysics of morals and a metaphysics of nature. Works on both topics subsequently appeared. Later, Kant saw the need for the metaphysics of morals to be preceded by its own propaedeutic, a *Critique of Practical Reason*. The new arrangement is that the first *Critique* paves the way for a metaphysics of nature, while the second *Critique* prepares us for a metaphysics of morals. Why the need, then, for a third *Critique*? Kant attempts to answer this question in the Introductions to the *Critique of Judgement*.[4]

Kant argues almost entirely from architectonic considerations of analogy and completeness that a third *Critique* is needed. Though the arguments may not seem very compelling, read as reports of the creative processes that led Kant to conceive the project, they shed much light on his intentions. Briefly, Kant came to believe that his account of the 'topology' of the human mind in the first and second *Critiques* was incomplete.

In the earlier *Critiques* the mind is divided broadly into two functions or 'faculties'—cognition and desire, each having a 'higher' or formal component, and a 'lower' material component, where the former pertains to the intellect and the latter pertains to the senses. The collaboration of these formal and material components produces sentence-like 'judgements', and these sentence-like entities then enter into various inferential relations with each other. What differentiates the functions of cognition and desire is the role played by the lower element, and the relationship between the sentence-like product, and action. When the function is cognition, the material element contributed by the senses serves a purely informational function. The product of the collaboration of the higher and lower, of the intellectual-formal and the sensory-material, is a meaningful *statement* that represents how things stand in the empirical world. With desire, the lower sensory-material element contributes (though not exclusively) a motivational element. The collaboration of the intellectual-formal and the sensory-material is an *instruction* that leads to intentional bodily behaviour

---

[4] Kant wrote an earlier draft of the Introduction he regarded as ready for publication, but subsequently withdrew due to its excessive length. This 'First Introduction' was subsequently published. It is generally regarded as equally reliable at discerning Kant's systematic intentions as the briefer 'Second Introduction' that appeared with the work. Though the First Introduction appears as a posthumous work in Academy vol. xx, whereas the published text of the third *Critique*, along with the Second Introduction, appear together in Academy vol. v, I will cite both Introductions as parts of the *Critique of Judgement*.

or action. Kant's interest in these respective models of cognition and desire is to see if he can extract an '*a priori*' element from the contribution of the higher, intellectual-formal element. In the first *Critique*, this extraction is meant to isolate a body of metaphysical truths about (and only about) the empirical world: the contents of the Analytic of Principles. In the second *Critique*, what gets extracted is a rational reconstruction of folk morality.[5]

In both the function of cognition and the function of desire, the formal contribution divides into three aspects or components; I will illustrate this with cognition first, where Kant's views can be more readily grasped. The ultimate goal of cognition is to produce a theoretical edifice. Within the empirical sphere, Kant identifies this edifice with Newtonian mechanics (though we would have to qualify this claim to fit biology into the structure of knowledge). To produce a theory, besides the raw sensory data, Kant believes we need to accomplish three further tasks.

First, the content of the sensory data must produce claims or statements. This task involves two further components. To have a statement in the first place, one needs rules of syntax for guiding and constraining the correct concatenation of subsentential elements. The faculty that contains these rules, which is active in assembling the claims under their guidance, Kant calls 'the understanding'. However, transforming data intake into syntactically correct statements is insufficient. For once we have organized the data into classes, such as APPLES, PURPLES, and REDS, we must connect the right classes. The syntactically correct claim 'the apple is red' needs to be produced instead of the equally well-formed 'the apple is purple', which subsumes the subject into the wrong class. The faculty of correct class subsumption, Kant calls 'judgement'.

Finally, the total body of statements must be further organized in relation to each other. Statements that can be grouped together as entailments from more general statements should be so grouped; these more general statements themselves must also be produced. Statements that are inconsistent with other statements must be evaluated, and the inconsistencies found in the total set of statements eliminated by pruning away some statements. Further statements that can be inferred from currently endorsed statements must be produced and

---

[5] I use the expression 'folk morality' deliberately to highlight a parallel between the way Kant thinks about ethics, and contemporary discussions in philosophy of mind. Recent figures in philosophy of mind claim that human beings share a tacit explanatory theory, 'folk psychology'. Similarly, Kant assumes that we all share a tacit normative theory that it is his task to make explicit, systematize, and defend. Strawson classifies Kant as a 'descriptive' as opposed to a 'revisionary' metaphysician. This fundamental commitment to description (or 'analytic' as Kant calls it) and rational reconstruction pervades Kant's thought, and is not just limited to his metaphysics.

retained. In short, Kant identifies the correct inference-drawing faculty with the scientific theory producing faculty; he calls it 'reason'.[6]

A parallel account of how the three 'higher' faculties collaborate is central to Kant's theory of action, where the product is rational instructions for guiding behaviour. Empirical data, syntactical form, and subsumption all play a role in producing desires, which are much like statements, albeit in the imperative rather than in the assertoric mood. To achieve goals, one's *reason* systematizes these imperatives into complex plans, much as it systematizes empirical truths to yield scientific theory. The result is action informed by the constraints of morality. For Kant, morality is the natural offshoot of the attempt to achieve generality and consistency in the organization of one's own behaviour.

We can now see how Kant came to believe that there ought to be a third *Critique*. First, Kant notes that the first two *Critiques* have disclosed *a priori* principles associated with two of the three higher faculties of cognition. Understanding has *a priori* principles of the metaphysics of experience associated with it. Reason has *a priori* principles of morality associated with it. It would be peculiar if the third of the three faculties, judgement, did not have its own *a priori* principle or principles (*CJ*, Ak. xx. 202).

Second, Kant introduces for the first time a third function, distinct from the functions of cognition and desire: the feeling of pleasure and pain (*CJ*, Ak. v. 177/Ak. xx. 205–6). Kant regards the faculty of pleasure and pain as distinct, on the one hand, from sensibility, and on the other, from desire. Sensibility, as Kant characterizes it, provides us with data concerning (and, given his transcendental idealism, from which we construct) empirical objects; episodes of entertaining a proposition or harbouring a wish are also empirical objects, the subject matter of empirical psychology. The feeling of pleasure (or pain) for Kant is not a *component* of any empirical object, but rather is the mind's reaction to its own states (*CJ*, Ak. xx. 222). This seems plausible enough for observation: the pleasure I experience in eating an apple is in me, not in the apple. For introspection, matters are more complex. What Kant seems to want to say here is that episodes of introspection of my states that have propositional form do not contain feelings of pleasure as their components. If I entertain the statement 'George Bush will probably be the next President' while entertaining the wish 'I want it to be the case that George Bush is the next President' I may *react* with a feeling of pleasure. The feeling, however, is not a part of the thoughts. Kant

---

[6] In all these processes, Kant sees something like a drive toward cognitive completeness. Hence his association of reason with actual infinity in the Antinomies. Kant's usage is not perfectly consistent; at times he uses the expression 'reason' interchangeably with 'cognition' (as opposed to desire) or with the higher faculties of cognition (i.e. excluding the contribution of sensibility).

does not identify pleasure with preference-satisfaction (and it is crucial both to his ethics and his aesthetics that he *not* do so). Getting my way may lead me to react with a feeling of pleasure, but the feeling of pleasure is distinct from getting my way. Only in this fashion can Kant contrast wanting to do something because it will give you pleasure and wanting to do something because it is right. From considerations such as these, Kant claims that the feeling of pleasure is a faculty in its own right (*CJ*, Ak. xx. 206–7).

Again, architectonic considerations become suggestive. Of the (now) three basic functions of the mind, cognition, desire, and feeling, the first two again have *a priori* principles. Cognition, again, has the principles of the metaphysics of experience in the first *Critique*; desire, again, has the principles of morality in the second *Critique*. It would be remarkable if feeling did not also have its own *a priori* features, its own 'higher' employment, or if this *a priori* aspect did not coincide with the *a priori* element yet to be discovered in the faculty of judgement (*CJ*, Ak. v. 178–9/Ak. xx. 208).

Kant was also concerned with how to approach aesthetics, and whether there might be any objectivity to the claims of taste. Kant had initially assumed that objectivity was not to be had in aesthetics, precisely because finding something is beautiful is partly a matter of finding the object pleasurable (*CJ*, Ak. xx. 222). Yet what one finds pleasurable surely must vary from person to person; unanimity in response to aesthetic objects can only be due to sensory physiology and shared socialization. Such unanimity, even if it existed (and clearly it does not), could be at most contingently universal, just as the desire for happiness is contingently universal. For Kant, what is contingently universal is no proper basis for an ethics that would claim to be truly binding on agents.

In all likelihood, it was precisely this comparison between ethics and aesthetics that led Kant to abandon his earlier aesthetic subjectivism.[7] For similar considerations in ethics did not compel him to adopt an ethics of contingently universal human interests; the involvement of a 'higher' faculty, reason, which also plays an important role in cognition, had made deontology available. Perhaps pleasure, like desire, could be somehow connected with a higher faculty associated with cognition and what is necessary for it. 'Necessary' desires yield morality; perhaps 'necessary' pleasures would yield *taste*.

These considerations are scarcely more than intimations, associations, and potentially fruitful thoughts. Kant does attempt to fashion them into some sort of argument in the Introductions to the *Critique of Judgement*. The important point is that once Kant had laid his architectonic commitments next to the

---

[7] Kant makes the similarity between ethics and aesthetics explicit at *CJ*, Ak. v. 351–4.

problem of aesthetic judgement, the parallels between aesthetics and ethics suggested a solution. Taste would turn out to be judgemental pleasure, just as morality had turned out to be rational desire. Transforming these intimations into an articulate and defensible philosophical project faced one important hurdle.

For Kant, reason's requirements must be *a priori*. Given the number of different tasks Kant assigns to reason, this is not entirely clear, but at least in its central tasks of weeding out inconsistency and regulating inference, the apriorism of reason's constraints on cognition and action are straightforward. In what sense does judgement, which Kant conceives as the faculty of subsuming individuals into classes, contain an *a priori* element? In empirical judgements, the function of subsumption seems to take all its *a priori* elements from the understanding, which regulates what form a judgement is to have. The content of an empirical judgement appears to be entirely a function of the empirical data it expresses. It is this *a posteriori* element that determines what individuals will get subsumed into which classes.

Now there is nothing about judgement as a faculty of straightforward subsumption that will yield any transcendental principles. All that judgement does when it subsumes a familiar case under a familiar class is concatenate. To be sure, transcendental principles are employed, though these are not native to judgement itself.

It is here that Kant, inspired perhaps by the dual sense of the term 'judgement' in ordinary language, comes up with the idea of *reflective judgement*. For while philosophers (including Kant) have used the expression 'judgement' to denote propositions and the acts that produce them (and my frequent recurrence to 'sentence-like' entities follows this sense), it is also linked to the notion of knowing what is appropriate to say and do under circumstances underdetermined by rules. In this sense, we say that someone who approaches a new situation and responds to it wisely possesses 'good judgement'. Kant then tries to unify the two senses together by implying that the latter kind of judgement is much like the former—both kinds involve concatenation of expressions into sentence-like wholes, but the underdeterminedness of 'good judgement' is due to a missing expression, to wit, the very expression needed to make the good judgement good. Thus he annexes to the notion of judgement not only the notion of concatenation by subsumption, but also the notion of seeking (and producing or discovering) missing class concepts. Thus Kant divides the function of judging into *determinative* judging, the act of subsumption, and *reflective* judging, the act of seeking a missing term for later subsumption (*CJ*, Ak. v. 179/Ak. xx. 209–10).

45

If this were all, however, we could not say that there were two different types of judgements in the sense of propositions or sentence-like entities. Furthermore, there is little basis in the above considerations for calling the act of seeking missing classes 'reflecting'. I will propose, then, that we regard Kant as claiming that there is a second class of judgements (propositions, sentence-like entities) that represent the act of seeking itself. Presumably, when the search is over and the missing term found, the result will be as much a determinative judgement as if no search had been called for. We can express this idea in the following way. The act of seeking the missing class presents itself to the seeker as a judgement of the form: I cannot help but think that there is a class somewhere which subsumes this individual. This way of putting things could be fairly represented as a judgement concerning the as-yet unsubsumed individual. It could also be characterized as a judgement of reflection on the subject's own mental states: the state of seeking the missing term.

Having said that judgement might very well contain *a priori* principles, Kant goes on to look for them. Such *a priori* principles will not come from the conditions of the possibility of determinative judging. The only *a priori* elements there are the rules of concatenation—the logico-syntactical forms of the understanding. So if there are to be any *a priori* principles, they must pertain to reflective judging.

For Kant, to discover *a priori* principles 'critically' is to show that such principles are the conditions of the possibility of experience. It has sometimes been suggested that Kant's use of the term 'experience' is somewhat equivocal. Experience might be a state of conscious awareness, awareness that is minimally structured, or the ability to produce empirical theories. Here, Kant's sense is much closer to the last of these. Kant had already shown to his satisfaction, in the first *Critique*, that 'experience' requires the forms of intuition, the categories, and the principles. Now he observes that these are not sufficient for empirical theory, 'experience' in the richest sense: empirical theory must represent not only the sheer existence of substance(s) in causal interaction, but many types of individuals obeying many different causal laws. These individuals can be organized into an elegant and perspicacious taxonomy. The laws too can be hierarchically arranged so that more general laws (e.g. Newton's) subsume more specific laws (e.g. Kepler's). Nothing in the first *Critique* demands that this be so. For all we know, we might find that a certain degree of messiness in natural science cannot be overcome (*CJ*, Ak. v. 183, 185/Ak. xx. 209–10, 212). If we fail to assume that messiness in nature is merely apparent, Kant thinks we will not seek more elegant systematizations of natural science. The conviction that such messiness is merely apparent is a transcendental principle:

it is a condition of the possibility of natural science (*CJ*, Ak. v. 185/Ak. xx. 213–15).

So the principle he finds is merely the heuristic: nature is as if designed to be comprehended by human cognition. This principle does not legislate to nature, thus guaranteeing that nature will have this characteristic, rather, it legislates to cognition, requiring that cognition seek what design-like order it can find (*CJ*, Ak. v. 185–6). It may be helpful to the reader to call to mind here Daniel Dennett's notion of the intentional and design 'stances'. For what Kant is claiming here is that approaching nature from the design stance is a prerequisite of doing natural science at all. It is not that we must regard the world as having some discernible purpose apart from our cognitive interests: rather, we must regard the world as designed to serve our cognitive interests (*CJ*, Ak. v. 186/Ak. xx. 216). Kant is not saying that it *is* so designed. This is merely the *stance* we must take toward it if we wish to grasp what order there is in it.

This principle is reminiscent of Kant's ethics in two respects. First, it represents a form of self-regulation analogous to the categorical imperative. Second, in its transcendental aspect, as a condition of the possibility of natural science, it resembles the practical postulates of God's existence and our own immortality. In the second *Critique*, Kant argued that we need to have practical faith that our moral efforts will succeed to be sufficiently motivated to pursue them. The truth of such postulates, however, is in no way guaranteed. Similarly, the transcendental principle of judgement merely provides a motivation to seek systematicity in nature without in any way guaranteeing that it will be found.

Thus we can see in what sense judgement, like reason and the understanding, contains *a priori* principles. However, just as the higher faculties of cognition all have their *a priori* aspect, so too should the three basic functions, cognition, desire, and feeling, be regulated by the same. In what sense, then, does judgement relate to the feeling of pleasure (and pain)? The short answer will be that pleasure arises when a faculty satisfies its function; with judgement, the discovery of design-like properties in the objects of experience and their relations to each other produces its satisfaction: this is the occasion for pleasure (*CJ*, Ak. v. 184, 187).

But if this is the connection between pleasure and judgement, in what way is this specific to judgement? There are many different faculties—why do they not all give rise to the feeling of pleasure upon satisfying their functions? With the other cognitive faculties, Kant's answer is that without some resistance, without some possibility of failure, the feeling of pleasure (or pain) cannot arise; but with the understanding, which legislates to cognition, there is no possibility of failure, and hence no resistance, no overcoming of resistance and no pleasure (*CJ*, Ak. v. 187). Judgement, by contrast, has a function (find and subsume; seek evidence of design) which is not guaranteed of success. For while the failure of the understanding to perform its function would lead to the absence of experience, and hence we could not experience its failure, judgement *can* fail, and be experienced to fail. The order it seeks is, from its own perspective, contingent and in no way guaranteed.

But then what of desire? It is patent that the satisfaction of ordinary desires leads to pleasure (*CJ*, Ak. xx. 206). Kant also allows that though pleasure cannot serve as a motive for moral action, pleasure does follow on the knowledge that one has comported oneself morally (*CJ*, Ak. xx. 206–7). Here, the possibility of failure, resistance, and success all are present; practical reason is hardly guaranteed of discharging its function, 'holy wills' excepted.

These anomalies are not oversights. Rather, they are points Kant himself stresses when he discusses the difficult notion of 'transition' in locating the third *Critique* within the Critical edifice (*CJ*, Ak. v. 196). Judgement is connected to the feeling of pleasure, thus linking it with the faculty of desire, and to the search for hierarchical order in nature, thus linking it with the faculty of cognition. This is what induces Kant to speak of the third *Critique* as a 'transition' between the first and the second. I suspect that this notion of transition was important to Kant not simply because it was an appealing formal pattern in his thought. Beyond that, it revealed the possibility of an underlying *unity*: a unity in the world between phenomenal nature and the noumenal domain of freedom, and a unity in human nature between the various faculties. This unity was obscured by his previously sharp distinction between theory and practice. There is more than a hint that the underlying unity that makes this 'transition' possible is God (*CJ*, Ak. v. 196). Excluding the God of rational theology from the Critical system leaves cognition with nothing to do but natural science. Nonetheless, an *intimation* of the divine is suggested by judgement's inescapable demand that nature, constructed by the understanding, form an as-if-designed system. Yet this undiscussable source of design must surely be identified with the God postulated by practical reason. Again, we cannot know there is a God, but we must posit one, lest we despair of realizing the moral law within the phenomenal world. Perhaps more important is the hint Schiller detected in the third *Critique* that Kant had moved beyond the unhappy, bifurcated philosophical anthropology implied by the first two *Critiques*. Previously pleasure, while connected with our natural selves, played no role in our understanding of nature, and while connected to our agency, served to disrupt our moral vocation. The third *Critique*, however, brings a new dignity to pleasure by the role it plays in aesthetic judgement. Aesthetic judgement, in turn, possesses an intersubjective validity reminiscent of the moral law, and finds its most suitable object in the contemplation of nature. What is more, for Kant, the experience of aesthetic pleasure is due to a felt 'harmony' between the faculties. Inner war has given way to inner concord. At heart we are beings capable not only of joy, but of a 'higher' joy that embraces and incorporates our seemingly divided status as knowers and agents: we are 'aesthetic' beings (*CJ*, Ak. v. 344, 353).

Aesthetic judgement

The activities of judgement produce pleasure as a side-effect, much as the activities of practical reason produce pleasure as a side-effect. Pleasure follows on finding design-like order in nature, whether this be discovering an elegant taxonomy, subsuming a specific natural law under a more general one, or grasping the design of an organism. However, there is another kind of pleasure which is different. For whereas these preceding pleasures are all 'side-effects', another kind of pleasure cannot be conceived as a side-effect of any other ulterior purpose, cognitive or practical. And this is, of course, aesthetic pleasure.[8]

The problem, again, was to discover a sense in which judgement legislates to pleasure.[9] Judgement is related to pleasure because when it fulfils its cognitive function of discovering order of a certain sort, it produces pleasure as a side-effect. However, judgement does not 'legislate' to pleasure in the exclusive sense that we can say that reason legislates to desire or the understanding legislates to cognition. For the relationship between judgement and pleasure to be legislative, judgement's activities must produce pleasure *autonomously*, and not as the side-effect of achieving another cognitive or practical aim.

---

[8] Kant discusses cognitive pleasure at *CJ*, Ak. v. 187. He differentiates aesthetic pleasure from practical pleasure at *CJ*, Ak. v. 203–11.

[9] Kant characterizes the experience of the beautiful as a 'free play' between the imagination and understanding (*CJ*, Ak. v. 287). This is quite apt, once we see the role these faculties play in its genesis. However, talk of 'free play' may lead one to believe that it is inappropriate to characterize any faculty as 'legislating' to pleasure. My point, however, is that the involvement of judgement in the genesis of aesthetic experience suggests that there are higher and lower forms of pleasure. Judgement discriminates between these. This legislation does not resemble the legislation of the understanding, where illegality is impossible. Rather it resembles the legislation of practical reason, which demands that actions take a particular form, though there is no guarantee that they will.

The First Reading

Aesthetic pleasure, however, satisfies this condition. As we shall see, judgement's involvement in aesthetic contemplation has no ulterior purpose at all. Thus the pleasure that emerges from aesthetic experience cannot be said to be a side-effect—in this sense, it is entirely autonomous.

The yield for Kant's aesthetics comes not from the fruitfulness of his accounts of the different forms of aesthetic experience, let alone in criticism of specific art works. Kant's primary concern, beyond the architectonic issues outlined above, is to secure the intersubjective validity of aesthetic judgements (*CJ*, Ak. v. 288). Once other means of generating pleasure (satisfying preferences, discovering order in nature, obeying the moral law) have been removed, what remains is the pleasurable effect objects have on us by virtue of the mind's transcendental structure: that we synthesize data under forms of intuition and the categories to produce experience and well-formed, meaningful judgements about them. But having this structure is a necessary condition of the possibility of experience. All experiencers who confront the objects in question, by virtue of being experiencers, will feel pleasure. This is because those who would be justified in dissenting would be only non-experiencers, and there cannot be dissenting non-experiencers. Therefore the judgement that 'this object, by virtue of its design, necessarily produces pleasure in experiencers' is intersubjectively valid. This is all that saying 'this object is beautiful' comes to for Kant. Of course, this account of intersubjective validity depends crucially upon his account in the first *Critique* of the cognition of empirical objects. However, we must defer a detailed discussion of this to Chapter 5.

There is a possible difficulty in basing an account of aesthetic experience in the third *Critique* on the more basic account of experience in the first *Critique*. In the third *Critique*, Kant seems to characterize aesthetic experience as a *defective* product of the experience-generating process, one in which concepts do not play a role (*CJ*, Ak. v. 226–31). This is linked to Kant's claim that aesthetic judgements, being reflective, involve not the application of a concept, but rather the search for one (*CJ*, Ak. v. 179). This means that, at the very least, the final phase, in which conceptual contents are descried in the object, cannot occur—perhaps even that the entire process of imposing syntactic form on experience and thought does not occur. Yet Kant argues in the first *Critique's* Transcendental Deduction that such a process is a condition of the possibility of experience.

Paul Guyer has proposed that this difficulty can be resolved by distinguishing between the psychological and the epistemological aspects of the Transcendental Deduction.[10] But I think that we need not employ this distinc-

---

[10] Guyer, *Kant and the Claims of Taste*, 85–8.

tion here, for two reasons. First, on my view, the process by which the understanding legislates to the imagination is *not* necessary for consciousness. Only the process by which the imagination produces spatiotemporal phenomena is minimally necessary. Rather, the legislation of the understanding is only necessary for judgeable experience, consciousness of unified empirical objects, embedded in states of affairs or facts, and ready to be represented in the language of thought. What I would characterize as animal consciousness is still in principle available to human beings. So one possible claim Kant might be making is that aesthetic experience is subconceptual and animal-like.

This is unlikely to be what Kant has in mind. For rather than characterizing the imagination as entirely free of any relationship with the understanding, Kant speaks of a 'free play' between them, a 'harmony of the faculties'. This relationship resembles, but is significantly different from, the one that obtains when the understanding legislates to the imagination in ordinary human experience (*CJ*, Ak. v. 287). Rather, I think we must interpret aesthetic experience as analogous to a process of what Kant calls 'recognition' gone wrong (*CPR*, A 103–10). Each faculty is doing its job, but when the time comes to plug in the relevant expressions to complete the representation of the object, these expressions are missing. It is as if they were 'on the tip of one's tongue'. This does not mean that syntactical elements or empirical concepts are entirely absent, but that they are unable to play their normal role in generating complete experiences and thoughts. The process of experience-generation culminates in a penultimate stage in which the object is ready to be 'recognized' and subsumed under some class. In ordinary cases, this happens readily enough, and the result is a determinative judgement about the object. In the aesthetic case, however, no class concept is readily available to subsume the object under. Metaphorically speaking, the mind scans the object, in response to intimations of patternedness in it, seeking its unifying design. This design, once grasped, should yield the concept under which the object is to be subsumed. But this attempt fails, with the consequence that judgement cannot be made. If that were all, then a faculty would have failed to discharge its function, and the result would be pain, not pleasure. However, the persistent intimation of unifying design, however elusive, holds the faculty of judgement in suspense, preventing it from abandoning the object as an uninterpretable chaos (*CJ*, Ak. v. 220–1, 279). Rather, the faculty of judgement reflects on its own state and judges that it can't help but feel that there is a unifying design to the object.[11]

[11] My interpretation suggests that aesthetic experience happens by accident in cognitive contexts. But are we more likely to have an aesthetic experience after a day of frustration at the laboratory than when we are in the museum? While I do think that aesthetic experiences can take us by surprise in this

The First Reading

This judgement may very well be true enough, even if the mystery of the object persists. But in having produced the reflective judgement, the faculty of judgement has discharged its function of producing judgements, and thus in satisfying its aim, produces a feeling of pleasure (*CJ*, Ak. v. 218). As in Kant's theories generally, this 'processing' takes place off stage, unconsciously. What we as experiencers are conscious of is finding an object beautiful and judging that this is so. An analysis of what judging something beautiful *means* (the Analytic of the Beautiful), coupled with an explanatory theory of how the mind produces such judgements, yields the above account.

This introduces a further problem into Kant's theory of taste. It seems to make bad taste impossible, for if you can experience it, you must experience the beauty of it. Kant himself insists that an aesthetic judgement merely claims that everyone should find an object pleasurable, not that they necessarily will (*CJ*, Ak. v. 214, 216). Kant has available a reply, though it is one which many will no doubt find dissatisfying.

We can conceive of the gap between good and bad taste as analogous to the gap between competence and performance in something like Chomsky's sense. The capacity to make correct aesthetic judgements, on Kant's model, must be inborn, given the way he connects it to the transcendental structure of the mind. But even if the capacities are there, it should be possible to produce a bad performance of aesthetic judgement by introducing 'noise' into the system. This is how Chomsky explains grammatical errors, despite the innateness of grammar: by reference to slips of attention, tiredness, etc. In Kant's case, however, the noise must be limited to only those effects which can allow the continued possibility of experience. This condition is met by the existence of interfering pleasures deriving from cognition or desire (*CJ*, Ak. v. 223–6). Kant focused his attention exclusively on the latter, but parallel points could be made about cognition, and are perhaps more apposite now than in Kant's day. If the prospective aesthetic object pleases because it in some way satisfies my other preferences ('my clients will be impressed by how expensive this work of art was' or 'this painting is a great investment' or in even cruder ways, as with pornography), then I may mistakenly judge the work beautiful. The work might even satisfy the same preferences in everyone. Again we see the parallel

way, another way to bring about aesthetic experience would be to take recognition 'offline' by a gentle act of will. Refusal to recognize could be Kant's version of what it is to *adopt* an aesthetic stance toward an object. Similarly, institutional settings like museums may be aesthetic settings, not by social fiat (as the post-Dadaist 'institutional theory of art' would have it) but rather because these institutions uphold certain norms, perhaps including the norm 'no "recognizing in a concept" encouraged here'.

with Kant's ethics. Similarly, a work of art might give a critic pleasure simply because it represents a great interpretative puzzle. This pleasure might obscure the fact that it is otherwise not very pleasing at all. In both such cases, misapprehending non-aesthetic pleasure as aesthetic pleasure leads to appreciation of bad works—bad taste. Of course, just as the shopkeeper in the *Grounding for the Metaphysics of Morals* gives correct change because it is good business, someone lacking good taste, i.e. lacking the capacity to discriminate between the various sources of pleasure, might accidentally judge a good work good because it incidentally pleases in other ways as well.

This interpretation seems to conflict with the claim that an aesthetic judgement does not guarantee that a spectator will take pleasure in an object, but merely that she should. Kant's point there is that the normative claim is part of what is meant in making an aesthetic claim. The aesthetic claim might be false for all that. Then there might very well be others who do not react to the object with pleasure, lacking the interested grounds for doing so.

The problem with this theory is that while it may account for some types of bad taste, surely it cannot account for all. It places too much of the burden of aesthetic competence on an ability to ignore irrelevant pleasures (*CJ*, Ak. v. 294). The real difference between good and bad taste (whatever epistemological status it may have) is surely bound up with the capacity to acquire complex sensitivities and discriminatory capacities that must be learned like any other skill. Those with bad taste are not so much self-indulgent as blind.

The damage done to Kant's theory by rejecting his account of bad taste is dramatic, but not complete. In effect, good taste can only be partially accounted for by Kantian mechanisms; the remainder will be due to other contingent (probably social) factors. This means that the grounding of intersubjective validity on transcendental conditions is unsuccessful, and a certain measure of aesthetic relativity unavoidable. However, this need not mean that the explanatory job of the theory must be abandoned because it proves unable to carry the epistemological burden placed on it. In the appropriate cultural contexts, appealing to Kantian mechanisms might still be illuminating in the interpretation of aesthetic experience.

Kant's aesthetics is complicated by the fact that he distinguishes two basic types of aesthetic experience: the beautiful and the sublime. His analysis of the latter differs from the former in many respects. The sublime, in turn, is further subdivided into the mathematical sublime and the dynamical sublime. The sublime differs from the beautiful in being 'counterpurposive' and involving feelings of pain that are bound up with and lead to an ultimate sensation of pleasure. As such, they require a different analysis, albeit one which shows that they are also reflective judgements.

The mathematical sublime can be treated quickly, as it will not play a significant role in Nietzsche's aesthetics in *Birth of Tragedy*. The mathematical sublime is 'mathematical' because the aesthetic effect is primarily achieved by the impression of immense magnitude. Kant's explanation for the effect of such experiences parallels his explanation of beauty. With the beautiful, the imagination and understanding collaborate much as they do in the generation of ordinary experiences and our judgements about them. With the mathematical sublime, the imagination and reason collaborate much as they do in reason's theoretical employment (*CJ*, Ak. v. 256, 258). It may seem peculiar to invoke *reason* in this context. Kant's theoretical reason is no mere regulator of inference. In the first *Critique* reason is also involved in satisfying other cognitive desiderata of theory, especially the desideratum of *completeness*. This can lead to various pathologies of the intellect described in the chapter 'The Antinomy of Pure Reason'. These pathologies all involve attempts to conceive of infinite or infinitesimal magnitudes as *completed* totalities, which Kant believes to be incoherent. Kant claims that with the mathematical sublime, the object presented to sense is too large to be circumscribed as a manageable object; theoretical reason, with its interest in completeness, attempts to regard it as a perceptible yet infinite totality to be circumscribed (*CJ*, Ak. v. 254–5). Reason fails in its attempt to legislate to the imagination that the object is to be represented as both perceptible and yet also infinite. As a result the object presents itself to us as finite but 'too big' (or in Kant's expression, 'absolutely large' (*CJ*, Ak. v. 248)). Again we have an operation analogous to cognition, but one in which no cognitive goal vis-à-vis the object is achieved. This the mind experiences as pain (*CJ*, Ak. v. 257).

The pain, however, becomes transmuted into pleasure, for when I reflect upon my own states, the very awareness of failure to master the object produces an awareness of reason itself, and the way that it is designed to introduce unity and completeness into my experiences (*CJ*, Ak. v. 257–8). Felt awareness of my own reason's design, then, occupies the same place that awareness of the design of the object occupied with the beautiful. Again, awareness of design produces pleasure occasioned by the object. This pleasure is expressed in a reflective judgement about my own faculties' relations to each other in the presence of the object. But the judgement appears to be about the object itself, as in 'the Grand Canyon is sublime'. This recoil from pain to pleasure during reflection is Kant's attempt to make sense of the pleasure involved in the experience of awe. Again, given that in all experiencers, reason and imagination are type-identical, the intersubjective validity of sublimity judgements is assured (*CJ*, Ak. v. 280).[12]

Kant's analysis of the dynamical sublime is, however, very important for our interpretation of Nietzsche. After Nietzsche read the *Critique of Judgement* in 1867–8, his meditation on the difference between the beautiful and the (dynamical) sublime led him to the Apollinian and the Dionysian. As the Dionysian is a crucial component in our experience of tragedy, Nietzsche's likely reading of Kant's account of the dynamical sublime could have inspired his conception of tragedy. And the tragic, for Nietzsche, was not merely a particular form of aesthetic experience, but the vehicle for a kind of wisdom. Since tragic wisdom returns to the centre of Nietzsche's mature thought after a hiatus in his middle period, his encounter with the dynamical sublime takes on a special importance.

As with the mathematical sublime, the faculties involved are reason and the imagination. Here, however, reason is in its practical, not theoretical mode (*CJ*, Ak. v. 247). The data to be synthesized into an experience suggest not great magnitude, but rather great danger (*CJ*, Ak. v. 260). Again, the aesthetic experience can be understood in terms of a normal mental process gone awry: the process of recognizing something as dangerous and acting for one's own self-preservation. Such experiences are 'counterpurposive' for the faculty of desire in the same way that experiences of the seemingly infinite magnitude of certain objects are 'counterpurposive' for cognition. With the dynamical sublime, however, either the spectator occupies a position of safety or the object is a harmless representation of a danger. Consequently the faculty of desire is taken 'offline' and the pseudo-dangerous object or situation can be contemplated (*CJ*,

---

[12] Kant claims that judgements of beauty concern the object—a peculiar claim given his classification of judgements of beauty as reflective. Judgements of sublimity by contrast only concern the subject (*CJ*, Ak. v. 279–80). I dispose of this difficulty below. However, there is another, related difficulty.

In my interpretation of the beautiful and of the sublime, I ascribe the peculiarities of aesthetic experience to a certain form of cognitive failure, ultimately made good by judgement's turn to reflection: the inability of judgement to find the appropriate classification for the object, or the inability of judgement to represent the infinite to itself perceptibly. The pain of cognitive failure is part of Kant's explanation for the negativity involved in awe but not in the beautiful. Still, we should expect some trace of pain to be involved in the apprehension of the beautiful as well. Otherwise, why does cognitive failure produce pain in the one case but not the other?

Arguably, this either speaks against my interpretation of the beautiful, or else against Kant's account of it. However, there *is* an element of 'pain' involved in the experience of the beautiful as well. It manifests itself to us in a sense of the mysteriousness of the beautiful object. Mysteriousness has the advantage of being a recognizable component of at least many aesthetic experiences. We might speculate that it admits of degrees and is subtly present even in cases where it does not seem to be. It is recognizably related to cognitive frustration, on the one hand, and pleasurable fascination, on the other. Kant himself emphasizes that tediousness is incompatible with beauty (*CJ*, Ak. v. 242–3).

Ak. v. 261). The apparent dangerousness of the object is the source of pain; the actual harmlessness of the object neutralizes the propensity towards action by the faculty of desire. When this condition of suspense is then reflected on, it produces pleasure, just as with the mathematical sublime.

Why? Kant's ingenious answer: the experience of being moved to act and not acting (to attack, flee, protect oneself) brings the faculties of imagination and practical reason into a relationship much like when we are torn between the promptings of irrational desire and the dictates of the moral law, and then accede to the law (*CJ*, Ak. v. 262). (Recall that for Kant, the moral law simply is the product of the proper functioning of reason in its practical mode.) Kant's suggestion here depends not on the substance of his moral theory, but on a certain phenomenology of moral experience it is designed to explain. When one is tempted, the law presents itself to consciousness as peremptory and threatening; when one has resolved oneself in favour of the law, the danger the temptation is associated with is neutralized or mastered. If I am poor and tempted to steal, I rise above my fear of the consequences of my poverty when I resolve to eschew theft because it is wrong. I realize that what really matters is being a good person. By contrast, whether one starves or not is insignificant. Thus I raise myself above my own servitude to my desire for food. In this condition, I will then feel invulnerable to merely natural threats, and conscious instead of my own absolute freedom. I am not merely a phenomenal creature but also have a foot in the other, noumenal world, where the principles of order are not those of nature but morality. This is why Kant associates the experience of the moral law with freedom. Freedom is not only the presupposition of morality. It is also an experience of a certain invulnerability to nature's vicissitudes (*CJ*, Ak. v. 261–2, 269).

The dynamical sublime, then, simulates the experience of moral temptation and self-overcoming. By so doing, it symbolizes[13] to me my status as a more than natural being. I am a free being possessing not only a certain dignity and value that merely natural objects cannot possess, but also a certain invulnerability. Whatever we may think of the metaphysical, moral, and religious assumptions built into Kant's analysis here, we recognize the experience he describes, at least by proxy. For though it is to be hoped that no readers have experienced, for example, torture for their political convictions, it is the case that many of us are inexplicably inspired by stories of people who have clung to their convictions in the face of political repression, torture, etc.

---

[13] Kant himself does not claim that the sublime symbolizes noumenal freedom. However, he would be within his rights to do so, given the theory of symbolism he offers at *CJ*, Ak. v. 351–4.

and that part of our response, our *pleasure* at the sight of great moral courage, involves an aspiration to transcend the kind of dependency on the whims of nature and others characteristic of dogs, and sadly, of so many human beings as well.

Thus Kant offers a solution to the problem of why a certain aesthetic experience we value, the experience of the sublime, involves pain. While explaining the sublime, Kant shows how the sublime can give us a kind of indirect access to our noumenal nature as free beings (*CJ*, Ak. v. 261–2, 269), again without transgressing the limits placed on cognition in the first *Critique*.

Kant shows how our aesthetic interests, experiences, and sensitivities dovetail and harmonize with both our cognitive and practical interests. For in the experience of the beautiful we are reminded of the 'aesthetic' desiderata cognition brings to bear on its attempts to grasp nature in theory (*CJ*, Ak. v. 186–8/Ak. xx. 213–14), while we experience in the universality of our judgements of taste the possibility of a community of shared feeling for the beautiful whose harmony is analogous to the harmony of a society governed by the moral law (*CJ*, Ak. v. 293–8). In doing this, Kant suggests that at the basis of the complex interplay of our faculties there is an underlying, albeit inexplicable, unity of the self, and a corresponding unity to the natural and moral domains in which the self is embedded. This unity is in one sense already there as a supersensible substrate to the faculties. It also stands before us as a task of culture: to harmonize our cognitive, moral, and aesthetic activities within the phenomenal realm, thus perfecting nature and human nature (*CJ*, Ak. v. 344, 353).

Kant provides us with a quasi-Romantic account of the genius as that individual who brings forth new beautiful and sublime forms creatively. Kant's account of genius transcends the opposition between classicist and Romantic accounts of artistic production. According to classicist accounts, production becomes merely the imitation of pre-given, objective aesthetic norms, in which case there can be no creativity. According to Romantic accounts, the artist invents subjective norms along with her new aesthetic objects, rendering the distinction between good and bad taste unintelligible, in which case there can be no beauty. Kant's theory of genius allows that the productions of genius can be radically new, since there are no pre-given standards (if there were, aesthetic judgement would be determinative). Yet it also allows that these objects, once produced, serve as the objects of reflective judging and can be assessed by the nature of the pleasures they produce, thus preserving the idea of standards (*CJ*, Ak. v. 307–20).

Finally, the third *Critique* grounds all these claims on a vision of the supersensible as an understanding whose relation to nature is the same as ours, but whose intuition is active and intellectual instead of passive and sensible.[14] As moral agents who are also the beings responsible for nature, we are given reasonable assurance that human ends, as far as they are moral, are realizable within nature. Human beings, because they are moral agents, possess infinite worth. Therefore nature as a system can be conceived as designed to provide a site for the realization of human aims, again, as far as they are moral. Such a vision raises the problem of evil in a particularly acute form. Kant proposes that the suffering imposed by nature and immorality be understood as means for developing human capacities over time. Thus not only does nature prove to have a meaning; history too is given a narrative structure in which the evils of nature continually challenge us to cultivate ever more powerful science and technology, while the evils of human misconduct continually challenge us to devise ever more adequate social and political arrangements (*CJ*, Ak. v. 425–36).[15]

The unity of the concept of reflective judgement

Kant's *Critique of Judgement* has long been regarded as a central text in classical modern aesthetics. However, the text, as is well known, contains two parts, a discussion of aesthetic judgement and a discussion of teleological judgement. Many readers of Kant have concluded that the latter half's concern with questions of divine design have been rendered otiose in the wake of Darwin. They have chosen to appreciate the third *Critique* more as a torso than as a full figure.

This reading is at odds with Kant's intentions. The third *Critique* was meant to establish the scope and limits of a single function, judgement, which manifests itself in four different 'products': theoretical judgements, moral judgements, aesthetic judgements, and teleological judgements. The first two types of what Kant calls 'determinative' judgements are, in his view, adequately dealt with by the first and second *Critiques* respectively. However, it later dawned on Kant that there is a further genus, 'reflective judgements', of which

[14] Given the affinities between Kant's account of the relationship between nature and the mind as I have interpreted it, and Berkeleian idealism, it should come as no surprise that the relationship between God and nature should prove, on my interpretation, to be broadly Berkeleian as well. Once we cut through the thickets of Kantian terminology, the picture that emerges is that the thing-in-itself (the data source) which is the substrate of empirical objects is, in the end, God.

[15] Kant's attempt at historical theodicy in the third *Critique* and in the essays 'Idea of a Universal History' and 'Perpetual Peace' influenced Hegel. Hegel also attempts in his lectures to develop a narrative account of history as the unfolding of freedom over time. Hegel, of course, rejected Kant's claim that the endpoint of history would be the creation of international political institutions.

aesthetic and teleological judgements form the sole species. When we read the work as a torso of aesthetics, we fail to fully come to grips with Kant's systematic intentions, not only for the *Critique of Judgement*, but for the Critical edifice as a whole. To the extent that Kant's account of the judgement of taste depends upon his more general claims about the nature of judgement, we fail to apprehend the contours of Kant's aesthetics when we ignore its larger context.

That said, an attempt to read the work as a whole has come up against considerable difficulties. To be blunt, the various accounts of reflective judgement, and the applications Kant makes of the notion, appear incoherent. Worse, the very distinction between reflective and determinative judgements is itself a shaky one, often seeming to break down on closer inspection. The difficulty is ultimately the difficulty that seems to infect all of Kant's philosophy—the systematic ambiguity that seems to attach to the notion of transcendental idealism. Kant wants to hold that we can distinguish between claims that are subjective and those that are 'objectively valid'. Yet he wants to maintain that the latter are not absolutely valid but merely 'ideal', merely valid for us. This apparent ambiguity is expressed by the first *Critique's* fourfold distinction between the empirically real, the empirically ideal, the transcendentally real, and transcendentally ideal. A similar difficulty attends the Kantian distinction between theoretically and practically valid claims. The claims of transcendental philosophy, mathematics, and physics are theoretically valid. Other claims, like the belief in immortality or a moral God, possess merely 'practical' validity, as discussed in the second *Critique*.

Objectivity cannot be secured by correspondence to things in themselves. One way then to make sense of Kant's distinction between subjective and objective is to suggest that objective validity is something like universal, necessary, and intersubjective validity.[16] This notion of objectivity introduces considerable difficulties for making sense of the distinction between reflective judgements and determinative judgements. For Kant seems to wish to draw a distinction between claims that are objectively valid (determinative judgements) and those that are merely intersubjectively valid (reflective judgements) (*CJ*, Ak. v. 385–9).

Worse, Kant differentiates between the two types of reflective judgements by suggesting that aesthetic judgements are 'subjective' while teleological judgements are 'objective' (*CJ*, Ak. v. 193). Moreover, Kant claims that judgements of taste concern objects in a way that judgements of sublimity do not (*CJ*, Ak. v. 279–80). This seems to imply that there are grades or degrees of objectivity with

---

[16] Kant discusses the notion of intersubjectivity at *CJ*, Ak. v. 293–6.

the various types of judgements occupying various positions on a spectrum thus: judgements of sublimity; judgements of beauty; teleological judgements; theoretical and practical judgements. The basis for this gradation, couched as it is in the language of a sharp contrast between the subjective and objective, proves to be quite elusive. Matters are made almost intractable by Kant's remarks that teleological judgement involves concepts and aesthetic judgement concerns only feeling (*CJ*, Ak. v. 193, 228). On the face of it, a feeling does not seem to be the sort of item appropriately characterized as a type of 'judgement' at all.

As daunting as these difficulties may seem, coherent sense can be made of most of Kant's claims about these various types of judgements. Given Kantian assumptions, there is an overlooked faculty, reflective judgement, which demands its own *Critique*. In what follows, then, I propose that there *is* a cogent, unitary notion of reflective judgement underlying the various claims and implications of Kant's text.[17]

What is it that makes a reflective judgement reflective? On the face of it, one would suppose that it involves in some sense a reflection upon one's own states. Yet both types of reflective judgements involve objects other than our states. Teleological judgements concern objects in the natural world which strike us as resembling designed artefacts (organisms). Aesthetic judgements concern objects which arouse an aesthetic response in us. Yet Kant is quite clear that reflective judgements are not *about* their objects in any straightforward sense.

The text is consistent with the proposal that we read reflective judgements as (a species of) propositional attitude statements. The logical peculiarities of such statements, in particular, failure of substitution, have long been noted in the literature of analytic philosophy. For example, 'Tully was Cicero' and 'Cicero denounced Catiline' entails 'Tully denounced Catiline'. However, 'I

---

[17] From this point I proceed without reliance on previous interpretations of reflective judgement, and my interpretation will no doubt strike the reader familiar with this literature as peculiar. Discussions of reflective judgement divide into three camps. First, there are those who emphasize the 'seeking a missing class' aspect. They see Kant's theory of reflective judgement as a theory of empirical concept formation addressed to the same sorts of questions as Locke's theory of abstract ideas. For an example of this sort of approach, see Hannah Ginsborg, 'Reflective Judgment and Taste', *Nôus*, 24 (1990), 63–78. Second, there are those who emphasize that these are judgements of reflection, judgements *about* one's own mental processes. For an example of this sort of approach, see John H. Zammito, *The Genesis of Kant's Critique of Judgment* (Chicago: University of Chicago, 1992), 64–88. Third, there are those who emphasize the role of feeling in aesthetic judgements. For an example of this sort of approach, see Jean-François Lyotard, *Lessons on the Analytic of the Sublime*, trans. Elizabeth Rottenberg (Palo Alto: Stanford University Press, 1994), 1–49. What I have tried to do, in my analysis, is to do some justice to all these aspects while preserving and clarifying the unity of the notion (i.e. what aesthetic and teleological judgements have in common). However, in the end, the most important part of my analysis is to make sense of the peculiar epistemological status that reflective judgements appear to have (which is especially clear with teleological judgements) of appearing to allow a transgression of the first *Critique's* constraints on judgements vis-à-vis things-in-themselves without actually doing so.

believe that Tully denounced Catiline' and 'Tully was Cicero' does not entail 'I believe that Cicero denounced Catiline'. After all, I might believe that Tully was Augustus, or another person. Failure of substitution is because propositional attitude statements are not, ultimately, about the referents contained within the embedded proposition at all. Rather, they are about the person entertaining the embedded proposition. 'I believe that Tully denounced Catiline' is not primarily about Tully or Catiline. It is about me, in particular, about my beliefs.[18] It has also often been noted that what a person believes may not be something that person is immediately aware of in the way that one is aware of a sensation. What I believe may only become clear to me as I respond to an interlocutor's various eliciting acts. Consider the example of believing that there are at least two camels in Saudi Arabia. I believe it but have never experienced an episode of thinking, 'My goodness, there are at least two camels in Saudi Arabia'. Rather, I assent to the statement if asked to. My disposition to assent, which has been present long before I was questioned on the matter, constitutes my belief if anything does. In short, we may have to reflect to discover our cognitive commitments. However, a report on those commitments is not the same thing as a report expressing those commitments. The former is reflective—it is about me. The latter is determinative—it determines the content of what I believe.

So my first suggestion is this: determinative judgements take objects directly and make assertions about them, whereas reflective judgements embed reference to their objects in propositions, and take the subject related to the proposition as the topic of assertion. Such a reading makes sense of what Kant says about teleological judgements, which contain reference to, while not making straightforward assertions about, organisms. However, Kant needs more than failure of substitution. Consider the statement, spoken by Bob, 'I think that the lung is for absorbing phlogiston', and the statement, spoken by Sally, 'I think that the lung is for absorbing oxygen'. Both statements, as far as they accurately reflect the respective speakers' beliefs, are true and thus do not conflict with each other. How are we to capture the implied demand for intersubjective consensus that Kant clearly intends a reflective judgement to entail, without transforming it into a determinative judgement about lungs? The problem, of course, is that Kant believes that functional claims about organisms, if read determinatively, must be read as claims about the intentions of nature's designer. This must be, for Kant, inscrutable.

This is why Kant introduces 'necessity'. Recall that for Kant the mind is not merely a passive recipient of data which might have been otherwise. Nor is the

---

[18] The example is taken from W. V. O. Quine, *Word and Object* (Cambridge, MA: MIT Press, 1960), 212–16.

mind entirely free to determine its own states. Rather, there are features of how the mind 'processes' its data which are necessary if it is to experience with that data at all. Transcendental conditions on experience, precisely because they are necessary conditions, impose certain characteristics on the experience of all minds. Necessity (established by transcendental argument) guarantees universality.

If one's response to an object is conditioned both by the data it is constructed from and by constraints on cognition that must be satisfied to experience it at all, then one is assured that similar experiencers will respond similarly. Thus, a better approximation of a teleological judgement might look like this: 'I can't help but think that lungs are for absorbing oxygen, given the way minds have to work if they are to experience at all'. The phrase 'can't help but think' is implicit in the assertion by virtue of transcendental conditions. The claim, though referring only to the thoughts in the person doing the asserting, nonetheless implies that all similarly constituted minds can't help but think similarly. Notice how much stronger the assertion has now become. In particular, it can no longer be true unless the felt requirement to respond to the data in a particular way is due, in part, to transcendental conditions. If the speaker is mistaken in this, the claim will prove false. For example, the speaker may have mistaken associative compulsion for transcendental necessity. Thus, teleological judgements are testable, and not merely by reference to how the speaker happens to be thinking. We can disagree in our reflective judgements about objects. We can resolve that disagreement by testing rival claims in light of the data and the known transcendental conditions all experiencers share. Yet such claims, though testable, will remain not, ultimately, about their objects at all. By contrast, objects of inquiry by physicists, though mind-dependent for Kant, can serve as the target of assertions *simpliciter*. 'Bodies fall toward the centre of the earth at 32 ft. per sec. per sec.' is straightforwardly a testable claim about bodies. It is, of course, a further fact about bodies that they are, for Kant, mind-dependent. Nonetheless, assertions about bodies are not assertions about our thoughts. Assertions about organ functions *have to be*, for Kant. For if they were not, they could only be assertions about the relationship between organs, and divine intention. Since we can know nothing about the latter, it would follow that we could know nothing about the former, and there would be no science of biology (*CJ*, Ak. v. 360–1). On this basis, we could say that the deep structure of a teleological judgement is:

[I] { [can't help but] [think that] ([this] [is designed to be synthesized as a unity]) }

The content of the curly brackets is predicated of the subject 'I'—it is this which makes the judgement *reflective*. The contents of the parenthesis give us the proposition which, if it were to stand alone as a determinative judgement, would transgress the boundary separating the sensible from the supersensible. This would render the claim's truth-value unknowable. 'Can't help but' expresses the element of transcendental necessity which must be the partial source of the judgement's truth. 'Think that' shows the faculty, cognition, the reflective judgement is reporting about. 'This' refers to the sensible object the judgement *seems* to predicate design-related properties to (though it does not).

At this point, an obvious objection would have occurred to the careful reader who knows the third *Critique*. The analysis offered above is fine for teleological judgements. Kant scholars often claim that Kantian reflective judgement was inspired by Kantian teleological judgement. But the entire notion of a reflective judgement collapses when we try to adapt the judgement of taste to this scheme. For judgements of taste, Kant claims, are 'subjective' while judgements concerning teleology are 'objective'. This distinction is impossible to make if the common denominator of reflective judgements is to be about the subject making the judgement, and if the validity of such judgements is underwritten by universal, intersubjective features of the mind's activities. Both aesthetics and teleology are 'subjective' for the former reason and 'objective' for the latter reason. Even worse, we have statements by Kant suggesting that teleological judgements involve concepts, whereas aesthetic judgements are concerned merely with our feelings. It is tempting to think that aesthetics concerns, so to say, intersubjectively valid feelings. Thus it does not, strictly speaking, involve judgement (since judgements must deploy concepts and combine them predicatively) at all.

Kant's terminological thicket has bogged him down unnecessarily. The distinction he wishes to make between the two species of reflective judgements is tolerably clear. It is not the epistemic status of the two types of judgement that distiguishes them. What distinguishes them is which faculty produces an inner state used by judgement. This state, then, is the 'object' which the judgement asserts something about. According to the Introductions, there are three broad faculties or functions of the mind: cognition, desire, and the feeling of pleasure or pain. Kant tells us that the third *Critique* concerns this third faculty, the other two having been handled adequately by the first and second *Critiques*. What I propose is that we analyse the judgement of taste as follows:

[I] { [can't help but] [feel that] ([this] [is designed to be synthesized as a unity]) }

The suggestion that we are dealing with two species of a common genus is brought out by the remarkable similarity of the two types of judgement-structure. The only difference is that the faculty of feeling occupies the position which the faculty of cognition occupied in the analysis of teleological judgements. The difficulty involved in Kant's claim that teleological judge-ments involve thought, whereas aesthetic judgements only involve feeling, is dissolved. Both kinds of judgements are thoughts, of course. How could a Kantian judgement be anything *but* a thought? The former, however, is a thought about my thoughts. The latter is a thought about my feelings.[19] This structure also allows us to preserve all the features of teleological judgements that made us wish to take them as paradigms of reflective judgements more generally. We see analogous features in the aesthetic judgement. The aesthet-ic judgement, too, is not about the aesthetic object, but rather about myself. Nonetheless, the aesthetic judgement is testable in relation to the object. The involvement of transcendental conditions rules out aesthetic claims owing to 'interested' pleasure, for such pleasure is due to contingent, non-transcenden-tal features of the appreciative subject. A merely personal association between the object and some former pleasurable experience would not serve as the basis for a judgement of taste.[20] Thus, the intersubjective validity of aesthetic judgement is captured as well. Finally, we get a sense of what formal features within the object are responsible for aesthetic pleasure: the intimation of designedness (*Zweckmäßigkeit*),[21] as opposed to mere order—order that pre-sents itself as if it were intentional.

It is the intimation of design that distinguishes Kant's aesthetic theory from a purely formalist one. This also explains why Kant, after discussing the har-monious functioning of the imagination and the understanding in the Deduction of Aesthetic Judgement, goes on to invoke the supersensible in the Dialectic of Aesthetic Judgement (*CJ*, Ak. v. 339–47). For it is not merely form,

---

[19] This interpretation may seem to contradict Kant's claim at *CJ*, Ak. v. 218 that in aesthetic judge-ments, judging precedes the feeling of pleasure. However, given our model of aesthetic judgement above, the conflict is only apparent. First, the mind seeks a concept to subsume the perceptual mani-fold: this is the judging that precedes pleasure. This attempt, given the formal properties of the object, produces pleasure. Subsequently, we report on this process that, in the face of this object, I cannot help but feel pleasure.

[20] Matters are more complex if the association is to another art work that gives pleasure because of the right transcendental conditions. Think of a painting of a Roman scene I enjoy because it brings to mind my recent Roman vacation.

[21] Throughout my discussion of Kant's third *Critique* and Nietzsche's reading of it, I translate '*Zweckmäßigkeit*' idiosyncratically as 'designedness'. I also strive consistently to render all related expressions involving '*Zweck*' with expressions involving 'design'. This is admittedly peculiar: '*Zweck*' is closer to 'purpose' while '*Absicht*' is closer to 'design'. I am deliberately exploiting an ambiguity here that I believe is more evident in Kant's text than in the standard English translations. One way to express the notion of something done intentionally is to say that it was done 'by design'. Yet we also use the expression 'design' to refer to the structure of something, without explicitly conjuring up the presence of intention. Thus 'designedness' captures both the quasi-formalist character of Kantian aes-thetics, while reminding us of the quasi-intentionalist aspect as well. Of course, the allusion to 'the Argument from Design' is quite deliberate.

but *designlike* form that provokes the response of the faculties; to descry design-like properties in the object necessarily involves a reference to a designer, even if a bracketed reference. Guyer's interpretation, by contrast, eliminates the reference to intimations of design from his account. This renders the discussion of the supersensible otiose and the concept of reflective judgement as encompassing both aesthetic and teleological judgement inexplicable. My interpretation avoids these difficulties.

Notice that just as we need not identify any genuine divine intentions in identifying the function of a body organ, we need not rely on an actual artist's intentions in clarifying the meaning of a particular art work. Appeal to intentions as fictions may be inescapable, as when we speak of the 'message' of a novel without committing ourselves to it being the *author's* message.

What are we to make of Kant's claim that judgements of sublimity are more subjective in some sense than judgements of beauty (*CJ*, Ak. v. 279–80)? The key, I believe, lies in the nature of the embedded proposition. For whereas the judgement that this is beautiful has, on my reading, the underlying form:

[I] { [can't help but] [feel that] ([this] [is designed to be synthesized as a unity]) }

The judgement that this is sublime has a *double* reference to the subject, thus:

[I] { [can't help but] [feel that] ([I] [am designed to be synthesized as a unity]) }

Kant's claim that beauty is 'objective' whereas sublimity is 'subjective' is preserved by noting that with the beautiful, it is the object about which we have intimations of designedness. With the sublime, it is the subject about which we have these intimations.

One remaining difficulty confronts our interpretation. I have substituted a reference to *cognition* and *feeling* for Kant's reference to *objective* and *subjective* reflective judgements. This avoids the difficulty of speaking of subjective–objective judgements and subjective–subjective judgements; reflective judgements are all 'subjective' by representing my mental states, but only some concern my feelings. Kant tells us that there are two broad types of reflective judgement, teleological judgements and aesthetic judgements. One version of the distinction between objective and subjective seems to correspond to the distinction between teleological and aesthetic. However, if we follow my reconstruction, there ought to be, not two, but three broad types of reflective judgement. There are not two, but three basic faculties in the third *Critique*'s architectonic: cognition, desire, and the feeling of pleasure and pain. If my reconstruction is correct, Kant has overlooked the demand symmetry makes on him to discover a third type of reflective judgement: the reflective judgement of desire. Desires that are in some sense obligatory for me, desires I must have, form the cornerstone of Kant's ethics. However, Kant makes it clear that ethical judgements are determinative, not reflective. Furthermore, reflective judgements appear on the surface to make an assertion about an object, not a command to act in a certain way. Now one possible response to this 'demand for symmetry' is to insist that it need not always be met. After all, Kant's division of judgements into analytic or synthetic, and *a priori* or *a posteriori*, does not yield the four types that symmetry would demand: there is no such thing as the analytic *a posteriori*.

Is there anything in Kant's writings reminiscent of such a reflective judgement of desire? In the second *Critique*, Kant argues that practical reason allows us to commit ourselves in some sense to assertions that we are not licensed to believe on theoretical grounds. Not only are we allowed to commit ourselves, for example, to the existence of God and the immortality of the soul. We are positively required, as moral agents, to so commit ourselves (*CPrR*, Ak. v. 124–48; Kant repeats the discussion at *CJ*, Ak. v. 442–61). Yet it is awkward for Kant to regard such commitments as cognitive commitments. For if I unconditionally ought to believe them, then it would appear that I am unconditionally justified in regarding them as true. If the moral law genuinely binds me, and it follows that there is a God, then we should be able to assert without qualification that there is a God. But this interpretation clearly does not capture Kant's intentions, for practical faith is not supposed to amount to knowledge.

A reflective judgement of desire might seem to capture what Kant has in mind here. Wanting something to be true does not make it so. We say that people ought not to believe something simply because they very much want it to be true. However, if we can't help but want some proposition to be true, and it is at least possibly true, are we not entitled to believe it? As long as it did our cognitive interests no harm, while furthering our practical interests, it would seem so.

These considerations help to show that the idea of reflective judgement has its origins, initially, in Kant's thought, in the notion of practical faith in the second *Critique*. That Kant chose not to re-baptize practical postulates as a third form of reflective judgement was no oversight, however. For though a reflective judgement always represents the subject's own states, there must be, embedded within the entertained proposition, some 'this' which is to be synthesized as a unity from data. What data could we possibly be presented with which, if synthesized, would yield an intuition of ourselves as immortal? In reflective judgement, the 'this', whether it is the object (teleological judgements and judgements of taste) or the subject (judgements of sublimity) is always that which is designed. The practical postulate that there is a moral God, by contrast, concerns a designer. Reflective judgements all point to, allude to, a designing God; but none ever speak his name. However, we have strayed beyond the confines of the text as it has been given to us. We must reluctantly conclude that the reflective judgement of desire, like the analytic *a posteriori* judgement, is an empty cage in the Kantian zoo.

Kant had good reasons to claim that reflective judgement demanded its own *Critique*. His claim that there was a structural similarity between aesthetic claims and teleological claims is plausible. This similarity vindicates Kant's claim for an overarching unity to the third *Critique*. Kant's seemingly free attributions of 'subjectivity' and 'objectivity' to different types of judgement does *not* rest on a mass of confusions. Rather, it reveals a quite complex, nuanced, and plausible account of the different ways we can judge and their objectivity.

Teleological judgement

Having set up the similarities and differences between beauty, sublimity, and teleology, we can now present Kant's theory of teleological judgement. My purpose is to set up a transition to Nietzsche's reading of the third *Critique* out of his desire to resolve difficulties in his own conception of teleology. However, a word should be said about the contemporary status of Kant's theory.

A superficial reading of the 'Critique of Teleological Judgement' might lead one to conclude that Kant is retracting his earlier repudiation of 'physico-theology' in the first *Critique*. There, Kant had argued that empirical facts might very well suggest the idea of a Designer or Architect of the world. This would suggest that the Deity is the noumenal cause of the phenomenal realm. However, such reasoning depends upon previously establishing that what lies in the noumenal realm is the sole necessary and sufficient condition of the phenomenal realm. That cannot be established by any means other than the successful deployment of the Cosmological Argument, an argument which is itself unsound. Yet in the third *Critique*, Kant seems to argue that the existence of organisms or the elegance of the system of nature give us reason to believe there is a God after all. But Kant is *not* retracting his earlier position. To see exactly where Kant's thought stands in the wake of Darwin, we need to get his claims more clearly in view.

Suppose that you are walking down the beach, past some magnificent cliffs. You are suddenly confronted with what looks for all the world like a giant image of the Virgin Mary, carved into the rock. There are many possible continuations of this scenario. One is that, upon showing the site to others, they respond to it as to a Rorschach inkblot. You are thus led to believe that your perception of it was idiosyncratic. If you were to believe despite this that there was religious import in the image, you would be considered self-deceived. Call this the Foolish Believer Scenario. Another possibility is that all who see the image agree that it is indeed an image of the Virgin Mary. In one such scenario, a careful examination of the cliff surface reveals chisel marks and other signs of human labour. Call this the Unproblematic Immanent Design Scenario. Alternatively, a team of geologists confirm beyond any question that the image could not have been produced by natural erosion or by human labour. It is as if, millions of years ago, the parts of the cliff that do not resemble the Virgin Mary simply jumped into the sea, violating all known physical law. Call this the Miraculous Transcendent Design Scenario. Finally, there is the case that would concern Kant: the shape of the cliff face can be entirely accounted for by the forces of erosion—the sea itself has carved this image, entirely according to known laws of hydraulics, erosion, etc. The only problem is: why does the cliff look like the Virgin Mary? Call this the Mysterious Transcendent Design Scenario.

A Deist could argue that God had established the initial conditions of the universe, and the relevant physical laws, to make this image. Here, we would have two overlapping explanations—one in terms of erosion, and another in terms of God's intentions.

Kant's view is closely related to the Deist view, though his God of course does not appear at the beginning of the universe in time. He is outside the universe and time altogether. For Kant, the intentionalistic explanation, 'God wanted us to see the Virgin Mary', and the mechanistic explanation in terms of hydraulics and erosion, are not competing explanations. They differ in that, for reasons made clear in the first *Critique*, the intentionalistic explanation is forever unconfirmable, since we cannot examine the relationship between the physical universe, stretched out in space and time, and God, who is outside it.

Of course, Kant's theory of teleology is concerned not with mysterious artefacts, but with the functional articulation of organisms. Kant does, on occasion, express scepticism about the competence of mechanics to provide adequate explanations for biological phenomena. However, his claim that there will never be a 'Newton (of a) blade of grass' (*CJ*, Ak. v. 400) rests not on an unwarranted pessimism about the future development of physiology, biochemistry, and molecular biology. Rather, he is claiming that there could never be a reduction of functional claims about body organs to any conjunction of claims in physics or chemistry. This is so even if the latter should prove competent at providing complete explanations on their own terms.[22] Kant's additional scepticism that the sub-biological sciences will provide such explanations is thus beside the point. Why does he think that such functional claims cannot be reduced?

His answer, in brief, is that functional claims involve a tacit reference to normativity. One cannot say what something is for without saying what it is supposed to do. For Kant, normative claims cannot have content independent of the preferences and intentions of agents. There is no fact about what is supposed to happen if there are no agents with preferences; if there were no agents, then there would only be what happens, not what is supposed to happen. To say that something is supposed to happen is to say that it embodies or expresses someone or other's intentions. This is so even with moral obligation, for Kantian morality is nothing more than the form that desire takes when it is rational. If there were no desires, there would be no rational desires. In this sense, the moral order, like the natural order, is constructed from elements immanent to the subject; it is crucial to Kant's anthropocentrism, his 'modernism', to have divested the world of intrinsic purposes, things that are just supposed to happen without reference to our purposes and our freedom to determine them.

Intentions need not have moral significance. When I use a hammer, what makes it a hammer, for Kant, is that I take it up as an agent and use it with certain purposes in mind. I prefer being sheltered, see building a house as a means to that, and see inserting nails into wood as a means to that in turn. My taking up this handled hunk of metal and pounding it makes this thing a hammer with the function of hammering. If, by the blind forces of nature, some metal deposits in the heart of a large rock took a hammer-like form, it would not be a hammer.

All that is clear enough. However, Kant also claims that we have no other concept of function than the concept of something put to a certain use intentionally. The appearance to the contrary is because when we apply functional analysis to non-tools, we suppress reference to the intentions of a designer. Still, our very description of a system in functional terms contains implicit reference to design by virtue of what functional expressions mean. However, when we do this, we may for whatever reason suppress this fact. But even to be able to conceptualize a lung as a respiratory organ we must think in terms of what respiration is for. This requires that we adopt intentionalistic concepts, however bracketed.

---

[22] Of course chemistry was quite undeveloped in Kant's day, which is why he speaks of a Newton of a blade of grass. The point remains untouched, since the relationship between chemistry and physics today is a paradigm of the reduction of one science to another.

The First Reading

What Kant is claiming, then, is that when we say that a lung is for respiration, this claim can only be read in one of three ways. First, it could be read as a shorthand for a long conjunction of things that lungs typically do, expressed in the language of physics (and chemistry). This will not do, however. We will then be unable to capture an important difference between what lungs do when filled with air and what lungs do when filled with water. Second, we could say that claims about lungs' functions are simply claims about God's design intentions. This is unacceptable to Kant, and rightly so, because, as Kant observes, the functions of organs are discoverable, and God's intentions are not.[23] This leaves only one remaining possibility: that functional claims are reflective judgements. If, given the constitution of the human mind, I cannot help but think of the organism as if designed, then I am licensed to say so. I must simply bear in mind that I am only making a report on what, in the face of this object, I can't help but think. Such claims will not be about the object directly, and will enjoy the same epistemic status that aesthetic judgements enjoy: merely intersubjective validity.

Thus we can see that the link between God and biology is not that the latter gives us evidence for the existence of the former. Kant explicitly rejects this (*CJ*, Ak. v. 381, 395–7). It is that the latter is conceptually linked to the former. Where does this leave Kant, in the wake of Darwin? Here I think matters are far more ambiguous than is commonly thought. If Kant is not claiming that true functional claims give evidence of a designing God, then God, not being deployed for explanation in the first place, cannot be displaced by another explanatory posit. When Darwinism claims to supersede physico-theology, this means that it is as if nature, the blind watchmaker, designed organisms, rather than a Deist or Kantian God. Now Kant's response would be that this *is* to make a reflective judgement that organisms, though not literally designed, must be interpreted as if they had been. Kant would disagree with Darwin only in saying that if the phenomenal world is all the world there is, then these Darwinian reflective judgements are useful fictions. Though they would retain their intersubjective validity, they would lose what Kant gives them: the possibility that the embedded claim of designedness is literally true. Instead, a Darwinian functional claim would read: I can't help but think that this is

---

[23] From within a religious framework in which this option seems a live one, this may seem like a strange claim. We can never establish God's intentions by the sorts of means we would employ to discover a human being's intentions, because whereas the behaviour of a human being in relation to its environment is discernible, God's behaviour, if He exists, is not observable, so there is no foothold for interpretation of it to reveal His intentions. The objection that God might express his intentions directly by way of miracles has little attraction for Kant, and it looks like his account of causality, if successful, would preclude the very possibility of a miracle in the traditional sense.

as if designed to be synthesized as a unity, but I know it wasn't. Rather, to displace Kant's analysis of functional claims, we would need a rival, non-intentionalistic analysis. Such may very well be available (though I am sceptical). But the truth of Darwin's theory is irrelevant here.[24]

The tension with Darwin exists at a different level. Kant never meant to suggest that our attitude toward organisms be understood in terms of what I called above a Miraculous Design Scenario. Had that been the case, then further advances in physiology, embryology, genetics, etc. would suffice to demolish any attraction that an appeal to a designing God might have here. Rather, we are to understand the functional articulation of organisms in terms of the Mysterious Design Scenario. Everything is explained, and yet a nagging sense of the inexplicable remains, to be satisfied by rational faith that there is hidden design after all.

However, Darwinism does essentially change the picture that prevailed under Newtonian mechanism. Evolution via natural selection can completely explain the phenomenal facts. A nagging sense of the inexplicable does not license us to have faith that there is hidden design after all. Unlike the Virgin Mary story's Mysterious Design Scenario, post-Darwin, no *mystery* remains. Natural selection is a filter, and the existence of functional articulation is no more mysterious than the existence of coffee in your coffee maker. If we assume a Kantian distinction between phenomena and noumena, it is possible that what appears to us as unintentional is the product of metaphysical conspiracy at another level. There is just no reason to think this.

As we have seen, Kant's account of teleology, and his critically purified physico-theology of the third *Critique* are much more complex and subtle than commonly thought. Darwinism does significantly change how this part of Kant's thought should be received. However, it need not affect his central claim that teleological judgement is essential to biology and that teleological judgements are reflective judgements.

Thus Kant offers a solution to the problem of how we can speak of teleology in a mechanistic world using reflective judgement. Once we have the notion of reflective judgement available, the way is open to make legitimate metaphysical statements about the supersensible without transgressing the limits laid down in the first *Critique* against making determinative judgements about it. Kant claims that it is necessary if we are to have natural science that we do

[24] There are many possibilities here, but I will consider just one. Ruth Millikan provides an ingenious analysis of functional claims that reduces them to claims about a thing's evolutionary history couched in strictly Darwinian terms. However, Kant would regard this not so much as an attempt to explicate functional language as to abandon it. See her *Language, Thought and Other Biological Categories* (Cambridge, MA: MIT Press, 1984), 17–38.

precisely this. This was the transcendental principle of judgement that we must conceive of nature as purposive for cognition.

The message of the *Critique of Judgement*

Kant's third *Critique* is now largely regarded as a text in aesthetics, offering an intersubjectivist alternative to either subjectivist or objectivist theories of taste. It achieved this goal by offering a psychological theory that does not inflate our ontology with aesthetic properties or our epistemology with the capacity to apprehend them. Also, by rooting the pleasures of art in the transcendental structures of the mind, Kant avoids the subjectivist conclusion that art is whatever happens to please. He thus saves the possibility of aesthetic evaluation. But it was meant to be far more than that. For once we piece together its various elements, we can see the contours of a grand metaphysical vision, this 'adventure of reason' as Kant called it. It was a vision that inspired Goethe, Schiller, Schelling, and Hegel. As we shall see in the next chapter, it was a vision that also moved the young Nietzsche, which he creatively appropriated and transformed into the exercise in Romantic theodicy he titled *Birth of Tragedy*.

Early Nietzsche and the *Critique of Judgement*

3

Why Nietzsche read the *Critique of Judgement*

It is sometimes said that, though there are many Kantian themes in Nietzsche, he understood Kant badly, having only read (perhaps only portions of) the *Critique of Judgement*.[1] Three things need to be said here. First, claims that others have not understood Kant well are hostage to one's own interpretation of Kant, and Kant scholarship is a notoriously conflict-ridden area. Second, a more plausible view is that it was Nietzsche's reading of the *Critique of Practical Reason* that was decisive for his understanding (or misunderstanding) of Kant. Nietzsche discusses that work and copies out passages from it several times in the *Nachlaß* of the 1880s. Its impact on the *Genealogy of Morals* is plain: the three discussions of equality, autonomy, and otherworldliness respectively target the Kant of the second *Critique*. Third, one needs to ask: *only* read the *Critique of Judgement*? Only? The third *Critique* is among the most profound of Kant's writings, a view echoed by various twentieth-century figures from Arendt to Lyotard. Kant himself regarded it as crucial to unifying and completing the Critical system, by harmonizing the claims of theoretical and practical thought. Given the importance of the third *Critique* for Schelling and Hegel, it seems that, if anything, a concern with the third *Critique* puts Nietzsche in very good company.

---

[1] Werner Hamacher, 'Das Versprechen der Auslegung. Zum hermeneutischen Imperativ bei Kant und Nietzsche', in Hamacher, *Entferntes Verstehen. Studien zu Philosophie und Literatur von Kant bis Celan* (Frankfurt a.M.: Suhrkamp, 1998), 49–112.

The First Reading

Surprisingly, then, we find that there is almost no discussion of the third *Critique* in the Nietzsche literature, and the following questions remain unanswered. Why did Nietzsche decide to read the *Critique of Judgement* in 1868 and what expectations did he bring to that reading? What was he looking for? What did he find in it? How did his reading of the third *Critique* shape his views in *Birth of Tragedy* and the associated texts of the early period? The early Nietzsche's interest in questions concerning the conditions for a healthy culture, our relationship to the Greeks, and the significance of Wagner are all well documented. However, core philosophical questions in metaphysics, epistemology, ethics, and aesthetics continued to press on him as he developed his responses to these other issues.

Nietzsche read Kant to solve a problem he had squaring his Schopenhauerian commitments of 1865 about teleology with his sudden awareness of Darwinism after reading Lange in 1866. Kant's notion of reflective judgement seemed tailor-made to address this difficulty, but it did more than that. Once Nietzsche approached Kant, reading him through Lange's instead of Schopenhauer's eyes, he discovered a wealth of unexpected material. Kant reinforced Nietzsche's reluctance to join Schopenhauer's dogmatic philosophizing about things-in-themselves; devastating critiques of Schopenhauer's metaphysics appear in the *Nachlaß* just when Nietzsche reads the *Critique of Judgement*.

The third *Critique* also made available to Nietzsche a new, non-Schopenhauerian way to do transcendent metaphysics without transgressing Kantian constraints on determinative judgements. As we saw, reflective judging enables the individual legitimately to commit to claims, including transcendent metaphysical claims, which, though intersubjectively acceptable, are nonetheless not objectively valid. Such claims are ultimately rooted in our aesthetic sensitivity, for the very faculty that enables us to be sensitive to artistic value in objects also enables us to make reflective judgements regarding the functional structure of organisms and the hierarchical structure of the natural world. Kant's transcendental principle of judgement, that we must judge the world to display an elegance satisfying our cognitive interests, is the beginning of the early Nietzsche's conception of the world as a work of art. The embedded claims of reflective judgements are themselves the product of our aesthetic sensitivity. Since they are not asserted any more than the claims of fiction are, we can see here the beginnings of the early Nietzsche's conception of philosophy as edifying myth.

Nietzsche's own edifying myth was that this world is the product of something called the 'Dionysian world-artist'. The myth itself owes more to

Kant's notion of a divine transcendent understanding which projects an empirical world than to Schopenhauer's atheistic cosmology of a mindless 'will' that 'objectifies' itself in phenomena. Both the content of Nietzsche's metaphysics and the epistemology that licenses us to think it are thoroughly Kantian. What is neither Kantian nor Schopenhauerian is Nietzsche's suggestion that the world is *justified* as an aesthetic (as opposed to moral) phenomenon. What has escaped most interpreters of *Birth of Tragedy* is that the key to grasping how the world is justified lies in realizing that the phenomenon is not for *us*. This suggests that the 'theodicy' theme in *Birth of Tragedy* may be meant quite literally. If so, the later Nietzsche's talk of the death of God may not have been so much an axiom for him as a lived experience.

Since this interpretation is a radical departure from the received view of *Birth of Tragedy*, we must do more than document Nietzsche's encounter with the *Critique of Judgement*. The strongest support lies not in the notebooks in which Nietzsche copies out whole passages from the third *Critique* on teleology four years before *Birth of Tragedy* was published. The strongest support comes from the way that Kantian commitments make sense of Nietzsche's early corpus. For in the notes before *Birth of Tragedy*, Nietzsche sceptically rejects Schopenhauer's metaphysics as clearly as he does one year after *Birth of Tragedy*, in *Truth and Lie*. I read the early Nietzsche, not as indecisively careening from scepticism to dogmatic metaphysics and back again, but as consistently holding a unitary view.

The argument will depend upon the new interpretation of the *Critique of Judgement,* which showed the unity of the aesthetic and teleological topics Kant analysed. Aesthetics and teleology fit together for Kant such that organisms, people, and even the world itself become works of art. Nietzsche's debt to Kant is in that area where he seems most un-Kantian: his aestheticism. It is ironic that while Kant looked to aesthetics to integrate the theoretical and the practical, early Nietzsche used aesthetics to incorporate and annihilate them both.

Schopenhauer on teleology

When Nietzsche read Schopenhauer in 1865, he quickly embraced both the metaphysics of the will and the speculative account of teleology that flowed from it. But Nietzsche's early enthusiasm for Schopenhauer's metaphysics soon dimmed, and with it, his ability to make sense of teleology. In 1868, Nietzsche turned to Kant's third *Critique* to make good this loss.

Schopenhauer had accepted Kant's arguments in the Transcendental Aesthetic that space and time are mere forms of intuition. Thus, like Kant, Schopenhauer believed that primary qualities (e.g. shape, extension) as well as secondary qualities (e.g. colours, pains) are mind-dependent. Therefore the physical world, which is in space and time, must also be mind-dependent.

However, also like Kant, Schopenhauer contrasted the *phenomenal* and the *noumenal* domains, the former as the domain in which spatiotemporal predicates are satisfied and the latter where they are not. Like Kant, Schopenhauer believed that the mind organizes its experience further in terms of categories and principles. However, he pared down Kant's profusion of these to causality. We introduce causal connections into our experience, rendering the principle 'every event has a cause' true *a priori*. From space, time, and causality, we then construct material substance and the theories that characterize it. Natural science rests on features of our experience for which we ourselves are responsible. The result of the sum of these operations is the 'world as representation subject to the principle of sufficient reason'. This aspect of the world can be known by a combination of scientific inquiry and transcendental reflection.

For Schopenhauer, as for Kant, human beings tend to regard the 'world as representation' as not merely objective, but as existing independently of the contribution of human cognition. Furthermore, this 'realistic' tendency manifests itself in the inclination to regard the world as representation as all the world there is. On such a view, natural science gives us (at the limits of inquiry) a complete and correct description and explanation of reality. For Schopenhauer, this is a profound mistake, for not only is this aspect of the world mind-dependent, there is still more world beyond our experience to deal with: the world 'uncontaminated' by our cognitive interaction with it, the world as will.

At this juncture we must exercise caution, for there is potential confusion latent in Schopenhauer's use of the appearance/reality contrast. Schopenhauer's frequent reference to the Hindu idea of *Maya* suggests that he identified the epistemological notion of deceptive appearance with the metaphysical notion of mind-dependent appearance:

Now as Kant's separation of the phenomenon from the thing-in-itself, arrived at in the manner previously explained, far surpassed in the profundity and thoughtfulness of its argument all that had ever existed, it was infinitely important in its results. For in it he propounded, quite originally and in an entirely new way, the same truth, found from a new aspect and on a new path, which Plato untiringly repeats, and generally expresses in his language as follows. This world that appears to the senses has no true being, but only a ceaseless becoming; it is, and it also is not; *and its comprehension is not so much a knowledge as an illusion.* (*WWR* i. 419, emphasis mine)

Kant wished to avoid this conclusion:

I am saying, then, that the intuition of external objects and the self-intuition of the mind both present these objects and the mind, in space and in time, as they affect our senses, i.e. as they appear. But I do not mean by this that these objects are a mere *illusion* . . . I am not saying that bodies merely *seem* to be outside me, or that my soul only *seems* to be given in my self-consciousness. (*CPR*, B 69–B 70)

Schopenhauer seems to have identified mind-dependence with error. In this respect, Lange was closer to Kant's epistemic respect for the empirical world. In an important sense, however, Schopenhauer's use of the term 'illusion' is appropriate. If we naively regard the spatiotemporal world as independent of our cognitive contribution to it, and as all the world there is, we do mistake appearance for reality. If I am watching a movie and say 'Leonardo di Caprio is about to drown', my assertion is correct if I understand that it is only a movie. However, if I were hallucinating and believed that Leonardo di Caprio was in my presence the same way the other theatre patrons were, then my statement would be false. In the latter case, it seems as if di Caprio is in front of me, but he really is not. This kind of distinction depends on our ability to make an intelligible contrast like the one I made between di Caprio *qua* movie image and the other theatre patrons. If no such contrast is available, the claim that there is something wrong with believing that di Caprio is in front of me becomes questionable. For Schopenhauer, the intelligibility of the contrast depends on (and is not the source of) an antecedently clear distinction between the phenomenal and the noumenal. The basis for this contrast is the presence or absence of metaphysically mind-dependent features, e.g. spatial extension. The empirical world *qua* representation *is* spatiotemporal, and in its own mind-dependent way, it exists. However, Schopenhauer also believed in a mind-independent reality. From our preceding account of science and its role in describing the phenomenal world, clearly such a non-phenomenal world is not open to scientific description.

Though the noumenal world is mind-independent for Schopenhauer, our access to it is rooted in a certain kind of experience, even if one not mediated by thought or sensibility: the experience of desire. Schopenhauer identifies the character of the noumenal with what it is like to be a desiring being. Thus if there were no desiring beings (and desire is surely a manifestation of mentality) there would be no noumenal realm and no access to it. In this peculiar sense, one could say that, for Schopenhauer, the noumenal is mind-dependent after all. This point was important to him: he thought it immunized him from the objection that his metaphysics and epistemology were pre-Critically dogmatic.

The First Reading

It is a matter of some controversy just how Kant understood the terms 'noumenal' or 'thing-in-itself'. For Kant, reality and possibility are categories, and the very concept of an object is only a rule for synthesis: thus, the notion of a possibly real non-empirical object is of questionable intelligibility. At times he refers to noumena negatively, not as an unknown reality, but as border-concepts, delimiting the limits of empirical knowledge. However, Kant also uses this concept to save the possibility of freedom crucial to ethics from the deterministic commitments he thought so important to natural science. In the Third Antinomy in the first *Critique*, Kant defends a kind of compatibilism, using the noumenal realm as a place to make free will safe from natural law. We can be phenomenally determined, yet noumenally free. Such a use of the concept of the noumenon goes quite beyond the purely negative use that Strawson endorses.[2] For if the point of such a use is to salvage morality, then the concept of the thing-in-itself must possess at least the possibility of being instantiated. Schopenhauer redeploys this positive conception of the noumenal.[3]

Using Kant's solution to the Third Antinomy, Schopenhauer argued that the nature of reality beyond appearances is *will*. First, Schopenhauer endorsed the positive use of the concept of noumena that Kant employed in the solution to the Third Antinomy. Second, Schopenhauer argued that we are introspectively aware of our own agency. It is not that Schopenhauer thought we are introspectively aware of our own freedom, for he did not even think that *qua* individuals we have free will; as individuals we are phenomena, empirical objects subject to the reign of determinism. When we observe the motions of things in the world as representation, we are often able to predict how they will behave, by formulating and testing hypotheses about them. Our own bodies are also things in the world. Yet my belief that I am about to move my arm is not, according to Schopenhauer, empirical knowledge on a par with my beliefs about other physical objects. I know what will happen because it is within my power to bring it about, and I intend to do so. Consequently, with our own bod-

---

[2] Peter Strawson, *The Bounds of Sense* (London: Routledge, 1966), 15–44.

[3] A third strand in Kant's use of the concept of the thing-in-itself is that it is the source of the data from which we construct the phenomenal world. This raises the difficult question: has Kant violated his own restrictions on the proper use of the concept of causality? Nonetheless, it is inevitable that he appeal to something other than the data, from which we receive data. This guarantees that a plurality of experiencers all share a common, even if 'virtual', experience given type-identical transcendental characteristics. If there was only one experiencer, it would suffice to say that there is data in relation to which the subject is passive; the question of where the data came from need not arise. It is only with a larger population that the thing-in-itself becomes inevitable. If this is correct, then despite Nietzsche's late rejection of things-in-themselves, there must be *some* sort of reality to anchor the plurality of experiencers into one world.

ies, we have an additional source of information that is 'internal' in some sense, which we do not have about other physical objects. According to Schopenhauer, our knowledge of our own acts does not involve applying the causal principle to an observed spatiotemporal object; such knowledge is therefore 'not representational'.

Schopenhauer might be right that knowledge of our own intentions differs from empirical knowledge. However the slide from 'not external' to 'not representational' is illicit. For Kant, we have 'inner sense' which enables us to observe datable psychological events such as episodes of thinking or choosing. Presumably, episodes of trying to move my arm would be objects of the inner sense, and thus entirely phenomenal.

Schopenhauer seems to endorse the argument from analogy as the solution to the problem of other minds, though he can also be read as regarding other minds as an indemonstrable but inevitable assumption. In either case, he says that when we observe the bodily movement of other people, we may assume an inner agency is at work in them as well.

Finally, Schopenhauer considered the characteristics of noumena required by his quasi-Kantian commitments. The existence of space and time is the precondition of our capacity to individuate things as separate from each other and as constituting a plurality. But space and time are features of the world as representation. If agency is characteristic of human beings as things-in-themselves, then *qua* things-in-themselves, we are non-spatiotemporal, and therefore cannot be individuated. From these considerations, Schopenhauer concluded that there is really only one undifferentiated agent manifesting itself in the actions of the plurality of phenomenal people.

Empirical objects like rocks and trees and animals are as empirically real as human beings' bodies are. There must be some noumenal 'substrate' for them as well. Given the remarks on space and time above, there can still only be one noumenon, since the conditions for individuation (space and time) are not available. They too must be manifestations of the underlying will. Given the various disanalogies between the 'behaviour' of rocks, trees, and animals, and the behaviour of human beings, Schopenhauer's characterization of 'willing' must be broadened. The willing subject is to be regarded as ultimately identical with not only all human beings, but with all empirical objects. Think of your phenomenal self as paired off with a noumenal self. You must regard other phenomenal objects as either lacking a corresponding noumenon, or else as paired off with the same noumenal self, making all things identical. Opting for the latter alternative, Schopenhauer arrived at the undifferentiated underlying reality: the world as will.

Schopenhauer then deploys his view of nature as the expression of noumenal will to help resolve the mystery of teleology. How can various systems and processes in nature seem to be the product of intelligent design without being so? Attributing such design-like characteristics to God's intentions would be incompatible with Schopenhauer's atheism. Instead he attributes them to a noumenal striving for ever greater degrees of formal complexity and vitality. Unfortunately, Schopenhauer's theory of teleology leads him to claims that are reminiscent of the worst excesses of physico-theology. Not only does he explain the design-like systematicity of individual organisms by appealing to the 'unity of the will'; he also claims he can describe the system of the world in means–ends relations. His examples are scarcely more plausible than the claim that God made cork trees that people might stop bottles, e.g.

the soil adapted itself to the nutrition of plants, plants to the nutrition of animals, animals to the nutrition of other animals, just as, conversely, all these again adapted themselves to the soil. All the parts of nature accommodate themselves to one another, since it is one will that appears in them all, but the time-sequence is quite foreign to its original and only adequate objectivity, namely the Ideas . . . (*WWR* i. 160)

The mystery of how organisms could seem designed to benefit organisms appearing later in time can be explained not by God's foresight, but by the will's atemporality. The one will then expresses itself in forms given by an array of Platonic Ideas, or as he also calls them, 'grades of objectification of the will'. Thus Schopenhauer's conception of the noumenal will ends up doing the same job, to all intents and purposes, that the old designing God did. Since the noumenal will is unintelligent, it must avail itself of designs already left lying around in Platonic heaven.

Lange, Darwin, and Kant

When Nietzsche read Schopenhauer in 1865, he appears to have initially thrown all his support behind the views that he found in *World as Will and Representation*. By 1872, Nietzsche had published *Birth of Tragedy*. Though the metaphysics, epistemology, and aesthetics (if not the account of tragic affect) of the two books seem similar from afar, closer scrutiny reveals important differences. Nietzsche's views on the thing-in-itself and our knowledge of it as well as his account of the plastic arts are simply not Schopenhauerian. The early Nietzsche must have emerged then between 1865 and 1872. What was Nietzsche reading at this time?

The first thing he read after Schopenhauer was Friedrich Lange, in 1866. A growing secondary literature ascribes more prominence to the encounter with Lange, with some arguing that Lange was a staple of Nietzsche's reading throughout his career.[4] In my view, Lange's influence was far more modest. Lange offered Nietzsche an alternative to Schopenhauer's early Neo-Kantianism; issues that were settled if one remained within Schopenhauer's orbit became open to reconsideration, once the differences between Schopenhauer and Lange became evident.

For our purposes, the significance of Lange for Nietzsche lies in one area: Lange impressed on Nietzsche the significance of Darwin's theory of evolution by natural selection. After reading Lange, Nietzsche began to subject Schopenhauer's quasi-teleological conception of the natural world to stringent criticism.

Nietzsche saw that the Darwinian revolution had rendered Schopenhauer's use of metaphysics to explain biological phenomena superfluous. Perhaps the moral, religious, and aesthetic phenomena Schopenhauer had attempted to explain using metaphysical hypotheses could also be explained by appealing to biological, social, and historical factors. All that would remain of the thing-in-itself would be a kind of beyond into which we could project our ideals. It would serve to regulate inquiry and moral conduct without providing knowledge.

Nietzsche read Lange's first edition of *History of Materialism* in 1866 and could not have read Lange's later, expanded editions then. Nonetheless, it is interesting that in the later editions Lange argued that Kant's theory of teleology was compatible with Darwinism. Lange interpreted Kant as saying that appeals to design do not compete with, but supervene on, Newtonian accounts of the same biological phenomena.

In the Kantian philosophy, therefore, which has sounded these questions deeper than any other, the first stage of teleology is directly identified with the principle which we have repeatedly spoken of as the axiom of the intelligibleness of the world, and Darwinism in the wider sense of the word, i.e. the doctrine of a scientifically intelligible theory of descent, not only does not stand in contradiction with this teleology, but, on the contrary, is its necessary presupposition. The 'formal' finality of the world is nothing else than its adaptation to our understanding, and this adaptation just as necessarily demands the unconditional dominion of the law of causality without mystical interferences of any kind, as, on the other hand, it presupposes the comprehensibility of things by their ordering into definite forms. [Lange admits in a footnote at this point that 'this

---

[4] Jörg Salaquarda, 'Der Standpunkt des Ideals bei Lange und Nietzsche', *Studi Tedeschi*, 22/1 (1979), 133–60, and George Stack, *Lange and Nietzsche* (Berlin: de Gruyter, 1983) both advance this view.

interpretation of Kantian teleology is indeed not the usual one', and expresses his debt to August Stadler's 1874 monograph, 'Kant's Teleology and its Epistemological Significance'.] Kant, indeed, goes on to lay down a second stage of teleology, the 'objective'; and here Kant himself, as in the doctrine of free will, has not everywhere strictly drawn the line of what is critically admissible; but even this doctrine does not come into conflict with the scientific taste of natural research. On this view we regard organisms as beings of which every part is throughout determined by every other part, and we shall thus be brought, by means of the rational idea of an absolute reciprocal determination of the parts of the universe, to regard them as if they were the products of an intelligence. Kant regards this conception as indemonstrable and as demonstrating nothing, but he wrongly regards it as at the same time a necessary consequence of the organization of our reason. For the natural sciences, however, this 'objective' teleology, too, can never be anything but a heuristic principle; by it nothing is explained, and natural science only extends as far as the mechanical and causal explanation of things. If Kant believes that in the case of organisms this explanation will never be sufficient, this view—which is, moreover, not a necessary part of the system—is by no means to be understood as if the mechanical explanation of nature can ever strike upon a fixed limit, on the other side of which the teleological explanation would begin; rather Kant conceives the mechanical explanation of organisms as a process running on to infinity, in which there will always be an insoluble residuum, just as in the mechanical explanation of the universe. This view, however, does not conflict with the principle of scientific research, even though men of science may be for the most part inclined to form other ideas on this point, which lies beyond our experience.   (Lange, iii. 70)

Lange correctly claimed that Kant never meant to suggest that organisms be understood in terms of a Miraculous Design Scenario. Had that been the case, further advances in physiology, embryology, genetics, etc. would suffice to demolish any attraction that an appeal to a designing God might have here. Rather, we are to understand the functional properties of organisms in terms of the Mysterious Design Scenario. Everything is explained, and yet a nagging sense of the inexplicable remains, to be satisfied by rational faith that there is design behind the phenomenal scenes after all.

More questionably, Lange claimed that Darwinism does not essentially change the picture that prevailed under Newtonian mechanism. Lange is wrong about this. Once we grasp that those properties we interpret as functional are understood to have arisen by Darwinian mechanisms, it becomes far more attractive to regard functions as useful fictions. No nagging sense of the inexplicable remains.[5]

---

[5] The late Nietzsche was committed to a similar view. This presents serious obstacles to interpreting his positive ethic in terms of an ethic of 'healthiness', for the very notion of healthiness as it is traditionally understood (i.e. each part performing its proper function) will be unavailable to a

What I want to suggest, then, is that in 1866 Nietzsche was unwilling to simply bite the bullet and embrace a straightforward Darwinian rejection of teleology. This refusal was in part supported by his Kantian unwillingness to regard mechanistic explanations of biological phenomena as anything more than the discovery of mind-imposed order on mind-dependent appearances. Yet he was no longer able to defend the arguments for his prior, Schopenhauerian philosophy of nature with a clear conscience. He then turned to Kant hoping to better understand the nature of teleology. Nietzsche did not know that, in later editions, Lange would propose Kant's own theory of teleology to reconcile functional description with Darwinism. He seems to have arrived at this notion independently, inspired by Lange's first-edition discussions of Kant and Darwin.

'On the concept of the organic since Kant'

In 1867, Nietzsche began to contemplate the abandonment of philology in favour of philosophy of biology. He began to prepare an outline for a doctoral dissertation, to be titled 'The Concept of the Organic since Kant'. During the planning stages of this project, he read Kuno Fischer's two volumes on Kant. It was at this point that he also read the *Critique of Judgement*.

Nietzsche wanted to clarify the concept of the teleological without transgressing the Kantian constraints against transcendent metaphysics. Who better to turn to than Kant himself? Kant had faced much the same problem of making sense, not of Darwinism and teleology, but of Newtonian mechanism and teleology. Yet the first thing that Nietzsche would have found in Kant's text is the claim that teleological judgements fit into a larger system of types of judgements. Empirical and moral judgements are, according to Kant, 'determinative' judgements; teleological judgements are, on the other hand, 'reflective' judgements. The purpose of the third *Critique*, then, was to clarify what a reflective judgement is, and what the grounds are for accepting one. The notion of a reflective judgement is first presented in the remarkable Introduction to the third *Critique*, where Kant provides a brief systematic overview of the entire Critical system. Most suggestively, however, Kant claims that there is another kind of reflective judgement: aesthetic judgement. One can easily imagine the young Nietzsche reading this with growing curiosity.

post-Darwinian thinker. As we shall see, Nietzsche's concept of a 'great health' reintroduces function consistent with Kant's account by making functions relative to individual not divine intention. Thus what makes my eye for seeing is that I need to see to paint, and that I *will* or intend that I be a painter.

The First Reading

The main source of information about Nietzsche's attempts to grapple with these issues is a *Nachlaß* fragment entitled 'On Teleology', dated October 1867–April 1868. The structure of the fragment is as follows:

1. Introductory remarks titled 'On Teleology' containing quotes from Schopenhauer's 'Criticism of the Kantian Philosophy', his discussion of the third *Critique* (*WWR* i. 529–34).

2. Historical remarks titled 'Teleology since Kant' under which we find the following headings and discussions:

    A. 'Nature-philosophical' containing three quotations from Schopenhauer, section 28 of the first volume of *World as Will and Representation*, where he discusses teleology (*WWR* i. 53–61).

    B. 'Designed' (*Zweckmaßig*)[6] containing one quotation from Lange, a reference to Strauss's remarks about Brockes, two quotes from the third *Critique* (*CJ*, Ak. v. 375–6), one quotation and one citation from Goethe (*Princeton Goethe*, xii. 31, 64), extensive quotation from Fischer's discussion of the 'Dialectic of Teleological Judgement', in volume two of his Kant book and two quotes from Schopenhauer's 'On Teleology' (*WWR* ii. 327–41).

    C. Brief notes titled 'Goethe's attempt' including one quotation from the third *Critique* (*CJ*, Ak. v. 384).

    D. A discussion of the conflict between mechanistic and teleological explanation titled 'A False Alternative' including four more quotes from Fischer's discussion of the third *Critique*.

    E. Nietzsche's own account of teleology, including two quotes from Fischer's discussion of teleology, and one quotation from Fischer's discussion of Kant's *Natural History Universal* in volume one, one quotation from Kant taken from Fischer, six quotes from the third *Critique* (*CJ*, Ak. v. 378–9, 381, 384), and one paraphrase (of *CJ*, Ak. v. 425, 2nd para.).

3. An outline or outlines of the proposed dissertation. I am inserting the title and possible reference to parts, deleting explanatory marginalia, and paraphrasing some chapter titles. Since the outlines for what I am calling 'Part I' and 'Part II' are separated by several chapters, perhaps 'Part II' was a fresh attempt at 'Part I'.[7]

---

[6] See Ch. 2, n. 21.

[7] The original texts, translated, look like this:

Ch. I.   concept of designedness. (as existence-ability)
Ch. II.   organism (the indeterminate life-concept, the indeterminate
             (misspelled) individual-concept. (missing close paren.)   *cont. /*

'On the Concept of the Organic since Kant'
(Part I or first outline)
Chapter 1. The concept of designedness
Chapter 2. The organism
Chapter 3. Mechanistic explanation
Chapter 4. Designlessness
(Part II or second outline)
Chapter 1. Teleological reflection and organic form
Chapter 2. Organic form and transcendental subjectivity
Chapter 3. Life force

The first outline seems to suggest that the first two chapters will provide an expository account of what designedness is and in what sense an organism possesses it. The third and fourth chapters appear to intend to discuss the reconciliation of mechanistic and teleological accounts, and also give an explanation of maladapted organisms. The second outline introduces the Kantian notion that teleological judgements are reflective judgements, and that organic form is thus in some sense projected into nature by the mind. Finally, Nietzsche proposes to discuss something he calls the 'life force', which, as we shall see, is something quite distinct from organic form.

4. The reading lists: early in the manuscript Nietzsche appears to begin listing further reading that might be of interest: Kant's *Natural History of the Heavens*, which we know he read at least in part shortly after that (it is quoted in *Philosophy and the Tragic Age of the Greeks*[8]), Kant's *The One Possible Proof*,

Ch. III.	the supp. (*angebl.*) impossibility of explaining an organism mechanically (what does mechanically mean (*was heißt mechanisch*)?)
Ch. IV.	the known designlessness (*Zweckloßigkeit*) in nature in contradict. (*Widerspr.*) with designedness (*KGW* i.4. 567 (1868))
Ch. I.	Teleological reflection is reflection on forms
Ch. II.	Forms (individuals) accompany and are inseparable from hum. organiz. (*menschl. Organis.*).
Ch. III.	life force. = (*KGW* i.4. 573 (1868))

The title is from the letter to Rohde; I have inserted it here. My summary use of the expression 'transcendental subjectivity' is non-committal as to idealist metaphysics; I am using 'transcendental' to mean 'concerning the necessary conditions for the possibility of experience' and 'subjectivity' to mean 'experiencer'. This is not to prejudge whether Nietzsche is 'naturalizing' the Kantian subject. I take up this issue below.

[8] Though part of the quotation (the famous 'give me matter and I shall build a world from it!') from Kant's *Natural History Universal* that Nietzsche provides in *PTG* 17 (at *KGW* iii.2. 361 (1873)) is also to be found in Fischer iv. 156, and we know that Nietzsche read this quotation in Fischer because he gives a page number reference, the complete Kant text that Nietzsche quotes in *PTG* is not in Fischer. Nietzsche must have followed Fischer's footnote citation and at least checked the quotation in the original Kant.

and works by Holbach, Hettner, and Moleschott (*KGW* i.4. 552 (1868)). Later in the manuscript (*KGW* i.4. 572, 576 (1868)) beyond further reference to the third *Critique* and Trendelenburg's *Logical Investigations* and Moleschott, we find a list of works by Schopenhauer, Treviranus, Czolbe, Virchow, an article by Trendelenburg, Ueberweg, Helmholtz, Wundt, Lotze, Herbert, Schelling (both the *System of Transcendental Idealism*, the *Ideas for a Philosophy of Nature* and Rosenkranz's lectures on Schelling), Herder, Bichat, Müller, Fries, Schleiden, Maimon, Oken, Carus. Most of these works concern either philosophy, Idealist philosophy of nature, or contemporary biology and medicine.[9] There is, of course, no reason to suppose Nietzsche read all these texts, since he abandoned the project shortly after conceiving it. 'This theme cannot be realized . . . unless one goes about it no less carefully than a fly', he says in a letter to Rohde, May 1868 (*KGB* i.2. 274). However, the text contains quotations from the first and third *Critiques*, and Kuno Fischer's two-volume study of Kant. Quotations from *both* volumes appear in the text. This is significant, because the commentary on the third *Critique* is in the second volume, while the commentary on the first *Critique* is in the first. This lends support to the notion that Nietzsche read Fischer on the first *Critique*. In addition, there are extensive quotations from Schopenhauer, and brief citations of Goethe, Hamann, David Strauss, and Lange.

The fragment begins by contrasting three successive conceptions of teleology from theology, philosophy of nature, and Darwinism. Nietzsche, referring to Kant, claims that it is no longer the case that we must *necessarily* conceive of organisms as designed. From the context, however, we can see that Nietzsche is not referring to the element of necessity involved in reflective judgement as such. Rather he is referring to the judgement that the system of nature must play a perfectly rational design. From such a judgement, we can then argue that there must be a God. This is made clear from the following remark: 'The necessity of which Kant speaks no longer exists in our time: remember however "that even Voltaire held [the] teleological proof [for the existence of God] irrefutable." '[10] Nietzsche is observing here that while Darwinism has undercut the teleological proof, it is not necessary, for 'against universal teleology one

---

[9] Another fragment with the heading 'On Teleology' contains a list of books (*KGW* i.4. 491–2 (1867–8)); given the various quotations throughout the text from many of these books, it is possible that this is a record of the books he had before him as he worked. All texts are German unless otherwise indicated: Trendelenburg, *Logical Investigations*; Gustav Schneider, *Of Aristotelian Final Cause* (Latin); Hume, *Dialogues Concerning Natural Religion* (English); Kant, *Critique of Pure Reason*; Kant, *Critique of Judgement*; Rosenkranz, *History of Kantian Philosophy*; Kuno Fischer, *Kant and his Doctrine*.

[10] Nietzsche is quoting from Schopenhauer (*WWR* ii. 339).

has the weapon: the proof of designlessness', an observation that had been available to Voltaire. That Nietzsche understands Kant's rejection of the teleological proof is evidenced by his quoting Kant with approval:

Thus if we introduce the concept of God into the context of natural science in order to make the designedness in nature explicable, and then in turn use this designedness to prove that there is a God, then neither natural science nor theology is intrinsically firm; a vicious circle makes both uncertain, because they have allowed their boundaries to overlap.   (*CJ*, Ak. v. 381, quoted in Nietzsche, *KGW* i.4. 567 (1868))

He goes on to observe that the evidence of designlessness suggests a modified view; there is an imperfectly rational, imperfectly powerful unconscious designer or design tendency:

With [designlessness] one only proves that the highest reason has only worked spora-dically . . . There is no unified teleological world: but there is a creating intelligence. The acceptance of such an intelligence is made after human analogy: why cannot there be a power which unconsciously creates the designed, i.e. nature . . . This is the standpoint of philosophy of nature. One no longer posits cognition outside of the world. But we remain stuck in metaphysics and must call on the thing-in-itself for assistance.   (*KGW* i.4. 550 (1868))

This is the view Nietzsche associates with Schopenhauer and Schelling, a view he rejects as firmly as he rejects the physico-theological view. Both transgress the bounds of empirical knowledge: 'Two metaphysical solutions are attempt-ed: the one, coarsely anthropological, places an ideal person outside the world, the other, still metaphysical, flees into an intelligible world, in which the designedness of things is immanent' (*KGW* i.4. 550 (1868)). Nietzsche also claims that even if we regard the source of design as imperfect, to account for imperfection in the system of nature, the very fact of pervasive competition and waste strains this idea to the breaking point. Presumably even a very imperfect designer would have found some way to avoid these defects: 'But the opposite of the whole theory is formed in light of the terrible struggle of individuals . . . and species. The explanation (for this competition and waste) presupposes an overarching teleology: which doesn't exist' (*KGW* i.4. 551 (1868)). Later, he quotes Schopenhauer's remark, 'this immense prodigality fills us with amaze-ment' (*WWR* ii. 328). Last, there is the only view that does not transgress these limits: the Darwinian. 'Finally, a resolution can be possible from a purely human standpoint: the Empedoclean, where designedness appears only as an instance among many designlessnesses . . . Designedness is the exception. Designedness is chance. This reveals (the) complete arationality (of the process). One must sever every theological interest from the question (of why there is organic form)' (*KGW* i. 4. 550 (1868)). We may take the appearance of designlessness, both in individual maladaptations and in the frequent lack of what Kant calls 'relative designedness', rational coordination between organisms, at face value.[11] 'Relative designedness is an illusion (*Täuschung*)' (*KGW* i.4. 553 (1868)). Having committed ourselves to Darwinism, we are now 'acquainted with the method of nature, how such a "designed" body arises, a senseless method . . . Chance can find the most beautiful melody. Secondly, we know the method of nature which would maintain such a designed body. With senseless frivolity' (*KGW* i.4. 553 (1868)). As a result, the appearance of design, which raised 'a multitude of questions which are (seemingly) insoluble, or have been until now' can be explained away, thus eliminating any need for an appeal to a 'world organism' or an explanation for an 'origin of evil' (*KGW* i.4. 553 (1868)).

In the section titled 'Designed', Nietzsche criticizes the conception of teleology. Where do we get the concept of designedness from? 'We see a method for reaching the goal, or more exactly: we see existence and its means and decide that these means are designed' (*KGW* i.4. 554 (1868)). We see some organic system persisting. We see that it would not persist if its parts did not function in the particular way that they do. We then go on to imagine that these parts were put there somehow *in order to* make the system persist. We do this only because the system is so complex that we cannot readily imagine how it could have come about except by design. 'We are astonished then at the complicated and conjecture (after human analogy) a special wisdom for it. What is wonderful for us is really organic living: and all means to maintain this we call designed' (*KGW* i.4. 554 (1868)). We do this only with living things because inorganic objects, though they may present themselves to us as unities, lack the appearance of systematicity, of functional articulation. Our inability to grasp how these organisms could have come about by way of a 'strict necessity of cause and effect [which] excludes goals' leads us to suppose that the source of organic form comes from 'motives lying outside [the phenomenal world of mechanical] causality, inserted here or there, through which even the strict necessity is continuously broken. Existence [conceived in this way] is perforated with miracles' (*KGW* i.4. 555 (1868)). But if we attribute organic form to conscious intervention in this way, we must then ask the further question, why this

---

[11] Some contemporary 'deep ecologists' (e.g. Arne Naess) seem to regard ecosystems, and even the biosphere itself, as organism-like, in 'healthy' balance or deviating from it. Such claims tacitly rely on some notion of 'relative designedness'. To talk of ecosystems this way requires normative notions whose use is problematic enough when restricted to individual organisms.

conscious intervention? The answers we might propose will have the character of 'pure arbitrariness' (*KGW* i.4. 555 (1868)).

When we describe an act of human production, we describe the causal conditions of the product under our control as means. '[We] call the conditions for the existence of the finished work designed after the fact' (*KGW* i.4. 555 (1868)). Then when we look at organic systems, we think of them as products and call them designed, which 'means only with the presupposition that they arose in the same manner as human works' (*KGW* i.4. 556 (1868)). Again, Nietzsche points out that a Darwinian approach undercuts this way of thinking, for the 'means' to existence can be given just as easily by chance as by design. 'When a human being draws a lot out of an urn and it is not death, (what is drawn) is neither designed nor undesigned, but, as one says, chance, that means without prior intention. However, the conditions of . . . further existence are given' (*KGW* i.4. 556 (1868)).

After two quotes from the third *Critique*, Nietzsche quotes from Goethe's 'On Morphology': 'No living thing is unitary in nature; every such thing is a plurality. Even the organism which appears to us as individual exists as a collection of independent living entities' (*Princeton Goethe*, xxii. 64).[12] Here we have an anticipation of Nietzsche's mature phase, in which he often claimed that unities like organisms are analogous to social unities. Goethe says that the organism appears to us as a unity, to which Nietzsche adds that this is because we impose organic form on an experienced plurality. The 'organism [does] not belong to the thing in itself. The organism is form. If we abstract away the form, it is a multiplicity . . . Organism as a product of our organization' (*KGW* i.4. 558 (1868)).

The concept of the whole, however, is our work. Here lies the source of the representation of ends. The concept of the whole does not lie in things, but in us. These unities which we call organisms are also only multiplicities. There are in reality no individuals, rather individuals and organisms are nothing but abstractions. Into these unities, made by us, we later transfer the idea of design. (*KGW* i.4. 560 (1868))

From this we can gather that Nietzsche sees at least three stages in our experience of an organism. First, whatever is necessary to enable us to experience it as a collection of material objects and processes must take place. These are the same processes Kant describes which yield experience of empirical objects generally. Second, we must impose a formal unity on the physical multiplicity by

---

[12] For translations I follow Johann Wolfgang von Goethe, *Scientific Studies, Goethe's Collected Works*, vol. 12, ed. and trans. Douglas Miller, 1st paperback edn. (Princeton: Princeton University Press, 1995), cited as *Princeton Goethe*, xii.

interpreting it as a system composed of interconnected parts. Finally, we must interpret the activities of the parts as if they were means to the end to the persistence of the whole. In all of this, the organic system is merely a creation of the human mind, a 'product of our organization'.

Again, Nietzsche links the later stages of this psychological process that yields the experience of organisms with a Darwinian account. 'The presupposition [is that] the living can arise out of the mechanical' (*KGW* i.4. 559 (1868)). Given that there is no obstacle to claiming that 'designedness arose as a special case of the possible: countless forms arise [by way of] mechanical assembly [and] among these countless [forms] there could also be some capable of life' (*KGW* i.4. 559 (1868)). 'With that we come closer to the solution of (the question of the origins) of the organism' (*KGW* i.4. 559 (1868)).

Nietzsche refers a second time in this section to Goethe, saying, 'Very important Goethe B 40 p. 425[13] about the origin of his natural philosophy out of a Kantian proposition' (*KGW* i.4. 556 (1868)). This reference is to Goethe's paper, 'Judgement through Intuitive Perception', which contains some of Goethe's remarks concerning the third *Critique*. These remarks are of sufficient interest to bear quoting at length.

In seeking to penetrate Kant's philosophy, or at least apply it as well as I could, I often got the impression that this good man had a roguishly ironic way of working: at times he seemed determined to put the narrowest limits on our ability to know things, and at times, with a casual gesture, he pointed beyond the limits he himself had set. He had no doubt observed man's precocious and cocky way of making smug, hurried, thoughtless pronouncements based on one or two facts, of rushing to hasty conclusions by trying to impose on the objective world some notion that passes through one's head. Thus our master limits his thinking person to a reflective, discursive faculty of judgement and absolutely forbids him one which is determinative. But then, after he has succeeded in driving us to the wall, to the verge of despair in fact, he makes the most liberal statements and leaves it to us to decide how to enjoy the freedom he allows us. In this sense I view the following passage as particularly significant:

But we can also conceive of an understanding that, unlike ours, is not discursive but intuitive, and hence proceeds from the synthetically-universal (the intuition of a whole as a whole) to the particular, i.e., from the whole to the parts . . . And (to make these points) we do not have to prove that such an *intellectus archetypus* is possible. Rather, we must prove only that the contrast [between such an intellect and] our discursive understanding—an understanding which requires images (it is an

---

[13] The reference is to *Goethes Sämmtliche Werke in vierzig Bänden* (Stuttgart and Augsburg, 1858), xl. 425.

intellectus ectypus)—and the contingency of its having this character lead us to that idea (of an *intellectus archetypus*), and we must prove that this idea does not involve a contradiction.[14]

Here, to be sure, the author seems to point to divine reason. In the moral area, however, we are expected to ascend to a higher realm and approach the primal being through faith in God, virtue and immortality. Why should it not also hold true in the intellectual area that through an intuitive perception of eternally creative nature we may become worthy of participating spiritually in its creative processes? Impelled from the start by an inner need, I had striven unconsciously and incessantly toward primal image and prototype, and had even succeeded in building up a method of representing it which conformed to nature. Thus there was nothing further to prevent me from boldly embarking on this 'adventure of reason' (as the Sage of Königsberg himself called it).   (*Princeton Goethe*, xii. 31–2)

It is striking that Nietzsche takes interest in this. For the passage represents the bridge that led German thought from Criticism to the Absolute Idealism of Schelling and Hegel. This suggests that Nietzsche's thought is not only contemporary with early Neo-Kantianism, but also seeks to establish nostalgic relations with German Idealism. As we shall see below, Nietzsche will end up identifying what he calls 'the life force' with Kant's intuitive understanding posited by reflective judgement.

The section 'Designed' is followed by a very brief section titled 'Goethe's Attempt'. Here Nietzsche alludes to Goethe's work in natural science, in particular his study of the metamorphosis of plants. Goethe had argued that one can discern in organic phenomena certain basic formal patterns; the great diversity of individual and specific forms are variations on more general themes. Goethe seems to have conceived of these basic patterns as Platonic Ideas which express themselves somehow in concrete cases. This was the source of Schopenhauer's notion of 'grades of objectification'. However, Goethe also seems to have thought of these basic patterns as like perpetually mutable forces, striving to express themselves in a diversity of circumstances and over time. Thus Goethe sees organic phenomena not merely in terms of the unfolding of a *telos*, but as a process by which that *telos* is itself constantly transformed, thus transforming those beings through which it acts. Nietzsche's only point in mentioning this mysterious notion is to say that for Goethe, 'metamorphosis belongs to the explanations of the organic out of the *effective* cause' (*KGW* i.4. 561 (1868)), that is, this process of forms working themselves out in particular cases and transforming themselves into related forms is a purely

---

[14] I have substituted Werner Pluhar's translation of the passage from Kant to maintain consistency in the translations from the third *Critique* throughout my text.

immanent and unintentional process, an empirical hypothesis concerning one possible type of efficient causality. Clearly, Nietzsche would prefer Goethe's descriptions of organic processes and forms to a Deist account. What makes Goethe's attempt merely an attempt is his failure adequately to appreciate the mind-dependence of organic form in the first place.

The next section discusses 'A False Antithesis', between the pervasiveness of mechanistic processes and the appearance of 'miraculous' designedness. Nietzsche reiterates that his combination of Darwinism with Kantianism allows him to get beyond accounts of nature as largely mechanistic, but with organic systems requiring special metaphysical explanation. Once we see that Darwinian processes can yield organic phenomena without appealing to special, non-mechanistic kinds of explanations, and that the functional interpretation of the system is projected into it by us, there is no further mystery to be solved. 'If only mechanical forces rule in nature, then the designed appearances being mere appearances, acquire their designedness only because of our *idea*' (*KGW* i.4. 562 (1868)).

The remainder of the fragment, before the outline for the study and the reading list, is titled 'Naturalistic Polemic'. Nietzsche entertains the notion that mechanical judgements, being determinative, have a special status or intelligibility that teleological judgements, being reflective, lack. This is because he is reading repeatedly in Kant and Fischer that teleological judgements are merely reflective, whereas mechanical judgements are determinative. A teleological judgement takes the form of the organism and interprets it as if it were the product of intentional design: 'teleological examination (is also) examination of forms. Design and form are in nature identical' (*KGW* i.4. 572 (1868)). In the end, however, he rejects this and thus parts ways with Kant in claiming that

one can only comprehend the mathematical completely . . . In all else human beings stand before the unknown. In order to overcome this [they] invent concepts, which only gather together a sum of appearing characteristics, which, however, do not get a hold of the thing. Therein belong force, matter, individual, law, organism, atom, final cause. These are not constitutive [i.e. determinative] but only reflective (*reflektirende*) judgements. (*KGW* i.4. 565 (1868))

In short, Nietzsche rejects Kant's claim that the claims of physics have objectivity, whereas the claims of biology have only intersubjective validity. *All* natural scientific claims have only intersubjective validity. Recalling our previous analysis of reflective judgements, this should be read as saying that intimation of design (patterns that are as if intentional) is involved in coming to grasp *any* natural phenomenon. Since the designedness cannot be taken literally, such judgements retain an ineliminable element of 'stance-ishness' or 'as-iffy-ness' and with it, relativity to human cognition.

This is an astonishing expansion of what Kant had originally licensed, which was broad enough already. For Kant had used the notion of reflective judgement to legitimate not only claims about function within organisms, but even claims about the systematicity of nature as a whole; the systematicity of phenomenal nature was to be understood as intelligently designed by a noumenal intellect. Here Nietzsche is reducing the entire sphere of human cognitive activity, apart from mathematics, to the enterprise of producing merely intersubjectively valid expressions of intellectual incapacity. As he would put matters in his later work, rationality is thinking according to a scheme that we cannot throw off.

There were even more questionable consequences. By lumping together the mundane results of physics with more speculative flights of fancy regarding intelligent design in the world, Nietzsche licensed himself to take such flights. So did Kant, to the extent that such speculation furthered our theoretical or practical interests, independent of his capacity to offer empirical evidence for such claims. After all, the posits of physics rest every bit as much on what we think. As he put it in *BT*, 'I feel myself impelled to the metaphysical assumption that the truly existent primal unity . . . also needs the rapturous vision . . . for its continuous redemption' (*BT* 4).

This was not Nietzsche's last word in his early philosophy of biology. 'What we see of life is form; how we see it, as individuals. What lies behind that is unknowable' (*KGW* i.4. 575 (1868)). What is this 'unknowable'? Nietzsche seems to think that something crucial has been left out of his account of life because he has focused on living things as *objects* for human experiencers; but we too are alive—we experience life 'from within' as well, from the subjective side. He fumbles about in an effort to characterize this. ' "Life" occurs with sensations: we consider the sensations as condition for the "organic." "To live" is to exist consciously, that is (it) is humanlike . . . We cannot conceive of "life," that is, sensate, growing existence, other than as analogous to the human' (*KGW* i.4. 575, 576 (1868)). Here we see the re-emergence of the temporarily suppressed Schopenhauerian notion of the will. For even if we cannot employ his notion of the will to illuminate the fact of design in organic objects, let alone in the system of nature, Nietzsche cannot resist Schopenhauer's notion of the will as action seen from the inside, and of identifying that with a kind of life force. Though from the outside we can only grasp life as organic forms we ourselves have projected into our experience, there remains phenomenology: what it is like to be alive. Nietzsche cannot put aside the vitalist intimation that in *being* a living being, something felt, some power or 'life force', operates in him and through him.

'On Schopenhauer'

Once we commit ourselves to Kant's theory of teleological judgements as reflective, we see that organic form is in a certain sense projected into our experience. To claim that something possesses organic form, we must use teleological judgements, which contain embedded reference to a transcendent source of order in nature. This source is modelled on our own understanding. We may not *assert* that such an understanding exists. If Nietzsche had adopted something like Kant's view concerning teleology, we would expect his own metaphysical and epistemological commitments to change in the following ways.

First, determinative judgements about noumena, such as those made by Schopenhauer, would be prohibited. Any attempt to argue from the character of phenomena to that of noumena must fall under Critical ban. Instead of determinative judgements about the thing-in-itself as will, we would expect Nietzsche to speak reflectively of a design-producing understanding in the supersensible realm, as Kant had. However, Nietzsche was not bound by Kant's belief that even seemingly undesigned phenomena must express a mysterious purpose. This claim rested not on any intrinsic feature of Kant's theory of teleology, but rather on his conviction that the supersensible designer must be conceived as the Deity. This God, being omnipotent, can be appealed to in making sense of design, but only at the cost of requiring that there also be design behind the seemingly undesigned. However, Kant's theory is also compatible with the view that the supersensible designer be conceived as inefficient and limited in the power to realize its intentions. Such a designer would be responsible only for what design in nature we can discern.

This is precisely what we find. There is a body of notes titled 'On Schopenhauer' dated October 1867–April 1868, the same date as the fragment 'On Teleology' documenting Nietzsche's reading of the *Critique of Judgement*. Here Nietzsche explicitly criticizes Schopenhauer's metaphysics along two different fronts. In these notes, Nietzsche is surprisingly sensitive to the ambiguity in Kant's treatment of the thing-in-itself. He recognizes that Kant's tendency to slip from the negative, 'limits of empirical knowledge' use of the concept to the positive, 'possibility of freedom' use unleashed Schopenhauer's own speculations. If we adopt stricter 'Kantian' principles than Kant himself employed, Schopenhauer's argument for the thing-in-itself as will becomes just another instance of pre-Critical dogmatic metaphysics. Whether Nietzsche endorsed Kantian constraints on knowledge (and I think he did), he could no longer use the *arguments* for Schopenhauer's metaphysics, since Schopenhauer was inconsistently committed to these very Kantian principles himself.

Nietzsche's first objection is that the concept of the thing-in-itself is nothing more than the concept of sheer thinghood coupled with the concept of mind-independence. Therefore it is neither unknowable nor very interesting. (Similar arguments against Kant can be found in Hegel.) 'The first and most general—aimed at Schopenhauer only in so far as he did not here, where it was necessary, go beyond Kant—aims at the concept of the thing-in-itself and sees in it, to speak with Ueberweg, only a hidden category' (*KGW* i.4. 421 (1868)). The second criticism is that Schopenhauer's arguments for the identification are unsound. The identification 'is only born with the help of a poetic intuition, while the attempted logical proofs cannot satisfy either Schopenhauer or us' (*KGW* i.4. 421 (1868)). Nietzsche does not tell us why he thinks that this is so. Kantian constraints on the legitimate domain for applying 'logical proofs' ought to have ruled out transcendent metaphysics already.[15] The third criticism is that Schopenhauer arrives at determinate knowledge of the noumenal realm by simply negating claims about the properties of the phenomenal realm.[16] 'We are compelled to guard against the predicates which Schopenhauer ascribes to his will, which for something simply unthinkable sound much too certain and all stem from the contradiction to the world of representation: while between the thing-in-itself and its appearance not even the concept of opposition has any meaning' (*KGW* i.4. 421 (1868)). The fourth criticism is that besides these negative properties, Schopenhauer imputes positive properties to the thing-in-itself, borrowed from the world of appearance.

Schopenhauer demands that something, which can never be an object, nevertheless should be thought of objectively: a path which can only lead to an apparent objectivity, in so far as a completely dark and ungraspable x is draped with predicates, as with colourful clothes, which are taken from the world of phenomena, a world foreign to it. The demand follows, that we take the draped clothes, namely, the predicates, for the

---

[15] Not all 'logical proofs' involving things-in-themselves will violate Kantian constraints. For example, claims like 'if there is a thing-in-itself, it is self-identical' and anything that can be inferred from it, would be legitimate.

[16] Nietzsche's rejection of this Schopenhauerian move is consistent with his endorsement of the 'neglected alternative' to transcendental realism and transcendental idealism about space and time. Trendelenburg had argued that we need not choose between them. For the space with which we are acquainted might very well be as Kant characterizes it. Yet there might very well be a mind-independent space with which we are not acquainted. Nietzsche's commitment to the 'neglected alternative' is present in every stage of his development. See Ch. 4 for further discussion.

thing-in-itself: for that is what the sentence means: 'if it is to be thought objectively, it must borrow its name and concept from an object.' The concept 'thing-in-itself' is then secretly removed . . . and another is pressed into our hands . . . The borrowed name and concept is the will . . . . All the predicates of the will are borrowed from the world of appearance . . . they are all indivisibly knotted together with our organization, so that it is completely doubtful whether they have any meaning (*Bedeutung*) outside the human sphere of knowledge. (*KGW* i.4. 423–5 (1868))

The last two objections are especially serious, since they bring out quite clearly the impossibility of Schopenhauer's enterprise: to make assertions about the unintelligible. Nietzsche raises the question of 'whether they have any meaning outside the human sphere of knowledge', foreshadowing his later rejection of the coherence of the concept of the thing-in-itself. Nietzsche allows that Schopenhauer's characterization of reality independent of human cognition *may* be correct, but denies that we can ever know this. Had Nietzsche claimed that these predicates are meaningless when applied outside experience, then all that would remain of the thing-in-itself would be the concept of thinghood plus unknowable predicates. Nietzsche was tempted by this approach, as shown by the above criticism that the thing-in-itself is only a 'hidden category'. If the concepts of thinghood and predication were only meaningful when applied within experience, then the entire Schopenhauerian project would collapse. Nonetheless, Nietzsche continues to affirm at this stage that the thing-in-itself as Schopenhauer describes it is a meaningful, if unknowable, possibility.

Despite these constraints, Nietzsche seems to regard himself as licensed to speak of a 'Dionysian world-artist' in *Birth of Tragedy* and contemporary *Nachlaß* material. However, the relationship between 'world-artist' and world is not at all like the relationship between the Schopenhauerian thing-in-itself and appearances. Berkowitz expresses this nicely:

The fact is that in the key exposition of the proposition that existence is justified only as an aesthetic phenomenon, Nietzsche presents the individual, even the genius, as a passive medium, the unwitting tool through which a mighty godlike power, 'the primordial artist of the world,' expresses its creative will (BT 5) . . . The consequence is to reduce the lives of flesh and blood human beings to 'merely images and artistic projections for the true author' (BT 5).[17]

For Schopenhauer the empirical world is the product of the objectification of the will conceived in entirely non-cognitive terms, and the experience producing effects of the individual's perceptual-cognitive apparatus. By contrast,

---

[17] Peter Berkowitz, *Nietzsche: The Ethics of an Immoralist* (Cambridge, MA: Harvard University Press, 1995), 44.

Nietzsche repeatedly characterizes the thing-in-itself as a perceiver whose relationship to the empirical world is that of a Kantian transcendental subject's relationship to its own experience. Since both metaphysics seem equally exotic, why would Nietzsche exchange one for the other?

Schopenhauer's account of the individuation of empirical objects is vulnerable to a fatal objection. He had claimed that individuation is not present in the thing-in-itself, but is the product of the mind's imposition of spatial and temporal form on experience. Schopenhauer assumes that there is a mind in this sense for every empirical person, apparently identifying the mind with the brain. According to Schopenhauer, the physical world is mind-dependent. Yet he also believed that mentality is a property of higher animals and human beings (animals have 'understanding', human beings in addition have 'reason'), and that these all arose at some point in time. Yet there are physical states of the world that long precede the appearance of mentality, animal or human. Schopenhauer explains, in response to the apparent difficulty, that the physical reality of these past states should be understood phenomenalistically. That is, if there had been a perceiving mind, it would have seen Precambrian plants and rocks. Schopenhauer says in *Parerga und Paralipomena*:

The geological processes that preceded all life on earth did not exist in any consciousness: not in their own, for they had none; not in some other: as there was none. Hence . . . these processes did not exist at all; for what could it mean to say that they were there? *At bottom, their existence is merely a hypothetical one; such that, if there had been consciousness in those primeval times, then the said processes would have represented themselves in it*; this is what the regress of appearances leads us to. (*SW* vi. 149, emphasis mine)

For Nietzsche, this 'phenomenalist' answer is incoherent.

But how, so we ask after these thoughtful remarks, was the emergence of the intellect ever possible? Surely the existence of the last stage prior to the appearance of the intellect is just as hypothetical as that of any that came earlier, i.e. it did not exist because there was no consciousness. Then, at the next stage, the intellect is supposed to appear, i.e. the tree of knowledge is alleged to have suddenly and abruptly blossomed forth from a world that does not exist. Moreover, all of this is *supposed* to have taken place in a realm devoid of time and space, without the mediation of causality: yet that which has its origin in such an unworldly world must—according to Schopenhauer's tenets—be a thing-in-itself: either the intellect is now a new attribute, forever combined with the thing-in-itself; or there can be no intellect, because an intellect could never have come into being. But there does exist an intellect: consequently, it could not be an instrument of the world of appearances, as Schopenhauer claims, but a thing-in-itself, i.e. a will. Thus Schopenhauer's thing-in-itself would be both *principium individuationis* and the ground of necessity: in other words: the world as it exists. (*KGW* i.4. 426–7 (1868))

The plurality and individuation of experiencers are left hanging. There must be another experiencer who generates a plurality of experiencers, who then in turn generate a plurality of empirical objects. Otherwise experiencers must somehow bootstrap themselves into existence and then produce empirical objects. Nietzsche rejects the latter alternative and argues that there is something about the thing-in-itself which produces individuation.

The other difficulties Nietzsche raised here are of the same order. Nietzsche was concerned that since the thing-in-itself (which, by his lights, is all that exists until the appearance of actual consciousness) is timeless, it is unintelligible how mentality could arise at some point in time without covertly assuming that the thing-in-itself exists temporally as well. Even if we accept that the thing-in-itself is temporal, it is supposed to be featureless in all other respects. If so, then there is no way to make sense of the sudden upsurge of mentality at one point in time as opposed to another. From this consideration, it follows that either the thing-in-itself is not featureless, or else mentality was always present, and thus did not have to arise at some point in time at all.

Furthermore, since causality operates in the world as representation only mind-dependently, there could have been no causality operative to cause the mind to come into existence. Nietzsche was also worried by Schopenhauer's quasi-teleological account of the will 'needing' to produce mentality. Such a need could only arise if there was something separate from the mind in question of which it needed to become conscious. Such a scenario presupposes plurality, which in turn presupposes spatiality or temporality and again a Kantian subject.

The Dionysian world artist

Nietzsche inferred that since the mind could not have arisen in this bootstrap fashion, either it does not exist or it is a characteristic of the thing-in-itself. Compare Ralph C. S. Walker on Kant:

the existence of the self, as subject if not as enduring and independent substance, is a condition of the possibility of experience. In the transcendental deduction appeal is frequently made to the part the self must play in synthesis; and this could not be simply the phenomenal self, even if Kant did not repeatedly make it clear that synthesis is the spontaneous activity of the self as it is in itself. The construction of the phenomenal world must be effected somehow; it could not be that the agent of the construction, and the act of constructing, belonged only to the world of appearances and were themselves constructions. One's bootstraps have only finite strength.[18]

[18] Ralph Walker, *Kant* (London: Routledge & Kegan Paul, 1978), 133.

The only way he could maintain that nature is mind-dependent was to posit a noumenal perceiver to produce the phenomenal world before the existence of animals and human beings, thus preserving his intuition that the world has a structure, cohesion, and intelligibility that transcends the plurality of individual experiences. This interpretative hypothesis is confirmed in a series of notes from 1870–1.

The cognitive faculty (of the will) by no means coincides with (that of) the human (cognitive faculty): this belief is a naive anthropomorphism. The only cognitive faculties in animals, plants (*sic*) and men are the faculties of *conscious* cognition. The immense wisdom of its creation is already the activity of an intellect. In any case, individuation is not the work of conscious cognition, but the work of that primordial intellect (*Urintellekt*). The Kantian–Schopenhauerian idealists have failed to recognize this. Our intellect *never* takes us beyond conscious cognition . . . (*KGW* iii.3. 115 (1870–1))

Nietzsche is also very clear about his reasons for postulating such a primordial intellect: 'I am reluctant to deduce space, time, and causality from our pitiful human consciousness; they belong to the will. They are the conditions of all symbolisms of appearance: now man himself is such a symbolism, now the state, and the earth also, yet this symbolism does not necessarily exist for the individual only' (*KGW* iii.3. 110–11 (1870–1)). Thus Nietzsche sets aside the Schopenhauerian model of an unindividuated thing-in-itself (the will) and the individuated experience of a Kantian human subject. Instead of the Schopenhauerian thing-in-itself, he speaks of the primordial unity (*Ur-Eine*) which is characterized in terms borrowed from Kant's account of a supersensible, intuitive understanding. The primordial unity 'projects' a world of appearance for itself to observe. Such a world is organized spatially, temporally, and causally because of the Kantian character of the primordial unity's 'intellect', not because of the character of finite human intellects. Nietzsche poetically characterized this process of 'projection' as if it were analogous to that of an artist who strives to overcome personal suffering through artistic creation. As he says in *Birth of Tragedy*:

For the more clearly I perceive in nature those omnipotent art impulses, and in them an ardent longing for illusion, for redemption through illusion, the more I feel myself impelled to the metaphysical assumption that the truly existent primordial unity, eternally suffering and contradictory, also needs the rapturous vision, the pleasurable illusion, for its continuous redemption. And we, completely wrapped up in this illusion and composed of it, are compelled to consider this illusion as the truly non-existent—i.e. as a perpetual becoming in time, space, and causality—in other words, as empirical reality. (*BT* 4)

But where and how does human subjectivity fit into this model? Schopenhauer's model of individual human subjects introducing space and time into their own experiential fields, thus producing a plurality of objects, is incoherent. These human subjects already represent a plurality. Nietzsche makes their plurality a function of the primordial unity's individuative act of projecting its own space and time. This reduces human subjectivity to just another episode within the phenomenal world. This, one might think, has the effect of suppressing human subjectivity altogether.

That, however, would be a mistake. For Kant, conscious experience is the product of operations by various faculties which are themselves unconscious. Consciousness and experience for Kant are not mysterious brute facts, but things that need to be assembled from preconscious materials. Kant's account of experience is essentially a functionalist one. We can liken the Kantian subject to a kind of computational machine generating experience by way of 'virtual reality' software. However, if that analogy is apt, then we can also liken finite human subjects to virtual machines running 'on top of' the machine, the primordial intellect, which generates nature. Of course, these metaphors were not available to Nietzsche. Yet they help us to see that there is nothing intrinsically paradoxical about a Kantian experiencer generating objects that function as experiencers embedded within the first experiencer. Since what the first experiencer, the primordial unity, projects is nature, the result is that the embedded experiencers must be purely naturalistic subjects. Yet their experiences are, in a sense, its experiences too. This is the only sense that I can make of the following passages: 'The primordial unity views the genius, who sees appearance purely as appearance: that is the most rapturous peak of the world' (*KGW* iii.3. 207–8 (1870–1)); 'In humanity, the primordial unity looks back upon itself by means of appearance: appearance reveals the essence. That means: the primordial unity views humanity, rather, the appearance viewing humanity, humanity which sees through the appearance' (*KGW* iii.3. 213 (1870–1)); 'our thinking is only an image of the primordial intellect, a thinking arising through the intuition (*Anschauung*) of the one will, which envisions a vision by thinking' (*KGW* iii.3. 216–17 (1870–1));[19] 'our intuition is only the image of the one intuition, that means, nothing but a vision begotten in every moment of one representation' (*KGW* iii.3. 216–17 (1870–1)); and finally, 'we are in one sense pure intuition (i.e. projected images of a completely enraptured being, which has the highest repose in this viewing), on the other hand we are

---

[19] My translation of *Anschauung* in Nietzsche as 'intuition' follows the standard practice of translating the term this way in Kant.

the one being itself' (*KGW* iii.3. 222 (1870–1)). These opaque passages, which have the thing-in-itself 'viewing', 'seeing', 'looking', 'intuiting', and 'envision-ing', simply make no sense if we restrict ourselves to Schopenhauer's meta-physics of the will.

This conceptual transformation of Schopenhauer's will into the 'Dionysian world-artist' in turn provided Nietzsche with a model of creativity he then could apply in his analysis of Greek tragedy. The tragic artist is himself not only a 'projection' of the primordial unity, and thus analogous to an artistic product; he also engages in an activity similar to the metaphysical 'activity' the world itself engages in.

He later described these early metaphysical ideas in these terms:

The world—at every moment the attained salvation of God, as the eternally changing, eternally new vision of the most deeply afflicted, discordant, and contradictory being who can find salvation only in appearance. (*BT* 5)

Once Zarathustra too cast his deluded fancy beyond mankind, like all afterworldsmen. Then the world seemed to me the work of a suffering and tormented God. Then the world seemed to me the dream and fiction of a God; coloured vapour before the eyes of a discontented God. Good and evil and joy and sorrow and I and you—I thought them coloured vapour before the creator's eyes. The creator wanted to look away from him-self, so he created the world. It is intoxicating joy for the sufferer to look away from his suffering and to forget himself. Intoxicating joy and self-forgetting—that is what I once thought the world. This world, eternally imperfect, the eternal and imperfect image of a contradiction—an intoxicating joy to its imperfect creator—that is what I once thought the world. (Z I. 3)

Compare the way that Kant characterizes the supersensible source of the sys-tematic order in nature in the *Critique of Judgement*.

Since universal natural laws have their basis in our understanding, which prescribes them to nature (though only according to the universal concept of it as a nature), the par-ticular empirical laws must, as regards what the universal laws have left undetermined in them, be viewed in terms of such a unity as (they would have) if they too had been given by *an understanding* (*even though not ours*) so as to assist our cognitive powers by making possible a system of experience in terms of particular natural laws. (*CJ*, Ak. v. 180, Introduction, emphasis mine)

Human beings, the early Nietzsche is claiming, are not responsible for the phenomenal world, but are episodes within it. If there is a metaphysics in *Birth of Tragedy*, it is not Schopenhauerian in argument or content.

Nietzsche thought his transcendent claims were more intelligible than Schopenhauer's. But this does not mean that he simply asserted these claims dogmatically. According to Kaufmann, Schacht, *et al.*, the metaphysical commitments in *Birth of Tragedy* were essentially no different from those in Schopenhauer. Only the account of tragedy and the 'tragic ethic' Nietzsche seems to endorse there differs from Schopenhauer's aesthetics and ethics.[20] Conversely, Paul de Man has argued that there is evidence in *Birth of Tragedy* that Nietzsche was not committed to *his own* metaphysical views as expressed in that text.[21] Though de Man goes too far, we have seen important evidence that the Kaufmann–Schacht view passes over. This evidence significantly alters our narrative of the early Nietzsche's development. As Kant does repeatedly in the third *Critique*, Nietzsche distances himself from the very content of his own metaphysics, implying that the tragic world-view itself cannot be straightforwardly asserted. For example, the tragic world-view is explicitly called an illusion on a par with the Socratic world-view:

the insatiable will always finds a way to detain its creatures in life and compel them to live on, by means of an *illusion* spread over things. One is chained by the Socratic love of knowledge and the delusion of being able thereby to heal the eternal wound of existence; another is ensnared by art's seductive veil of beauty fluttering before his eyes; still another by *the metaphysical comfort that beneath the whirl of phenomena eternal life flows on indestructibly* . . . These three stages of *illusion* . . . (*BT* 18, emphasis mine)[22]

Finally, there is evidence from *Truth and Lie* that Nietzsche did not believe that we can make dogmatic assertions about the thing-in-itself or its character.[23] In *Truth and Lie* (1873), one year after *Birth of Tragedy* was published, Nietzsche argues from Kantian premises to the conclusion that things-in-themselves are cognitively inaccessible.

---

[20] Schopenhauer's account of tragedy is that it teaches us resignation to suffering. His ethics are two-tiered. He recommends radical asceticism as a preliminary to world-denial in *WWR*; however, in *Parerga and Paralipomena*, recognizing that asceticism is likely to be dismissed as not a live option, he recommends Stoicism. In brief, happiness for Schopenhauer is unattainable. Setting aside salvation, how can one behave prudentially and thus reduce the damage that life inevitably does to us? Nietzsche's ethic in *BT* clearly coincides with neither a policy of asceticism nor prudential Stoicism, and he explicitly presents his early ethical proposals as alternatives to both. '[Schopenhauer's] twofold positive philosophy (it lacks a living nucleus)—a conflict only for those who no longer hope. How the future culture will overcome this conflict' (*KGW* iii.4. 222 (1873)).

[21] Paul de Man, *Allegories of Reading* (New Haven: Yale University Press, 1980), 79–102.

[22] Rejecting this as a mere slip, as Wilcox does, is unnecessary. See John Wilcox, *Truth and Value in Nietzsche* (Ann Arbor: University of Michigan Press, 1974), 109. The concept of reflective judgement allows us to make sense of the seemingly paradoxical notion of an 'illusion' to which one is committed. It leaves open the possibility that the 'illusion' is true, though unknowable.

[23] This claim is supported by *PTG*, where Nietzsche characterizes philosophy itself as a kind of poetry in concepts. Philosophy is neither art nor science. Its value lies in the exemplary character of the philosopher; what he says there about the 'Pre-Platonic' philosophers is an instance of what Nietzsche calls 'monumental history' in *UM* II.

The 'thing-in-itself' (which is precisely what the pure truth, apart from its consequences, would be) is likewise something quite incomprehensible to the creator of language and something not in the least worth striving for.   (*KGW* iii.2. 373 (1873)/ *TL* 1)

We should not presume to claim that this contrast (between individual and species) does not correspond to the essence of things: that would of course be a dogmatic assertion and, as such, would be just as indemonstrable as its opposite. (*KGW* iii.2. 374 (1873)/ *TL* 1)

The question of which of these perceptions [human as opposed to various animals] is the more correct one is quite meaningless, for this would have to be decided previously in accordance with the criterion of the *correct perception*, which means in accordance with a criterion which is *not available*. But in any case it seems to me that 'the correct perception'—which would mean 'the adequate expression of an object in a subject'— is a contradictory impossibility.   (*KGW* iii.2. 378 (1873)/ *TL* 1, emphasis Nietzsche's)

The rejection of Schopenhauer's arguments for identifying the thing-in-itself with the will is in the notes from 1867–8, *before* the composition of *Birth of Tragedy*. *Truth and Lie* continues *Birth of Tragedy*'s commitment to the superior value of art over science (see *KGW* iii.2. 381–4 (1873)/ *TL* 2). The following statement by Maudemarie Clark must be amended. '*BT* and *TL* differ only in relation to *BT*'s claim that Dionysian experience alone gives access to things-in-themselves. *TL* denies that we have any access whatsoever to things-in-themselves.'[24] *Birth of Tragedy* is cagey and unclear about access to things in themselves. The notes of 1867–8 and *Truth and Lie* of 1873 are pellucid: there is no such access. I conclude that these notes, *Birth of Tragedy*, and *Truth and Lie* all form the basis for a unified panorama. There is no contradiction between *Birth of Tragedy* and *Truth and Lie*. *Truth and Lie* presents in the starkest form both the Kantian restriction to phenomena and a Kantian constructivist account of how the mind produces phenomena; *Birth of Tragedy* presents reflective judgements concerning how we must think about noumena if we are to make sense of our experience of designedness in nature. The very passage in which Nietzsche's metaphysics is presented in *Birth of Tragedy* has the underlying form of a reflective judgement: 'For the more clearly *I perceive in nature* those omnipotent art impulses, and in them an ardent longing for illusion, for redemption through illusion, the more *I feel myself impelled to the metaphysical assumption that* the truly existent primordial unity . . .' (*BT* 4, emphasis mine). Design-like tendencies, available empirically, must be interpreted in terms of

---

[24] Maudemarie Clark, *Nietzsche on Truth and Philosophy* (Cambridge: Cambridge University Press, 1990), 90. Clark's book is controversial. Though her interpretation of *BT* must be rejected, her interpretation of *TL* is essentially correct.

the supersensible, though this interpretation is an 'assumption' we 'feel . . . impelled to'. If this is correct, then the 'early Nietzsche' is to be found throughout the texts preceding *Human, All-too-human*.

In short, the metaphysics of *Birth of Tragedy* can be derived from the metaphysics of the *Critique of Judgement*. There is a plausible, textually supportable narrative explaining how this could have come about. Furthermore, deriving this metaphysics from the *Critique of Judgement* is the only way to explain two differences between the early Nietzsche's view of the thing-in-itself and Schopenhauer's. First, the thing-in-itself, while associated with a Schopenhauerian 'life force', must also be understood on the model of a perceiver. This is just how Kant characterizes the supersensible: as an 'intuitive understanding'. Second, the concept of reflective judgement is the only way that we can make sense of Nietzsche's extravagant claims while simultaneously insisting that they can never be made under Kantian epistemological constraints.

The aesthetics of *Birth of Tragedy*

Today we are likely to regard Kant's journey into the supersensible with a smile, and focus our attention on what is salvageable in his aesthetics proper. Should we not do the same with Nietzsche? After all, Nietzsche describes *Birth of Tragedy* as a contribution to 'the science of aesthetics' (*BT* 1). The *Critique of Judgement* also exercised a decisive influence on Nietzsche's aesthetic thought, although showing this will be more roundabout a procedure than our preceding discussion of metaphysical biology. There are no quotations in the *Nachlaß* from the 'Critique of Aesthetic Judgement' before 1887. It is probable enough that Nietzsche had read the 'Critique of Aesthetic Judgement' at least as early as 1882–4. That is the point at which we begin to see Nietzsche's hostility to the idea of 'disinterested pleasure' emerge.[25] We do have a very early passage comparing Kant's account of procreation with the emergence of tragedy. This shows that Nietzsche had linked his reading of the third *Critique* with his own developing views in aesthetics.[26] Nietzsche had this text before him and read

---

[25] 'Since Kant, all talk of art, beauty, knowledge, wisdom is messed up (*vermanscht*) and soiled through the concept of "disinterestedness" ' (*KGW* vii.1. 251 (1883)). This passage is the earliest objection to Kant's aesthetics in the corpus; the first quotations from the 'Critique of Aesthetic Judgement' appear in 1887 at *KGW* viii.1. 275 (1886–7).

[26] *KGW* iii.3. 187 (1870–1). Nietzsche paraphrases Kant's remarks concerning the reciprocal designedness of the sexes for reproduction (*CJ*, Ak. v. 425) in 'On Teleology' without naming him at *KGW* i.4. 575 (1868). The point that we must regard the sexes as if designed for each other is repeated

half of it. The other half concerned matters in aesthetics. Given his interest in tragedy it is unlikely he let it sit unread. It is a mistake to limit ourselves to textual citation as the sole means of limning influence. How accurate would an account of the reader's own influences be if it was restricted to those manifested by quotations? Many books exercise a profound effect on us without producing copying or even note-taking as a response.

We need not merely speculate. For the only other explanation for Nietzsche's emerging views in aesthetics is that they are a variation on Schopenhauer's. This explanation is incoherent for two reasons, one concerning the Apollinian, another concerning the tragic. By contrast, an interpretation of Nietzsche's aesthetics drawing on Kant's is coherent and plausible. Since we know that he read the 'Critique of Teleological Judgement', we should accept the hypothesis that he was influenced by the 'Critique of Aesthetic Judgement' as well. As a preliminary to these two arguments, it will be necessary to say a few words about Schopenhauer's aesthetics.

Schopenhauer's explanation for the system of ends in nature is that the will provides the systematicity, and Platonic forms provide the designs for individual organisms. As in other sorts of Platonism (e.g. mathematical Platonism), ontological inflation inspires epistemological mystery. Schopenhauer must assume that besides the various mental faculties he has already discussed in Book 1 of *The World as Will and Representation*, there is a faculty for intuiting Platonic forms. Schopenhauer may have been trying to explain Goethe's highly intuitive work on the metamorphosis of plants. Having posited both the forms and our capacity to intuit them, Schopenhauer then concludes that this explains our capacity to appreciate the plastic arts. Beautiful works are beautiful because they participate in forms, and we can experience their beauty because we can intuit the forms in them.[27]

Is this the basis for Nietzsche's notion of the Apollinian? It cannot be if we interpret the notes of 1867–8, *Birth of Tragedy* in 1872, and *Truth and Lie* in 1873 as all of a piece. In *Truth and Lie*, where we have Nietzsche's clearest and most developed account of subjectivity in the early writings, we also have an explicit repudiation of the claim that there are Platonic forms. The very example he gives is a biological, not a mathematical one, thus suggesting that it is Schopenhauer's Platonism he rejects. Instead, Nietzsche proposes, in perfect

at *KGW* iii.3. 157 (1870–1), with Kant named. Then at *KGW* iii.3. 187 (1870–1), Nietzsche compares the tragic as offspring of Apollo and Dionysus with natural procreation by two sexes, and again Kant is named. He repeats the comparison in *BT* 1, without reference to Kant. Here we have an unbroken textual chain from the *Critique of Judgement* to *Birth of Tragedy*.

[27] For Schopenhauer's aesthetics of the plastic arts, see *WWR* i. 169–255.

agreement with his Kant-inspired remarks on organic form in 'On Teleology', that the very existence of organic form in organic phenomena is projected into them by our minds. *Truth and Lie* goes beyond this in the claim that it is because of a failure to grasp the mind-dependence of organic form that we then hypostatize it and fantasize it could exist independently of the organic phenomenon. This fantasy we then baptize with the term 'Platonic form'.

> Every concept arises from the equation of unequal things. Just as it is certain that one leaf is never totally the same as another, so it is certain that the concept 'leaf' is formed by arbitrarily discarding these individual differences and by forgetting the distinguishing aspects. This awakens the idea that, in addition to the leaves, there exists in nature the 'leaf': the original model according to which all the leaves were perhaps woven, sketched, measured, coloured, curled, and painted—but by incompetent hands, so that no specimen has turned out to be a correct, trustworthy, and faithful likeness of the original model . . . This means that the leaf is the cause of the leaves . . . We obtain the concept, as we do the form, by overlooking what is individual and actual; whereas nature is acquainted with no forms and no concepts, and likewise no species, but only with an X which remains inaccessible and undefinable to us. (*KGW* iii.2. 374 (1873)/ *TL* 1, ellipses mine)[28]

Again, the consistency between the notes before and after *Birth of Tragedy* is striking. The implications of this account of Platonic forms, however, is to leave Schopenhauer's entire analysis of the plastic arts in ruins. Surely Nietzsche could not have undercut the very possibility of a Schopenhauerian aesthetics with one hand and then helped himself to it with the other? Rather, I think we must assume that Nietzsche too, like Schopenhauer, linked questions of aesthetic form to those of biological form. Nietzsche was committed to the notion that biological form is *projected* into experience. It is hard to imagine him having any other view but that aesthetic form is projected into experience as well. This is consistent with Nietzsche's association of the Apollinian with dreaming (see *BT* 1). In dreams images and their forms are freely produced by the imagination without even the constraint of data.

If this is correct, then Nietzsche's conception of the Apollinian further develops *Kant's* conception of the beautiful. The reader's possible inclination to bristle at this suggestion may come from three sources. First, given Kant's own tame aesthetic preferences, it may seem incredible to link Kant's theory of taste with Nietzsche's much wilder late Romantic aesthetics. The answer is to reiterate that we are concerned with what Chapter 1 calls the 'skeletal' structure of

---

[28] The allusion to Goethe's 'Metamorphosis of Plants' is, no doubt, intended.

Nietzsche's thought, not its full flesh. Second, though Kant and Nietzsche may share the notion of projecting design-like form into experience, this at most makes Nietzsche an aesthetic subjectivist. Aesthetic subjectivism is such a common view that its alleged presence in Nietzsche would scarcely need explaining. What is distinctive about Kant's aesthetics is his attempt to salvage an intersubjective validity to claims of taste despite the absence of objective aesthetic properties. Does Nietzsche even have any interest in the epistemological dimension of aesthetics, in justifying the validity of claims of taste?

If Nietzsche was a pure subjectivist about aesthetic value, it is difficult to see how art could possess the importance *Birth of Tragedy* claims for it. Schopenhauer's dogmatic-Platonic means of securing the objectivity of judgements of taste is unavailable to Nietzsche. Having painted himself into this corner, Nietzsche should have availed himself of a Kantian analysis of the beautiful, because there is no alternative.

Does Nietzsche even care about the intersubjective validity of judgements of taste? How does this sit with the common view of Nietzsche as a champion of 'perspectivism' and creative self-expression? First, 'perspectivism' is really an issue for the late Nietzsche only. *Birth of Tragedy* wears its commitment to uniform standards of beauty on its sleeve. Second, throughout *Birth of Tragedy*, we see Nietzsche characterize the artist, not as expressing a personal, subjective experience, but as a vehicle through which the primordial unity operates. That Nietzsche is explicitly concerned with vindicating the intersubjective validity of aesthetic judgements, however, becomes evident in his analysis of lyric poetry.

Modern aesthetics, by way of interpretation, could only add that here the first 'objective' artist confronts the first 'subjective' artist. But this interpretation helps us little, because *we know the subjective artist only as the poor artist*, and throughout the entire range of art we demand first of all the conquest of the subjective . . . indeed, we find it impossible to believe in any truly artistic production, however insignificant, if it is without objectivity, without pure contemplation devoid of interest.   (*BT* 5, ellipses and emphasis mine)[29]

---

[29] In a footnote to his translation of this passage, Kaufmann, predictably, traces this claim to Schopenhauer, not Kant. It is true that Schopenhauer takes the notion of disinterested pleasure from Kant. Kant means by this 'pleasure not due to preference-satisfaction', a notion he then uses to secure the intersubjective validity of judgements of taste. Schopenhauer thinks he has no need to shore up the epistemological credentials of aesthetic judgements. Kant, however, would have found his reliance on Platonic forms and our intuition of them entirely objectionable. Misunderstanding Kant, Schopenhauer then transforms the notion of disinterested pleasure into the notion of 'quieting of the will', as if the plastic arts invariably had an anaesthetic effect. Nietzsche transparently opposes this claim about the arts. Though Nietzsche uses Kantian and Schopenhauerian formulae interchangeably here, his concern is with the epistemological credentials of an aesthetic judgement. This is a problem, given the idiosyncrasy of experience that lyric poetry expresses.

The First Reading

Nietzsche cannot regard aesthetic judgements as objective because this would commit him to independent aesthetic properties, and he has argued against this. But if he regarded aesthetic judgements as subjective, lyric poetry, an exemplar of subjective self-expression, would not be a counter-example requiring a special analysis. Nietzsche's Apollinian is thus neither subjective nor objective. If it is not intersubjective, it is nothing. Nietzsche's conception of the Apollinian was probably inspired by a reading of Kant's 'Analytic of the Beautiful'.

However, it is on Nietzsche's phenomenology of the tragic that his early claim to have set himself apart from Schopenhauer is thought to rest.[30] For Schopenhauer, representations of tragic episodes reveal humanity's basic condition, given the nature of the will and the destructive and pointless way that it expresses itself.[31] Tragedy, then, simply shows us the empirical facts about the impossibility of attaining ordinary happiness. This induces in us resigned weariness anticipating the 'denial of the will' upon which salvation depends.

Here, we must be quite careful, however, to note the limited role Schopenhauer's metaphysics plays in his account of tragedy. Schopenhauer classes tragedy as a type of poetry, one among many plastic arts. He ascribes its effects to its presentation of the Platonic form of human nature. The theory of the will only explains why human life is disappointing. The aesthetic effects of tragedy depend not, as in music, on some aesthetic mechanism essentially involving the metaphysics of the will. Instead tragedy reports the simple fact that we suffer, and the more contentious claim that there is no way around this. The metaphysics of the will serves to explain why human beings suffer, but not why we take pleasure in tragedy. The pervasiveness of suffering can be adduced without recourse to metaphysics. Unlike Aristotle, Hegel, or Nietzsche, Schopenhauer does not explain tragic affect at all. The question 'why does tragic suffering in an artistic frame please us when ordinary suffering outside the artistic frame does not?' does not interest Schopenhauer. Given his account, the effects of tragedy ought to be more efficiently produced by watching crime reports or natural disasters on the nightly news. Being a victim oneself would be still more efficient. Tragedy, like life, is just plain unpleasant, but at least it promotes resignation.[32]

---

[30] Note that the above already has impact on our interpretation of Nietzsche's account of the tragic affect, since the tragic for Nietzsche is a synthesis of the Apollinian and Dionysian.

[31] *WWR* i. 252–5.

[32] It is a commonplace that Schopenhauer's theory is flawed by its inadequate account of tragic affect, this being Nietzsche's central objection to it. The most unsatisfying aspect of his theory is that, despite his refusal to reduce tragedies to morality plays, the importance of tragedy for him is ultimately didactic: the right course of action is to give up acting. This confusion of moral with aesthetic aims seems entirely to be expected, given Schopenhauer's dogmatic-Platonic account of aesthetic experience.

Yet if we turn instead to Kant's analysis of the dynamical sublime, we can see that it already resembles Nietzsche's account of tragedy as 'the *sublime* as the artistic taming of the horrible' (*BT* 7, emphasis Nietzsche's). Recall that the dynamical sublime is an experience in which we are exposed to events and images which would be dangerous if real. The effect of pleasure is due, in the first instance, to the presence of the artistic frame, which neutralizes the danger. In Nietzsche's account of the tragic, there must also be an artistic frame. This is why the tragic involves the Apollinian as the representational form that the Dionysian experience must take. The Dionysian life force must be presented as a human character of beautiful form and also as the circumstances destroying her. This artistic frame of formal representation transforms staged events from dangers to objects of contemplation.

Furthermore, the dynamical sublime, like all aesthetic experiences for Kant, is ultimately pleasurable. Kant's explanation for the peculiarly stern but thrilling quality of that pleasure was that hostile images which leave us unharmed put us into a state analogous to the state we are in when reason overcomes moral temptation. This in turn reminds us that, as moral agents, we are not merely vulnerable phenomenal beings, but that we are also, as noumenal beings, ultimately indestructible. This is because the moral law demands the practical conclusion that we are free, and this is only possible if we are also noumenal. Thus scenes of destruction, paradoxically, evoke our own invulnerability.

Kant himself does not go beyond associating the dynamical sublime with our experience of nature, with its 'bold, overhanging and, as it were, threatening rocks, thunderclouds piling up in the sky and moving about accompanied by lightning and thunderclaps, volcanoes with all their destructive power, hurricanes with all the devastation they leave behind, the boundless ocean heaved up, the high waterfall of a mighty river' (*CJ*, Ak. v. 261). However some of his brief remarks on the sublime might very well have suggested to Nietzsche that human activities and interactions could be sublime as well. This would set the stage for interpreting tragic affect as a species of the dynamical sublime.

Hence, no matter how much people may dispute, when they compare the statesman with the general, as to which one deserves the superior respect, an aesthetic judgement decides in favour of the general. Even war has something sublime about it if it is carried on in an orderly way and with respect for the sanctity of the citizens' rights. At the same time it makes the way of thinking of a people that carries it on in this way all the more sublime in proportion to the number of dangers in the face of which it courageously stood its ground. A prolonged peace, on the other hand, tends to make prevalent a merely commercial spirit, and along with it base selfishness, cowardice, and softness, and to debase the way of thinking of that people. (*CJ*, Ak. v. 262–3)

The First Reading

The passage from the dynamical sublime to the Nietzschean tragic, however, must take us through several intermediate stages.

First, human activities must be substituted for natural forces. It is no coincidence that so much of the plot material of tragic drama involves war (or its domestic equivalent, as in *The Godfather* films) and its side-effects. It is in organized destructiveness that human beings most closely approximate the destructiveness of nature.

Second, the neutralized danger the spectator feels must be displaced onto a represented figure—the tragic protagonist. Instead of framed images that, if real, would endanger the spectator, as with painted thunderstorms, the spectator identifies with the protagonist, who, within the frame, absorbs all the danger. Displacement now does the work of neutralizing the danger, but the tension between danger and its neutralization is itself intensified, as the spectator has a proxy inside the frame.

Third, the protagonist must be synthesized by the spectator as a beautiful form; this is the Apollinian element that Nietzsche claims is essential to tragedy. It is here that Nietzsche's theory *is* in debt to Schopenhauer's remarks about tragedy presenting the Platonic form of humanity. We need not suppose that the experience involves intuiting forms, any more than dreaming, to which Nietzsche often likens the Apollinian, involves contact with a dream world. The experience of the protagonist as satisfying to our taste, on a Kantian analysis, does not require any such ontological inflation.[33]

Naturally, our response to the destructiveness of the tragic cannot be precisely modelled on the account Kant gives of the dynamical sublime. There appears to be nothing in Nietzsche's theory corresponding to the role Kant gives to practical reason. In Kant's account, the combination of an image of danger, with the frame which neutralizes the danger, produces a state in us analogous to the overcoming of moral temptation. This reminds us that we are not only phenomenal but (because we are potentially moral), also noumenal beings, invulnerable to the vicissitudes of phenomenal life.

There is, however, an implied ethic in *Birth of Tragedy*, though it takes some teasing out. In section 4, Nietzsche says:

---

[33] Nietzsche often seems to think that a tragedy is more satisfying if the beautiful form and the destructive force are the same character, as in, e.g., *Oedipus Rex*. However the locus of destruction can be partially displaced away from the beautiful form, as it is in *Othello*. Othello's destructiveness is dependent upon the destructiveness of Iago. In *Richard III*, our response to the protagonist is close to pure revulsion, while the beautiful forms, if any, must be sought in his eloquence or his victims. As this last suggestion regarding eloquence makes clear, the notion of form here is potentially a quite broad one.

If we conceive of it at all as imperative and mandatory, this apotheosis of individuation knows but one law—the individual, i.e. the delimiting of the boundaries of the individual, measure in the Hellenic sense. *Apollo, as ethical deity,* exacts measure of his disciples, and, to be able to maintain it, he requires self-knowledge. And so, side by side with the aesthetic necessity for beauty, there occur the demands 'know thyself' and 'nothing in excess'; consequently overweening pride and excess are regarded as the truly hostile demons of the non-Apollininan age . . .   (*BT* 4)

Nietzsche shows no interest in Kantian ethics in his early phase, and almost all his discussions of it subsequently are hostile. However, Nietzsche had already entertained the idea that the Dionysian human being is 'no longer artist, (but rather) has become a work of art' (*BT* 1). If we identify the Apollinian with Kantian beauty, section 4 implies that ethics is a matter of an imperative to give form to oneself.[34] Given what we have already seen of Kant's and Nietzsche's aesthetics, this claim need not have the disturbingly arbitrary implications it would have for most current readers. For the standards would be those of Hellenic taste, vindicated by appeal to intersubjectively valid standards. Kant himself speaks of intersubjectively valid standards as creating a community of feeling, a *sensus communis*, which parallels or anticipates the standards of a moral community. Rather than reinforcing reason's determinative moral standards, reflective judgements about the design of an agent's character, based on the pleasure this design gives to impartial spectators, would *replace* determinative judgements of practical reason. Conduct would be judged by its attractiveness, rather than by its conformity to objective rules.[35]

However that may be, it is clear from the passage above that this activity of giving form to one's own character involves imposing constraints on one's

[34] I am assuming that what the early Nietzsche takes here to be ethics for the Greeks would be for the early Nietzsche ethics *simpliciter*. The ethics I am attributing to the early Nietzsche is, in essence, Nehamas's account of Nietzsche's ethics, early and late; see Alexander Nehamas, *Nietzsche: Life as Literature* (Cambridge, MA: Harvard University Press, 1985), 142–234. My disagreement with Nehamas's aestheticism is that I find it most clearly expressed and committed to only in the early writings. Since Nietzsche is here committed to intersubjectively valid standards of taste, such a form of aestheticism proves to involve a notion of constraining social norms. Of course, such an ethics may still seem entirely unsatisfactory from a modern perspective. It would have to trace any requirements not to harm others to a prior requirement to self-restraint merely for the sake of giving the self a certain structure. We may not find such a view acceptable. Nietzsche is in good company, however, since this is also Plato's derivation of the prohibition against interpersonal harm in the *Republic*.

[35] This analysis raises interesting questions about the role of agent intentions in ethical judgement; though the concept of intentional action would be involved, just as it is in other reflective judgements, the attribution of intention would drop out of ethical judgement, to be replaced by what the judge can't help but feel was the 'as if' intention. There are areas of moral judgement, however, where this may not be far from what we do (two possible examples are judgements of culpable negligence and judgements of general character).

desires. This, in turn, is sufficient to give Nietzsche access to a conception of the dynamical sublime resembling Kant's, up to a point. The experience would now look like this: when confronted with images of danger, our faculty of desire is initially mobilized to flee in terror, but for the aesthetic frame that neutralizes the danger and assures us of our safety. This feeling of standing fast against temptation produces an aesthetic state paralleling what we experience when we give form to our conduct in accord with intersubjectively valid standards. Such giving form also requires us to stand fast in the midst of temptation. Thus would a Nietzschean dynamical sublime bring us into awareness of our own power of self-restraint.

Thus the Nietzschean tragic is, to all intents and purposes, a variation on Kant's dynamical sublime. Instead of the form-dissolving power of nature, we see the form-dissolving power of destructive human activities. Human beings are both the agents of the destruction and the exemplars of the beautiful forms being destroyed. This in turn leads to an invigorating awareness of our own capacity to give form to our own characters.

Life force

One problem remains: why should this awareness of our power of self-restraint convey to us the 'illusion' that 'beneath the whirl of phenomena eternal life flows on indestructibly' (*BT* 18)? As we have seen, there is no difficulty in generating the *idea* of an indestructible eternal life: this is simply the intuitive understanding which can and must be thought, though it cannot be known, if we are to be able reflectively to judge that organisms have functional articulation. Its unity and exclusive existence follows from the merely apparent character of the plurality of human subjects. We cannot conceive of plurality apart from its genesis in a single transcendental subject. This rules out the possibility of a plurality of human transcendental subjects.[36] The problem, instead, is why

---

[36] There is an apparent tension between these two stages of the argument. On the one hand we are being told that we may not argue from the phenomenal to the noumenal (though we can *think* the noumenal for various purposes); on the other hand, the argument regarding plurality suggests that the noumenal must be thought of as an isolated subject. The tension is merely apparent, because the argument regarding plurality only applies to the noumenal sphere if there is one. That argument itself does nothing to establish that there is a noumenal intellect. There is nothing to prevent us from being reasonable in our attempts to think it, while acknowledging that perhaps it does not exist. Such arguments would be compatible even with claiming that there is no noumenal sphere. Then they would resemble arguments concerning fictional characters (e.g. Hamlet must have been young if he had recently been in college).

would awareness of self-restraint lead to a state bringing to mind this notion that our individuality is merely apparent?

The experience of self-restraint, because it involves awareness of our desires, involves an awareness of our own life force. This alone does not take us beyond the phenomenal, since the experience of 'what it is like to be alive' is itself a phenomenal experience. This could only suggest the supersensible if Nietzsche assumes that we must identify the intuitive understanding with the life force. Not only has Nietzsche rejected any argument that could demonstrate the identity of the one with the other, in his critique in 'On Schopenhauer'; he has abandoned any rationale for even *thinking* the identity problematically. If we think otherwise,

The concept 'thing-in-itself' is then removed . . . and another is secretly pressed into our hands. . . . The borrowed name and concept is the will . . . [But] the predicates of the will are borrowed from the world of appearance . . . they are all indivisibly knotted together with our organization, so that it is completely doubtful whether they have any meaning outside of the human sphere of knowledge.   (*KGW* i.4. 424–5 (1868))

Now, of course,

There *may* be a thing-in-itself, however, only in the sense that in the subject area of transcendence, *anything is possible* which at some time was hatched in a philosopher's brain. This possible thing-in-itself can be the will. . . . [But] one could still object that the thinker who stands before the riddle of the world has no other means than to guess in the hope that a moment of heightened awareness will place the word on his lips.   (*KGW* i.4. 421–2 (1868), emphasis mine)

'Anything is possible.' Indeed. But this is a thin reed to rest the analysis of the tragic affect on.

The account of our relationship to things-in-themselves in *Birth of Tragedy* and in *Truth and Lie* is the same. In both works, for reasons that are essentially Kantian, determinative judgements about noumena are forbidden. Nietzsche's encounter with the theory of reflective judgement had given him an escape route: just as Kant had limited knowledge to make room for faith, so would Nietzsche. Nietzsche's faith would not be in a moral solution. He could not endorse a reflective judgement that moral goodness would be rewarded by an omnipotent and all-benevolent God hidden behind the veil of phenomena. When Nietzsche proposes instead an 'artistic' solution, he does not mean that art would provide soothing but subjective experiences that would make up for the pain of phenomenal existence; art was to provide meaningfulness for these experiences. This meaningfulness does not alter the balance of pain and pleasure, or of moral worth and unworth, to be found in the phenomenal world.

Neither did Kant's faith in noumenal rewards and punishments. Phenomenal experience is put in a different light by virtue of what the subject comes to believe is the case noumenally. This belief has no cognitive warrant at all; for Nietzsche, art does not serve to provide us with information about noumena. Art provides intimations, feelings suggesting cognitive claims without providing evidence for them, which can be made sense of if we make reflective judgements about the noumenal world. Nietzsche and Kant make very different reflective judgements about noumena. But they are both concerned to reassure themselves that the world is subject, however fitfully or imperfectly, to some sort of design. They both believe that a stern aesthetic experience (the dynamical sublime in Kant, the tragic in Nietzsche) provides us with an intimation of a supersensible being. This being lies at the basis of whatever design we discern in the world. It wants us to realize our freedom and dignity as creatures with one foot in painful nature and one foot in a realm beyond it.

We saw that the notes that precede *Birth of Tragedy*, *Birth of Tragedy* itself, and *Truth and Lie* all form a unitary view. All three are committed to the impossibility of determinative, but the possibility of reflective, judgements about things-in-themselves. However, there is something noteworthy about *Truth and Lie* that takes us beyond what we have seen so far in *Birth of Tragedy*. It is not the agnosticism about noumena or an account of transcendental subjectivity that makes nature into a mind-dependent appearance. Nor is it a certain evaluative hostility to science, given Nietzsche's linking of science in those works with transcendental realism. What *Truth and Lie* adds is a genealogy of the valorization of truth.[37] It is Nietzsche's first genealogical investigation, and in many respects, his most important one. Now it seems to me that the initial motive for this inquiry was to strengthen the Kantian critique of dogmatic metaphysics by casting doubt not only on our capacity for it (this being the point of the discussions there of perception and language) but also by casting doubt on the moral worth of the very desire for it.

---

[37] Many interpretative confusions surround *TL*, in particular, what to make of the apparent claim that truth is socially constructed. Nietzsche at most claims that the high value we place on truth, the 'drive' for it, is due to social and historical processes rooted in utility. These processes presuppose the prior existence of language. The unavailability of truth is established by appeal to Kantian considerations: the mind-dependence of appearances. Nietzsche tries to reduce literal linguistic meaning to metaphorical meaning. He then goes on to explain metaphorical meaning in terms of psychological processes couched in the same Kantian model that underwrites Nietzsche's scepticism. Literal linguistic meaning is also involved in practices which valorize truth-telling. The result is that most interpreters come to believe that Nietzsche is urging scepticism based on a social-constructionist account of what truth is. However, he never says this; the social-constructionist account is offered as a response to the question 'where does the *drive* for truth come from?' Of all interpreters, Maudemarie Clark is the only one I am aware of who gets this right.

Interestingly, most of these themes can also be found in *Human, All-too-human*. For we are told there, in 'On First and Last Things', that though we cannot avoid the notion of a thing-in-itself, we possess little capacity for knowing it. The constructivist account of the transcendental subject is still very much in place. (I will discuss below the problems raised by the 'naturalization' of this Kantian subject.) We are also presented again with the Schopenhauerian premiss: life is permeated with suffering, and the more clearly we understand this, the more urgently the question of the value of life becomes. This observation of suffering, incidentally, depends upon neither a knowledge of nor an intimation about the thing-in-itself—it is phenomenal knowledge. Nietzsche observes here, as in his account of Apollinian art in *Birth of Tragedy*, that perhaps pleasing illusion is the best response to such a world. Furthermore, as in *Truth and Lie*, he rejects the answer that we have a moral duty to prefer the truth, however painful, for genealogy has delegitimized such moral motives. What remains, then? Despair is one possible response to learning that life is suffering. Nietzsche suggests another response: to enjoy contemplative knowledge for its own sake and to abandon attempts to find happiness through this-worldly efforts. Commitment to phenomenal science, no matter how dispiriting its findings might be, can bring happiness to people of a particular temperament, by calming their passions, by 'quieting their will'. Remarkably, then, Nietzsche appears to have returned to Schopenhauer's solution to the problem of how to respond to life as a whole.

What, then, is different in *Human, All-too-human*? First, Nietzsche seems to have finally absorbed the lessons of the empirical realist side of Kant. If we link scientific knowledge to transcendental realism, we will inevitably be disappointed in our investigations, for they will lead us to 'empirical idealism', i.e. scepticism. This need not be the case once we accept the phenomenality of the objects of scientific inquiry. Commitment to transcendental idealism in this sense permits us to reaffirm our commitment to empirical realism and the success, within its Kantian limits, of the scientific enterprise. With his new-found appreciation for the empirical realist aspect of the Kantian enterprise, Nietzsche is now free to embrace scientific inquiry as a guide to the phenomenal world.

What Nietzsche rejects is the manoeuvre of baptizing one's wishful thinking with the phrase 'reflective judgement'. The discovery of genealogy, in *Truth and Lie*, had opened up a new, humiliating possibility. Kant had always said that noumena were unknowable, though thinkable. The claims of a reasonable religion could be true. The phenomenality of the empirical world helped to set aside empirical grounds for believing that they were not. We could make sense of our intimations, feelings, and desires, if the claims of reasonable religion were true but unverifiable. What genealogy revealed was that the very intimations, feelings, and desires suggesting reasonable religion could be as easily made sense of by appealing to phenomenal causes. Absent a detailed account of how this could be so, Kant could have said: 'yes, perhaps Newtonian mechanism could explain the feeling of the sublime, or the moral intuitions we have, or the appearance of design in biology. It has not delivered these goods. Perhaps we are presented with these things because the supersensible is God. As it is supersensible, you cannot prove that it is not.' Unlike Newtonian mechanism, Darwinian biology and Nietzschean genealogy can provide satisfying empirical explanations for these things. The lingering possibility that the supersensible answers to our wishes remains. But this makes reflective judgement appear to be nothing more than a confession of cognitive incapacity ('I can't help but think . . .') and cowardice. When Nietzsche overcame his wishful thinking, 'the phantom fled from me' (*Z* I. 3).

The cognitive situations Kant and Nietzsche found themselves in were not so very different—this was what made Nietzsche receptive to the *Critique of Judgement* in the first place. In the end, the difference between Kant and the later Nietzsche rested not on evidence, but on a difference of moral attitude. Or if one finds the language of morality objectionable here, one could say: it was, finally, a matter of taste.

PART TWO

The Second Reading: Reason
(1880–1889)

Space, Time, and Idealism　　　4

Space and time in Kant

Though it may seem peculiar to begin a discussion of the mature Nietzsche's thought with Kant's view of space and time, there are good reasons for beginning precisely here. If Nietzsche's theoretical philosophy and account of cognition is a reaction to Kant's, then we should begin where Kant did: with the nature of space and time. Kant's views about space and time form the basis for his account of cognition and the transcendental idealist metaphysics it entails. Conversely, Nietzsche's frequently mentioned 'naturalism' only comes into focus if we regard it as a commitment to the transcendental reality (properly understood) of space and time. Nietzsche's own account of cognition and his own metaphysics flow from an attempt to hold onto Kant's account of cognition while rejecting the transcendental ideality of space and time.

Kant's interest in space and time derived from the metaphysical foundations of physics. However, the account he gave of them connected this concern with the philosophy of perception and epistemological questions about *a priori* knowledge. As often happens in discussions of Kant, I will focus on space initially. Later, however, the nature of time will raise special problems of its own.

We refer to space as if it was a thing, yet if it is a thing, it is a peculiar one: intangible, imperceptible, massless. Despite this, Newton asserted that space was a substantial thing. This is perhaps the simplest view. Newtonian space appears characterless. It is perfectly homogeneous. Newton's claim that space is a thing is vulnerable to Leibnizian arguments which hinge on the principle of the identity of indiscernibles. If space is an independently real thing, then it would make sense to say that the entire physical universe might be moving in a particular direction relative to it. There would be no identifiable difference, however, between a universe at absolute rest and a universe in motion. The claim which permits the existence of a metaphysical difference without an identifiable difference is precisely the claim that space is a thing. Therefore, space is not a thing.

What the moving universe and the stationary universe have in common is that all the objects in them stand in the same spatial relations to each other. The only metaphysical difference is the additional presence of substantial space. So if we eliminate the substance (which makes no difference) all that remains is the set of spatial relations in which the various objects stand. From this, Leibniz concluded that space was nothing beyond the set of spatial relations in which the physical objects stand.[1]

Kant may have been initially sympathetic to the Leibnizian view of space for its metaphysical austerity. However, Kant was also aware of Newtonian objections to Leibniz's position, after reading Samuel Clarke's published letters to Leibniz. In the correspondence, Clarke showed that there were reasons for taking seriously the idea of the universe as a whole rotating or accelerating. Given the principles of Newtonian mechanics, such scenarios would have observational consequences after all. While reading the correspondence, Kant encountered an argument that proved to his satisfaction that Leibniz must be mistaken after all.

The relations between the parts of a right-hand glove to each other are isomorphic with the relations between the parts of a left-hand glove. On a relational view, if the universe contained nothing but a left-hand glove, it would be identical to a universe containing only a right-hand glove. Both universes would contain all the same parts and all the same spatial relations. The two universes are not identical: one is a left-handed universe and the other is a right-handed universe. Therefore, space must be something more than the sum of relations among physical objects.

For Kant the conclusion that space was a substance whose geometry was known *a priori* seemed intolerable. His resolution of the difficulty was to propose that our sensory processing or 'sensibility' imposes spatial and temporal form on our sensory data. Physical space and time are nothing beyond this sensory form. By getting to this processing directly (in some sense), we can have *a priori* knowledge of the geometry of space.

The product of the operations of sensibility is what Kant calls 'empirical intuition', which is immediate awareness of a particular individual, not a

---

[1] It would be a mistake, however, to identify Leibniz's concern with a verificationist scruple. Leibniz seems to think that the very idea of an indiscernible pair of non-identical entities is impossible as such, and that refusing to admit the existence of such in no way trades on our epistemic limitations.

sense-datum.[2] Kant's term for sensation is not 'intuition', but 'affection', a change in the subject's state passively undergone. Thus, when Kant calls space the 'form of intuition', he does not mean simply that we experience sensations as necessarily having space-like phenomenological properties. The space in question is one he means to identify with physical space. What he means is that awareness of individuals is bound up with being aware of them in physical space.

Not all Kantian intuitions are empirical. There are pure intuitions as well. A pure intuition would be direct awareness of a particular without any sensory affection.[3] When Kant uses the term 'pure' he means independent of sensory input. Therefore 'pure' and '*a priori*' go together; 'empirical' and '*a posteriori*' go together. Now Kant thinks that only one kind of intuition is pure: our awareness of regions of space, and of space itself (and similarly for time). So space and time are not only forms of intuition, a framework within which all awareness of empirical individuals must take place; they are also pure intuitions, individuals themselves of which we are aware.

Kant calls the object of an intuition an 'appearance'. This seemingly elementary point is significant. Interpreters of Nietzsche, in discussing his remarks about appearances versus things-in-themselves use these expressions very freely, often with paradoxical results. It is important to remind ourselves that the Kantian term 'appearance' is a term of art for transcendental philosophy with very specific uses. Consequently, things-in-themselves must be understood in contrast to *this* concept of appearance, and not loosely synonymous with 'truth' or 'reality' or some other deconstructionist bugbear.

'Transcendental Aesthetic', then, is the study of the *a priori* aspects of sensibility. We may discover what these are by imaginative subtraction. Take away

---

[2] As Kant explains in the Transcendental Deduction, awareness of an individual, whether empirical or non-empirical ('pure') involves being aware of something as an object. Objecthood is an intrinsically syntactical property, as I will argue in the following chapter, therefore something conferred by the understanding and involving the categories. In the Transcendental Aesthetic, Kant is setting aside this complication, as he explains later (*CPR* B 161, n. 305). Some animals have empirical awareness, which involves the capacity to be aware of the data of sense as arrayed spatiotemporally (or else how would they get by?), but as far as we know, only human beings can have *intuitions* of space and time, judge of them, and hence have what Kant calls 'experience'.

[3] This is not precise. Kant claims that when the mind interacts with the data, the result is extended nature. Without any data to interact with, I do not think Kant would want to say that we would simply experience empty space. We would experience nothing. Rather, there is nothing intrinsic to the data which contains information about the structure of pure space itself. Of course there must be something about the data which indicates, given some space-like framework or other, which data get assigned to where. Hence, the structure of pure space must be traceable solely to the subject. If that is right, then our intuition of space *does* require associated empirical intuitions, even if it is not reducible to relations between them.

everything concerning concepts and thought (this isolates the sensibility)—now take away everything empirical. Whatever is left is *a priori*. It turns out that what is left are space and time.

Sensibility divides into inner sense and outer sense. Outer sense concerns our awareness of things external to us: physical objects. Inner sense concerns our awareness of our own mental states as introspected. The form of outer sense is space; the form of inner sense is time. Physical objects also exist in time, so time must govern the outer sense as well.

The 'Metaphysical Exposition' tells us just enough about space and time to show that they are mind-dependent; the 'Transcendental Exposition' shows that this mind-dependence is a condition of the possibility of *a priori* geometrical knowledge.[4] Though much ink has been spilled trying to make sense of Kant's alleged efforts to prove conclusively that space and time are mind-dependent, I think the very expression 'exposition' suggests that these texts are better read as an attempt to provide an interpretation of space and time which can make sense of their metaphysical and epistemological or 'transcendental' peculiarities. We are free to reject the exposition, though it would be unwise to do so, if that would leave us stuck with less illuminating Leibnizian or Newtonian views.

Kant claims that I cannot acquire spatial concepts by abstraction from experience, because I must experience spatially to have experience at all. First, I cannot imagine the absence of space, though I can imagine the absence of anything occupying it. Second, the relationship between space and spaces is not the relationship between a concept and its instances; spaces are parts of space, not instances of space. The reason space is not a concept is as follows. Though a concept can have an infinite number of instances, a concept cannot have an infinite number of parts. The content of a concept could not be grasped if that content were infinitely complex. But space does have an infinite number of parts. Therefore, space is not a concept.

The 'Transcendental Exposition' of space is simplicity itself: geometrical propositions are synthetic *a priori*. This can only be explained if space is mind-dependent. Kant concludes that space is not a thing-in-itself, nor is it a set of relations between things-in-themselves. It is nothing but the form of outer appearances, knowable *a priori*.

At *CPR* B45, Kant says that he wishes 'to forestall an error: it might occur to someone to illustrate the ideality of space asserted above by means of examples such as colours or taste, etc.' This passage is sometimes taken to

---

[4] Kant also believes we have analogous *a priori* knowledge of time, which he calls 'phoronomy'.

imply that we misunderstand the doctrine of the transcendental ideality of space if we read it as implying the mind-dependence of space in some 'vulgar' sense. However, this passage is better read as indicating Kant's commitment to the Cartesian view of primary and secondary qualities, and the roles they play in the New Science. This is awkward given his insistence that space is in a certain sense subjective.

Descartes believed that colours, sounds, smells, tastes, and pains inhere in the mind, rather than in the objects associated with them. These experiential qualities are caused by the physical properties of the object that seemed to possess the experiential properties. For example, the redness of an apple is a sensory state in the mind caused by the apple absorbing or reflecting certain wavelengths of electromagnetic energy. Physics can characterize the reflective properties of the apple, and the intrinsic properties of the light wave without reference to colour as experienced. Physics models only the spatiotemporal and quantifiable properties of the system. One is tempted to infer that space, time, and matter are real (because they are referred to in physics) whereas redness is not real (because it is not).

What I think Kant is suggesting here is that we can have objective knowledge of appearances by, and only by, consideration of an object's primary qualities. This does not mean that primary qualities are not mind-dependent and secondary qualities are. Both are, but the latter cannot be the basis for objective knowledge of appearances. Kant says this to forestall the conclusion that objective knowledge is impossible simply because space is mind-dependent. The mind-dependence of secondary qualities had often been appealed to in an attempt to exclude them from the domain of scientific knowledge. Thus he argues that colours are subjective appearances. They are mind-dependent, but not necessarily the same for everyone. Spatiotemporal and physical properties are objective appearances. They are mind-dependent, but necessarily the same for all observers.

Space and time in Nietzsche

It is a safe assumption that Nietzsche began his thoughts about space in 1865 by accepting the views he found in Schopenhauer. Schopenhauer, as we saw, gave his unqualified support to Kant's claims in the Transcendental Aesthetic, thus making Nietzsche a Kantian initially, at least second-hand. The earliest first-hand acquaintance Nietzsche might have had with Kantian texts on this subject would be his probable reading of the *Prolegomena* in

1867–8;[5] there is also some indication of Nietzsche's familiarity with the first *Critique* as early as 1872–3[6] but Nietzsche had already abandoned Kant's theory of space well before this.

As we saw in 'On Schopenhauer', Nietzsche quite early argued that Schopenhauer's use of Kant's theory of space and time was unacceptable. Recall that for Schopenhauer, the mind which constructs empirical phenomena is the human brain, itself an empirical phenomenon. Nietzsche is quick to point out that this position leads to incoherence.

[The] intellect is supposed to appear, i.e. the tree of knowledge is alleged to have suddenly and abruptly blossomed forth from a world that does not exist. Moreover, all of this is *supposed* to have taken place in a realm devoid of time and space, without the mediation of causality: yet that which has its origin in such an unworldly world must—according to Schopenhauer's tenets—be a thing-in-itself: either the intellect is now a new attribute, forever combined with the thing-in-itself; or there can be no intellect, because an intellect could never have come into being. But there does exist an intellect: consequently, it could not be an instrument of the world of appearances, as Schopenhauer claims, but a thing-in-itself, i.e. a will. Thus Schopenhauer's thing-in-itself would be both *principium individuationis* and the ground of necessity; in other words, the world as it exists.   (*KGW* i.4. 426–7 (1868))

The collapse of Schopenhauer's view leaves us with only two possibilities. We can abandon Schopenhauer's identification of the Kantian intellect with the brain and return to a purer Kantian position which locates the human intellect outside nature. Alternatively, we can preserve the identification of the human intellect with the Kantian intellect, but reject the claim that the intellect produces the space and time of nature. If we take this latter course, then we have two further choices. We can continue to regard space and time as transcendentally ideal. If they are not produced by our own intellects, we must suppose they are produced by some other intellect. Or we can regard space and time as transcendentally real. Finally, if we regard space and time as transcendentally real, we will be faced with the return of the original problems which motivated Kant in the first place: are they to be regarded in terms of relations or as substances? How are we to account for our *a priori* knowledge of them?

Because Nietzsche was 'reluctant to deduce space, time, and causality from our pitiful human consciousness' (*KGW* iii.3. 110–11 (1870–1)), he initially responded to this conundrum with the daring and extreme expedient of con-

---

[5] Nietzsche quotes from the *Prolegomena*, Ak. iv. 261 in 'On Schopenhauer', at *KGW* i.4. 419 (1868).

[6] Nietzsche quotes from *CPR*, footnote on A 37, in *PTG* 15 at *KGW* iii.2. 351 (1873) and from *CPR* B xxx at *KGW* iii.4. 14–15 (1872–3).

sidering space and time as the mind-dependent projections of an intellect other than our own: the primordial unity, the primordial intellect, the Dionysian world-artist. This way Nietzsche can say we all share a common space and time, while evading the difficulties raised by identifying the brain with the human intellect. For now it was not the human intellect which, in producing space and time, produces the brain and therefore itself. Rather the primordial intellect produces space and time and by that produces the brain.

However, by 1873, in *Truth and Lie*, Nietzsche appears to be asserting the Kantian view:

[If] each of us had a different kind of sense perception . . . then no one would speak of such a regularity of nature, rather, nature would be grasped only as a creation which is subjective in the highest degree . . . All that we actually know about these laws of nature is what we ourselves bring to them—time and space, and therefore relationships of succession and number. But everything marvellous about laws of nature, everything that quite astonishes us therein and seems to demand our explanation, everything that might lead us to distrust idealism: all this is completely and solely contained within the mathematical strictness and inviolability of our representations of time and space. But we produce these representations in and from ourselves with the same necessity with which the spider spins. (*KGW* iii.2. 379 (1873)/ *TL* 1)

However, Nietzsche also seems to be asserting the paradoxical Schopenhauerian view that identifies the Kantian intellect with the brain. 'One might invent such a fable, and yet he would still not have adequately illustrated how miserable, how shadowy and transient, how aimless and arbitrary the human intellect looks *within* nature' (*KGW* iii.2. 369 (1873)/ *TL* 1, emphasis mine). I see no way of reconciling these strands within *Truth and Lie* other than by assuming that there are two different natures: the nature which is the object of natural science and the nature which contains the brain, nature as it seems to be and nature as it is. Such a view is compatible with the notion of the primordial unity that projects its own space and time. Nietzsche had expressed this notion in public one year earlier, in *Birth of Tragedy*, and in notes dating back even earlier. Such a view merely compels us to admit that we cannot know through natural science or geometrical intuition what the geometry of the primordial unity's space is. For all we know, it may be the same as the geometry of our own phenomenal space. Early Nietzsche, following Kant, links natural science (i.e. Newtonian physics) to our forms of intuition. Since our forms of intuition generate the space and time referred to in Newtonian theory, it follows that Newtonian theory does not give us access to nature as it really is, the nature within which we, and our brains, are embedded. Though real nature may be Newtonian, it may very well not be. We can never know if phenomenal space resembles nature's space.

The Second Reading

If this interpretation is correct, then we would expect to find Nietzsche endorsing Trendelenburg's famous 'neglected alternative' view of space and time: for all we know, the space and time that we are all *in* may coincide with the space and time I experience, though the converse may be true.

[If] the sciences are right, then we are not supported by Kant's foundation; if Kant is right, then the sciences are wrong. Against Kant, it must always be further objected that, even if we grant all of his propositions, it still remains entirely possible that the world is as it appears to us to be. (*KGW* iii.4. 47 (1872–3))

The forms of the intellect have very gradually arisen out of matter. It is plausible in itself that these forms are strictly adequate to the truth. (*KGW* iii.4. 55 (1872–3)).

This contrast between the two spaces, one known but imaginary, the other real but unknown, persists long after Nietzsche had disowned the 'artist's metaphysics' of *Birth of Tragedy*. 'Our space is valid for an imaginary world. Of the space, which belongs to the eternal river of the things, we know nothing' (*KGW* v.2. 398 (1881)). 'By my showing the subjective genesis, e.g., of space etc. the thing itself is neither refuted nor proven. Against Kant—' (*KGW* vii.2. 292 (1884)). The mature view differs from the view in *Birth of Tragedy* and *Truth and Lie*. First, as we have just observed, Nietzsche rejects the notion of the projection of a common space by the primordial unity. This appears to leave Nietzsche with a contrast between transcendentally ideal space and transcendentally real space. Second, though the notion of the Kantian intellect developing over time is one Nietzsche carried over from Schopenhauer and Lange, Nietzsche Darwinizes it. The specific character our forms of intuition possess is due to their selective advantage over equally possible competitors. Had rival intellects appeared, they would have perished, leaving the field to nature's favoured Euclideans.

The categories are 'truths' only in the sense that they are conditions of life for us: as *Euclidean* space is a conditional 'truth.' (Between ourselves: since no one would maintain that there is any necessity for men to exist, reason, as well as *Euclidean* space, is a mere idiosyncrasy of a certain species of animal, and one among many. (*KGW* viii.3. 126 (1888)/ *WP* 515, emphasis mine)

Now as the original formulation of the 'neglected alternative' thesis had it, the relevant contrast was between transcendentally ideal space and transcendentally real space, the space of things-in-themselves. In the final view, there is a significant departure from the 'neglected alternative' view. First, Nietzsche, rejects the intelligibility of a contrast between appearances and things-in-themselves. If the very idea of the thing-in-itself is unacceptable, then one would think that Nietzsche would be forced back into a strict Kantianism, for the very idea of a contrasting domain that might differ from the domain in which we find phenomenal space has lost all purchase. Matters are further confused by Nietzsche's repeated characterization of phenomenal space as a falsification. This not only suggests the existence of a contrasting domain, but even of some sort of access to it. We see assertions seeming to confirm this, as when he says 'I believe in absolute space as the substratum of force: the latter limits and forms. Time eternal. But space and time do not exist in themselves' (*KGW* vii.3. 285–6 (1885)/*WP* 545). In this last passage in particular, he seems to give with one hand what he takes away with the other: how can space and time be 'absolute' and 'not exist in themselves'?

We begin to get a clue to what Nietzsche has done with his Kantian inheritance in the following: 'Denial of *empty* space and the reduction of mechanics to the tyranny of the eye and the touch. Denial of *actio in distans*' (*KGW* vii.3. 439 (1885), emphasis mine). There is only one possible explanation for these Kantian themes in the late Nietzsche's view of space. The contrast is not between the space human beings construct versus the space of the thing-in-itself. The contrast is between the space we directly experience by virtue of our innate space producing psychological mechanisms versus the space our best empirical theory posits. This latter contrast does not commit Nietzsche to the claim that the space of natural science is mind-independent. I wish to leave open the possibility that nature as the late Nietzsche understands it is mind-dependent (i.e. is not to be identified with the Kantian thing-in-itself). Meanwhile we can still distinguish between the world as it appears in naive, uncorrected experience, and the world as it appears in scientifically corrected experience.

Matters are further complicated by the fact that Nietzsche is still highly critical of what *he* calls 'science' in his late writings. It is tempting to think that Nietzsche is still contrasting things-in-themselves and phenomena, where the latter are associated with the claims of scientific theory. Yet because Nietzsche describes phenomena, and our theories about them, as falsifications, this seems to commit him to knowing something about things-in-themselves (as Schopenhauer claimed). That knowledge would enable him to debunk the claims of natural science to have adequately described things-in-themselves. However, on my interpretation, Nietzsche never claimed to have knowledge of things-in-themselves, not even in his early phase; and in his late phase, he denies that there *are* things-in-themselves.

However, when Nietzsche criticizes the truth claims of 'science' he is often attacking Newtonian mechanism in favour of Boscovichian dynamism; the contrast is not between science and metaphysics, or between science and some postmetaphysical Nietzschean cosmology, but between one scientific theory and another, better one.

The evidence for this interpretation hinges on clarifying Nietzsche's views on the possibility of a vacuum. Nietzsche seems to have thought the space of nature invariably filled, as contrasted with phenomenal space, which contains empty regions. There are three possible reasons why he might have held such a view. First, there is a long tradition, dating back at least to Aristotle[7] and including Descartes, Spinoza, and Leibniz, which held that empty space is impossible; Nietzsche may have been aware of these discussions. He read the rationalists, and probably read Spinoza closely. There is no clear evidence in his texts of their influence on this issue though.

Second, the mature Nietzsche's commitment to Boscovichian dynamism can be read as entailing a commitment to a plenum cosmos for the following reason. According to Boscovich, there are fields of one force which manifest themselves at close distances as repulsion, but at greater distances as attraction. Boscovich's force, when repulsive, serves as his substitute for impenetrable matter; the same force, when attractive, behaves just as Newtonian gravity does.[8] Furthermore, Boscovich was a relationalist about space and time. Boscovich's cosmos consists, then, of movable, extensionless centres and the fields of the one force with which they are associated.[9]

When, then, if ever, should we say that Boscovichian space is empty? One possibility is that every point of space not occupied by a Boscovichian force-centre should be regarded as empty, including those points within a force-centre's repulsive field. This interpretation would have the world consist of far more empty space than a corresponding Newtonian world. However, this seems completely arbitrary. Another possibility would be to say that space is filled only as far as the field's repulsive region extends; once the force begins to manifest itself as attractive, we may regard the associated space as empty. This interpretation would have the world consist of exactly as much empty space as

---

[7] See *Physics* IV, chs. 6–9 in Aristotle, *The Complete Works of Aristotle*, trans. J. L. Ackrill, ed. Jonathan Barnes (Princeton: Princeton University Press, 1984).

[8] Ruggero Giuseppe Boscovich, *A Theory of Natural Philosophy*, trans. of *Philosophiae Naturalis Theoria Redacta ad Unicam Legem Virium in Natura Existentium*, 2nd edn. (1763) (Chicago, London: Open Court Publishing Company, 1922).

[9] Boscovich appears to think of the centres of his fields as movable, massless particles. However, given his relationalism, it is difficult to see the extensionless centre as anything more than an interior limit of the field; in that case, Boscovich's ontology would only consist of fields of force (which stand in various spatial and temporal relations to each other). This is a point Nietzsche seems to have grasped when he claims that Boscovich has done away with the notion of an atomic substratum of force.

the corresponding Newtonian world. There is also something arbitrary about calling space within which the force operates in one fashion 'empty' and space in which it operates in another fashion 'full'. By virtue of the inverse square law, gravity's effect diminishes over space continuously without ever stopping altogether. Given the existence of at least some 'matter' (on Boscovich's dynamist construal of it), Boscovich's force, in its gravitational, attractive mode, will reach to every region of space. We would describe the region in which the one force operates repulsively as 'full'. Given that it is only *one* force, it is more natural to describe those regions where it operates attractively as 'full' as well. If there is any 'matter' at all, the pervasiveness of gravity makes it natural to describe the entire Boscovichian cosmos as 'full'.

Nietzsche believed that the quantity of force and the number of Boscovichian centres of force in the cosmos were finite. '[The] world may be thought of as a certain definite quantity of force and as a certain definite number of centres of force—and every other representation remains indefinite and therefore useless' (*KGW* viii.3. 168 (1888)/ *WP* 1066). This appears to have been axiomatic for him, and I can find no place where he argues for it. Consequently, the world is 'enclosed by "nothingness" as by a boundary; not something blurry or wasted, not something endlessly extended, but set in a definite space as a definite force, and not a space that might be "empty" here or there, but rather as force throughout' (*KGW* vii.3. 338 (1885)/ *WP* 1067). Here, however, Nietzsche appears to have left Boscovich behind. For even if a Boscovichian cosmos only contained a finite number of centres of force, that force would radiate from those centres across an infinite extent of space. Though the intensity of the force would diminish with each unit of space traversed, since this diminution is continuous, it would never diminish altogether. If we are to regard space within which Boscovich's force operates, whether repulsively or attractively, as 'full', then a Boscovichian cosmos would be 'endlessly extended'. Thus, Nietzsche seems to have amended Boscovich's physics in some fashion so that this possibility is precluded. At some distance from a force-centre, the attraction exerted must drop to zero. Beyond the farthest reaches of the Boscovichian force, there is 'nothingness'. Yet in the very same passage, Nietzsche denies that there could be empty regions of space, which is precisely what this 'nothingness' would be, presumably. Again we are left with the apparently brute fact that space must always be filled.

Suppose that Nietzsche grasped that a Newtonian substantival account of space implied that it is possible that there could be a world containing Newtonian space and nothing else; such a possible world would be empty. Nietzsche may have confused the possibility of an entirely empty space with

the possibility of empty regions of space (which is what he appears to be denying at *KGW* vii.3. 439 (1885)). Of course one could be a relationalist about
space and still believe that there were empty regions, but I suspect that
Nietzsche did not see this. His denial of the possibility of regions of empty space
would then be due to rejection of substantivalism and a commitment to a relational view of space. This would explain why Nietzsche, having proposed that
the physical universe has a finite magnitude, felt compelled to characterize
what is beyond its extent as 'nothingness'. This nothingness is somehow to be
understood as distinct from a comparable region of empty space. For such a
region, being infinite, is almost like an entirely empty space; on a relationalist
view, there could not be an entirely empty space. Why did Nietzsche embrace
relationalism in the first place? Either he accepted the standard reasons offered
since Leibniz for such a view or he took it over from Boscovich. Ontological parsimony, Boscovich's likely motivation, probably loomed large for
Nietzsche as well.

Nietzsche believes, not that things-in-themselves are spatial, but that our
best empirical theory posits the existence of spatial relations among the parts of
a plenum cosmos. Space is nothing besides the relations obtaining between
parts of the plenum; if there was no plenum, there would be no space. Nietzsche
also seems to have understood that there is no reason to assume that this space
is Euclidean, for he canvasses the possibility that it is not: '[In] an indefinite
space [a state of equilibrium] would have to have been reached. Likewise in a
spherical space. The shape of space must be the cause of eternal movement'
(*KGW* vii.3. 258 (1885)/ *WP* 1064, emphasis mine).[10] This cosmology is not
meant to characterize things-in-themselves, of course; it is meant to characterize *nature*.

Within that nature, there are animals like ourselves, subject to selection pressures. Nietzsche regards our perception of the world as composed of stable
individual substances, an expedient falsification of what is actually continuous
and in flux; those who perceive this way enjoy a simpler, more tractable experience, to which they can respond quickly and effectively. What I propose is
that Nietzsche regards the latter falsification as interdependent with a falsification of space. Dividing the plenum into individuals also yields the empty space

---

[10] Another way to read the talk of being bounded by nothingness is to ascribe to Nietzsche a non-
Euclidean cosmology with a space of positive curvature, as Moles does. See Alastair Moles, *Nietzsche's
Philosophy of Nature and Cosmology* (New York: P. Lang, 1990). That which lies outside the curved
space would be 'nothingness'. That Nietzsche seems to have understood the possibility of a non-
Euclidean space seems implied by his reference to 'a spherical space' at *KGW* vii.3. 258 (1885)/ *WP*
1064. However, Nietzsche's references to non-Euclidean space seem to me far too sparse to serve as
an explanation for his belief that the physical universe is finite in extent.

between them; thus the experience of emptiness is a side-effect of an operation on the data of experience conferring selective advantages. Furthermore, projection of Euclidean space along with the carving out of many individuals is a condition of quantitative thought, with all the pragmatic advantages it brings in its wake. Finally, though I do not know if Nietzsche entertained this thought, imposing a Euclidean geometry on our experiences could be construed as simplifying as well. A Euclidean world is spatially isotropic: one region of Euclidean space is just like another. The space of nature is non-isotropic, but in ways lacking practical significance. There is no selection pressure for being perceptually sensitive to the ways one region of space differs from another.

In short, Nietzsche believed that Kant was right about the psychology of spatial perception. We have a faculty, sensibility, which organizes our experience. It arrays everything we perceive within a potentially empty Euclidean space whose geometrical properties can be known *a priori*. Kant was wrong only about the metaphysics and epistemology: the space of perception is not physical space, which may not be Euclidean, cannot be empty, and cannot be known *a priori*.

For Nietzsche our earlier empirical theory (Newton's) gave in to the temptation to reify this innate space of perception into a substance. Nonetheless it represented real progress over the physics of Aristotle. This very progress then paved the way for Boscovich's dynamist recasting of Newton's laws in terms of fields of force. Boscovich in turn urged on him that space was relational and not substantival as Newton had thought. This in turn made it possible to 'Darwinize' Kant's Transcendental Aesthetic and arrive at what Nietzsche regarded as the correct views of perceptual and physical space. The complete view is presented in *Human, All-too-human*:

That which we now call the world is the outcome of a host of errors and fantasies which have gradually arisen and grown entwined with one another in the course of the overall evolution of the organic being, and are now inherited by us as the accumulated treasure of the entire past—as treasure: for the value of our humanity depends upon it. *Rigorous science is capable of detaching us from this ideational world* only to a limited extent—and more is certainly not to be desired—inasmuch as it is incapable of making any essential inroad into the power of habits of feeling acquired in primeval times: but *it can, quite gradually and step by step, illuminate the history of the genesis of the world as idea—and for brief periods at any rate, lift us up out of the entire proceeding.* (*HA* I. 16, emphasis mine)

The invention of the laws of numbers was made on the basis of the error, dominant even from the earliest times, that there are identical things (but in fact nothing is identical with anything else); at least that there are things (but there is no 'thing'). The assumption of plurality always presupposes the existence of something that occurs more than once: but precisely here error already holds sway, here already we are fabricating beings, unities which do not exist.—Our sensations of space and time are false, for tested consistently they lead to logical contradictions ... (*HA* I. 19)[11]

The establishment of conclusions in science always unavoidably involves us in calculating with certain false magnitudes: but because these magnitudes are at least *constant*, as for example are our sensations of time and space, the conclusions of science acquire a complete rigorousness and certainty in their coherence with one another; one can build on them ... (*HA* I. 19)

So far this is also the view in *Truth and Lie* regarding the relationship between space and time as forms of intuition and the seeming objectivity of natural science. In *Truth and Lie* Nietzsche noted that we cannot help but perceive under the forms of intuition, and the evidence for any empirical theory is derived from such perception. From this he concluded that we are forever prevented from knowing empirically what space is really like. After reading Boscovich, Nietzsche recognizes another possibility:

[In Atomic theory], we continue to feel ourselves compelled to assume the existence of a 'thing' or material 'substratum' which is moved, while the whole procedure of science has pursued the task of resolving everything thing-like (material) in motions: here too our sensations divide that which moves from that which is moved, and we cannot get out of this circle because our belief in the existence of things has been tied up with our being from time immemorial.—When Kant says 'the understanding does not draw its laws from nature, it prescribes them to nature', this is wholly true with regard to the *concept of nature* which we are obliged to attach to nature (nature = world as idea, that is as error), but which is the summation of a host of errors of the understanding. To a world which is not our idea the laws of numbers are wholly inapplicable: these are valid only for the human world. (*HA* I. 19)

Nietzsche associates Kantian construction with an intellect that develops over time. He also associates Kantian construction with false physical theories which depend upon reification of the product of such constructive processes. But now, such theories are false not because of a contrast between phenomena and things-in-themselves, but because of a contrast between inferior (Newtonian) and superior (Boscovichian) empirical theories.

The heart of Nietzsche's naturalism is his commitment to the existence of two spaces and times. One pair is produced by the human intellect. The other pair is that space and time within which the human intellect is embedded. The central claim of Nietzsche's naturalism is that everything we are as individuals takes place in nature. Now it will be familiar to contemporary readers of

---

[11] I believe this to be an allusion to Kant's First and Second Antinomies (see discussion below).

analytic philosophy to identify nature with whatever it is that our best empirical theories posit as existing. For this sort of naturalism, a posit is acceptable if we can reduce the theory in which the posit appears to our best empirical theory (typically, physics).

This, however, is not the sense I wish to assign to Nietzsche's naturalism. In *Truth and Lie*, Nietzsche embeds human beings and their cognitive capacities within nature, while being a sceptic about natural science's ability to represent nature. Obviously then, for Nietzsche in *Truth and Lie*, nature cannot be identified with the posits of natural science. Rather, for Nietzsche to affirm naturalism is to affirm that if something exists, it exists embedded within space and time. In Nietzsche's early phase, he helps himself to judgements about the primordial unity or primordial intellect, which exists outside space and time. These judgements are merely reflective. Other entities outside space and time—transcendental subjects as Kant had conceived them and Platonic forms—are explicitly disowned as objects of determinative judgements. After Nietzsche abandoned his 'artist's metaphysics' even the primordial intellect dropped out as a topic for discussion. Then the space and time within which we are embedded became real and no longer dependent upon any subject, whether ours or the primordial intellect's. Nietzsche's naturalism is, in essence, what Kant called transcendental realism about space and time. Again, it is not that Nietzsche regards space and time as belonging to things-in-themselves, which is how Kant characterizes transcendental realism about space and time. According to Nietzsche, there are no things-in-themselves. Nietzsche parts company with Kant by refusing to identify physical space with phenomenal space, the space produced by our minds in organizing our sensory data. We discuss the relationship between Nietzschean nature and Kantian things-in-themselves below.

Yet thus far, we have seen no underlying reason motivating Nietzsche's departure from transcendental idealism in favour of naturalism. All the twists and turns of his thoughts on space go back to the original antithesis we mentioned above: the impossibility of reconciling a Kantian theory of space with a Schopenhauerian identification of the Kantian intellect with the brain. A reasonable conclusion would be to return to the original Kantian position: distinguish the Kantian intellect from the brain and allow the former to produce the latter without bootstraps. To grasp why Nietzsche believed that path was unavailable, we must turn to his views on time.

Time

Nietzsche also began his thoughts about time as a Kantian, given his Schopenhauerian starting point. While he came to regard Schopenhauer's naturalized Kantianism as unstable, he also concluded that Kant's theory of time fails on its own terms. The following passage from *Philosophy in the Tragic Age of the Greeks*, shows why.

If those adversaries however wanted to object 'in your thought there is, after all, succession, therefore your thought also could not be real and consequently also could prove nothing,' so would Parmenides perhaps answer as Kant did in a similar case, at the same objection, 'To be sure, I can say that my representations follow each other: however that is only to say that we ourselves are conscious of them as in a time-sequence, according to the form of the inner sense. Time is therefore not something in itself, also not an objectively adhering determination of things.' It is therefore necessary to distinguish between the pure thought, which is timeless like the one Parmenidean being, and the awareness of this thought; the latter has already translated the thought into the form of appearance, therefore into succession, plurality, and movement. It is likely, that Parmenides himself would have chosen this way out: incidentally the same objection ought to come against him then, that A. Spir (*Thought and Reality*, p. 264) brought against Kant.

> Now first, it is plain that I can know nothing of a succession as such, if I do not have the consecutive links together at once in my awareness. The representation of a succession is therefore not at all successive, consequently it is also altogether different from the succession of our representations. Second, Kant's assumption implies such apparent absurdities, that it takes a miracle to see how he could let them go unheeded. Caesar and Socrates are on this assumption not really dead, they live still even as well as they did two thousand years before and only seem dead to me because of the equipment of my 'inner sense'. Future persons now live already, and if they have still not stepped forward as living, for this too the equipment of the 'inner sense' is responsible. Here one must ask above all: How can the beginning and end of conscious life, together with all its inner and outer senses exist only in the apprehension of the inner sense? The fact is, one cannot deny the pervasive actuality of change. Throw it out of the window, it slips back in through the keyhole. One says 'it seems to me clear that conditions and representations change'— however, this appearance itself is something objectively existing and in it succession has undoubted objective actuality, inside it something really follows one after the other. Furthermore one must notice, that the whole criticism of reason could have rationale and legitimacy only on condition that our representations appear as they are. Then if representations had appeared differently than they really are, one would be able to make no valid claims about them, and therefore one

could erect no theory of knowledge and no 'transcendental' investigation of objective validity. However, it is beyond doubt that our representations appear to us as successive. (*KGW* iii.2. 351 (1873)/*PTG* 15)

Nietzsche does not explicitly embrace Spir's criticisms of Kant. However, he thinks that Parmenides' view of time is sufficiently similar to Kant's to be vulnerable to these criticisms. By implication, he would reject the Kantian account of time for the same reasons. The weak objection is that transcendental idealism about time is simply incredible if it means that 'Caesar and Socrates are on this assumption not really dead'. The stronger objection is that 'our representations appear to us as successive'. Even if we do construct appearances from our sensory data and impose spatial form on them in the process, sensory data themselves are presented to us in temporal succession. Therefore, there is at least one domain in which temporal succession is real: the domain of our own representations. What is more, any operations on our representations can only be conceived of as successive, and Kant's transcendental psychology is shot through with references to constructive *processes*; yet the very idea of an atemporal process makes little sense on the face of it.[12]

We have, then, a path from within Kantian thought to transcendental realism, at least about time. For even if we do not speculate about the character of the world outside the mind, transcendental realism about time gains a foothold within the mind itself. We have no choice but to embed the mind within a time extending before the existence of the mind and continuing long after its destruction. Having been forced to make this move, there seems little point in not embedding the mind within a transcendentally real space as well, at which point there are no further problems of *Kantian* origin to prevent the identification of the human intellect with the brain.[13]

There is an apparent problem with the interpretative claims we have made thus far. Recall that we said that Nietzsche rejects Kant's claim that the space and time of nature are the space and time our cognitive apparatus imposes on our sensations. Now, for Kant, there are really only two possible positions: that space and time are transcendentally ideal or that they are transcendentally real, where the former means that they are mind-dependent and the latter means that they are features of things-in-themselves. For Kant, the realm of nature is

[12] Kant might very well have bitten this bullet, as Wayne Waxman has proposed. My purpose here, however, is not to attack Kant, but to explicate Nietzsche. See Wayne Waxman, *Kant's Model of the Mind: A New Interpretation of Transcendental Idealism* (Oxford: Oxford University Press, 1991), 183–267.

[13] Obviously such an identification is not compulsory merely given the existence of intellects and transcendentally real space and time; it has its attractions when contrasted with the alternatives (e.g. Cartesianism).

precisely the spatiotemporal realm. So this question about the status of space and time, for Kant, just is the question of whether nature is mind-dependent or whether nature is real 'in-itself'.

Nietzsche agrees with Kant that our minds impose a spatial form on our sensations such that space appears to be Euclidean and in some regions empty. The same holds true for time. Though the 'geometry' of time is simpler by two dimensions, it does have a linear structure by which one can infer, e.g. that if t_2 is after t_1 and t_3 is after t_2, then t_3 is after t_1, etc. Also, just as regions of space can be empty, so too can moments of time. Nietzsche diverges from Kant in his refusal to identify this space and time with the space and time of nature. He is willing to posit a space and time of nature, which may differ from our intuitional space and time as to geometry, emptiness, etc. Consequently, in rejecting Kant's identification of these two spaces (and times), Nietzsche must also reject Kant's thesis that the geometrical properties of physical space are knowable *a priori*.

However, in Kant's terminology, this would be to reject the transcendental ideality of physical space and time, and to affirm their transcendental reality. For Kant, this is just to say that physical space and time (and whatever fills them) are things-in-themselves or transcendentally real relations between things-in-themselves. Notoriously, Nietzsche in his latest writings denies that the very idea of a thing-in-itself is coherent, and thus denies that there are any such things. Thus, one would think, if space and time cannot be transcendentally real (because nothing is transcendentally real, the very concept being incoherent and empty) they must be transcendentally ideal. This would collapse Nietzsche's position into something not unlike Kant's again.

Here, however, appearances can be misleading. Kant himself allows that natural science can posit entities, events, processes, etc. which are 'empirical' but unobservable for reasons relating to contingent limitations on our cognitive capacities. Even outside science, in the domain of ordinary life, there are countless cases of such 'empirical' speculation. We may never know the precise number of people who shot at President Kennedy; if there was more than one person, these other parties went (presumably) unobserved, left insufficient traces behind to confirm their existence, etc. Nonetheless, it is an empirical fact, not a noumenal fact, that the number of assassins was one (or two, or three). Historians and conspiracy theorists may posit the existence or non-existence of these additional assassins, based on available empirical evidence. In natural science, there are theoretical posits which may not be directly observable, which are posited based on available empirical evidence. Kant is not an instrumentalist about such posits. They fall within the domain of the phenomenal. They are no less a part of the world of empirical fact for being hidden, small, or far from observers. Whether this is the stance that Kant ought to have taken is a question I leave aside; the point is that, for Kant, quarks and genes would be 'empirically real and transcendentally ideal' despite being unobservable.

What I want to suggest, then, is that, for Nietzsche, the space (and time) of nature are empirically real but unobservable posits not unlike atoms. The fact that we cannot directly perceive the world in anything but Euclidean terms is analogous to the fact that we cannot perceive objects smaller than a certain size. However, based on the empirical evidence we possess, we can suppose that there are imperceptible quarks; similarly, based on the empirical evidence we possess, we can suppose that the space of nature is non-Euclidean. Whether our predisposition to perceive the world as Euclidean helps or hinders us in getting the geometry of physical space right is a physical question about nature. It is independent of whether nature as a whole is mind-dependent.

Nietzsche's understanding of what a thing-in-itself is *is* simply the notion of a completely mind-independent object; in denying that there are things-in-themselves, Nietzsche should be understood to be asserting a claim analogous to Berkeley's claim that to be is to be perceived. We must expand the scope of the perceived to encompass both the perceivable but not presently perceived. We should also include theoretical posits of the same general character as medium-sized objects, which for peculiar reasons are unobservable (the extremely small and the extremely remote). The sum of such objects, events, processes, etc. is what Nietzsche conceives nature to be. However, there is no obstacle to Nietzsche regarding the entire natural world as mind-dependent. Nietzsche's persistent claims to the effect that we falsify the world because our cognitive capacities have evolved under conditions which select for the expedient falsification, are completely independent of his metaphysical claims that the world is mind-dependent, or that the very idea of a mind-independent world is incoherent. The distinction between the falsified world and the not-falsified world should be made within the sphere of the mind-dependent.[14] The sphere of the mind-independent is empty.

One worry concerning the interpretation I have offered so far concerns the status of unperceived posits of our empirical theory. If we assimilate

---

[14] It is on this point that my interpretation diverges from what I take to be Maudemarie Clark's, to which I am otherwise obviously indebted. On Clark's view, eliminating the mind-independent world eliminates the basis for any contrast between falsified and unfalsified worlds. On my view, the 'falsification thesis' survives the rejection of things-in-themselves, carving a distinction between naive and sophisticated experiences of a mind-dependent world. See Maudemarie Clark, *Nietzsche on Truth and Philosophy* (Cambridge: Cambridge University Press, 1991), 95–158.

Nietzsche's view to Kant's, it seems we would have to regard Nietzsche as some sort of phenomenalist. We have already seen that when Schopenhauer defended his own idealism from incoherence, he fell back on quasi-phenomenalist construals of statements concerning unobserved objects. Yet Nietzsche rejected these construals in 'On Schopenhauer'. We have no further discussion of phenomenalism in his texts, so we must assume that this was a commitment he stood by. Without phenomenalism, how can Nietzsche distinguish a space and time produced by our sensibility from a space and time of nature? Such a nature is both mind-dependent in Berkeley's sense, and yet contains objects not currently perceived by us.

Nietzsche has available to him only the three options Berkeley had available to him: either some mind perceives all of nature (God, and therefore an option the late Nietzsche must reject), or the unobserved objects really do not exist (which is incredible), or there are enough finite minds in existence to guarantee that nothing we want to posit in our empirical theories goes unobserved. I believe that Nietzsche was committed to the third, peculiar view, though not in a completely arbitrary or *ad hoc* fashion.

According to Nietzsche, the cosmos is essentially as Boscovich characterized it: fields of force are the fundamental reality, and these fields permeate all of existence—where they are not, there is literally nothing, not even empty space and time. However, Nietzsche also appears to have endorsed a form of panpsychism regarding these fields of force. His reasoning for this is not our primary concern; he thought the idea of force makes no sense unless we understand forcing and being forced to be something undergone, felt, something (in our sense of the word) mental. Thus every field of force will have its corresponding 'feel' as it presses on other fields and is pressed upon in turn. If force possesses rudimentary awareness of its milieu, and force is pervasive, then the Berkeleian problem of unobserved items is solved. Everything is a perceiver because it undergoes influence from other fields of force. Also, everything is being perceived because there are fields of force upon which it expresses itself. Panpsychism thus allows Nietzsche to escape from the most untoward consequences of the *esse est percipi* principle. It allows Nietzsche to continue to affirm the existence of a nature within which we are embedded. Though it is permeated with mind, Nietzsche's nature transcends us. Our knowledge of it may well be imperfect, thus affirming a distinction between how things seem and what is so.

Some readers understand Nietzsche's perspectivism to be more fundamental than the thesis that the world is will to power. For them, it may seem that I have not done justice to Nietzsche's thesis that there is no thing-in-itself, that nature brings the thing-in-itself in through the back door. Conversely, one might think that calling Nietzsche's nature 'mind-dependent' stretches the meaning of that expression to its breaking point. I think the resolution of this difficulty is to see Nietzsche's concept of the thing-in-itself as meaning less than it is typically taken to mean.

A 'thing-in-itself' is an object whose characteristics obtain independent of all observers. To deny that there is such a thing does not mean that things become reduced entirely to episodes within the experiences of observers without residue. There is a difference between regarding things as collections of mental events, and regarding things as powers. An alternative to eliminating the thing altogether, or reducing it to the sum of observers' experiences, is to regard it as a locus affecting observers. The issue is not whether the thing has mind-independent qualities, but whether its mind-dependent qualities inhere in it or in its perceivers. It would be natural to ask the question, 'what, apart from the affections it produces in observers, is the object really like?' If one replies, 'well, the object surely has characteristics, but we will never know what they are', then one is committed to the object being a thing-in-itself. If, conversely, one says that the very idea of what the object is like apart from how it affects observers makes no sense, then one is denying that there is a thing-in-itself in Nietzsche's sense. However, clearly there is something out there, from which flows the sum of the effects; this something is nothing other than the locus. Nietzsche reinterprets things as complexes of power relations in which observers are always involved; he does not reduce things to sums of episodes within subjects. This view, I believe, is remarkably like Berkeley's in certain respects, as seen in the following passages.

A thing would be defined once all creatures had asked 'what is that?' and had answered their question. Supposing one single creature, with its own relationships and perspectives for all things, were missing, then the thing would not yet be 'defined'. (*KGW* viii.1. 138 (1885–6)/ *WP* 556)

The properties of a thing are effects on other 'things': if one removes other 'things', then a thing has no properties, i.e. there is no thing without other things, i.e. there is no 'thing-in-itself'. (*KGW* viii.1. 102 (1885–6)/ *WP* 557)

That things possess a constitution in themselves quite apart from interpretation and subjectivity, is a quite idle hypothesis: it presupposes that interpretation and subjectivity are not essential, that a thing freed from all relationships would still be a thing. Conversely, the apparent objective character of things: could it not be merely a difference of degree within the subjective? (*KGW* viii.2. 17 (1887)/ *WP* 560)

'In the development of thought a point had to be reached at which one realized that what one called the properties of things were sensations of the feeling subject: at this point the properties ceased to belong to the thing.' The 'thing-in-itself' remained . . . [If we reject this contrast, then] beings will have to be thought of as sensations that are no longer based on something devoid of sensation. (*KGW* vii.1. 691–2 (1883–4)/ *WP* 562)

Notice the strikingly Berkeleian character of these remarks. One could almost say that Nietzsche is reliving an earlier philosophical drama, and has cast Kant in the role of Locke and himself in the role of Berkeley. It is true that for Nietzsche, as for Kant, the mind is not a genuine substance. But it would be a mistake to think that because Nietzsche cannot believe that only mental substance exists, Berkeleian patterns of argument are not afoot. The rejection of a strong 'veil of perception' doctrine, a critique of the idea that a substratum of properties can be conceived independent of the properties it instantiates, the identification of sensible properties with sensory states, and the doctrine that the only causality possible is between minds, all bear the marks of deep Berkeleian commitments.

If we take this view, it is still easy to see how Nietzsche, like Berkeley, could think that his view mitigated sceptical difficulties considerably. It is not that we cannot be barred from access to reality because there is no reality to be barred from. It is that we cannot be barred from access to reality because there are no characteristics of reality apart from those which produce experiences.

This view, as I understand it, is reminiscent of Berkeley's in yet another way. For on Berkeley's view, it is not just that there are only experiences and experiencers. Rather, experiences are caused by something external to them that places them in us: God. God's intentions, then, occupy the same role that mind-independent things do in a realist view: they are not the experiences, nor the sum of experiences, but a locus that produces them. Nietzsche himself seems to see this similarity, when he makes the very Berkeleian remark that ' "Will", of course, can affect only "will"—and not "matter" (not "nerves", for example)' (*BGE* 36).[15] The difference from Berkeley, then, is not really at the level of fundamental metaphysics, but at that of theology. Where Berkeley has one God, Nietzsche has many gods, for that is what each 'thing' is: a *petit* Berkeleian deity producing experiences in the minds it affects.

---

[15] 'Now I desire to know, in the first place, whether, motion being allowed to be no action, you can conceive any action besides volition . . . and lastly, whether, having considered the premises, you do not perceive that to suppose any efficient or active Cause of our ideas, other than *Spirit*, is highly absurd and unreasonable?' George Berkeley, *Three Dialogues between Hylas and Philonous*, in *Berkeley's Philosophical Writings*, ed. David M. Armstrong (New York: Macmillan, 1965), 180.

The Antinomies

Kant's views on space and time are not exhausted by his remarks in the Transcendental Aesthetic, however. In the chapter of the first *Critique* entitled 'The Antinomy of Pure Reason', Kant argues that the concept of the infinite (and the infinitesimal) introduce further difficulties into our understanding of space and time, for which transcendental idealism provides a solution. The Antinomy is further subdivided into four separate sections. In each of these sections we are presented with a claim or Thesis, and its negation or Antithesis.[16] Kant then goes on to offer parallel proofs of each Thesis and Antithesis for each of the four Antinomies. The difficulty is that pure reason, when it attempts to discover *a priori* the magnitude of the world, can prove that this magnitude is finite or infinite. This cannot be. Kant's solution is to claim that the Thesis and Antithesis contradict each other only if the world being measured is a thing-in-itself. If we bear in mind, however, that the world is merely an appearance, the contradiction dissolves. Since regarding the world as an appearance is the only way to dissolve the contradiction, the Antinomies are *reductio* arguments against taking the world to be a thing-in-itself. Therefore they are indirect proofs of transcendental idealism. Each Antinomy resolves its contradiction in a different way. As the Antinomies seem not to have affected Nietzsche's views on the spatial magnitude of the world or its divisibility, I shall restrict myself to time as discussed by Kant in the First Antinomy.

The Thesis has it that 'the world has a beginning in time' while the Antithesis claims that 'the world has no beginning' (*CPR* A 426/B 454). The argument of the Antithesis is that the world beginning in time is inconceivable because such a beginning would be preceded by an infinite amount of empty time. Each of these empty moments would be indistinguishable from another; consequently nothing distinctive characterizes the moment preceding the beginning of the world that would explain why the world began then and not at any of the other empty moments.[17]

The argument for the Thesis is more difficult to explicate. If the world has no beginning, then an infinite amount of time must have elapsed up to the present

---

[16] Following tradition, I shall refer to them as the First, Second, Third, and Fourth Antinomies, though Kant himself does not.

[17] Nietzsche had already given an argument of his own against Schopenhauer reminiscent of the Antithesis of the First Antinomy (*KGW* i.4. 426–7 (1868)). Schopenhauer had claimed that the empirical world is mind-dependent, the mind is identical to the brain, and the brain arose at a moment in time. Yet without the mind, there could be nothing empirical; there would only be the undifferentiated thing-in-itself. Why then would mind appear at one point rather than another, if before there was

moment. But 'the infinity of a series consists precisely in the fact that it can never be completed by successive synthesis' (A 426/B 454). Kant thinks that to establish the magnitude of something, we must be able to measure it by some iterative counting procedure. The magnitude of something is then established by where you are when you complete the procedure. For example, if my steps are one foot in length, I can determine the length of an object by taking steps alongside it until I run out of object. Whatever number I reach in this procedure is the magnitude in feet. To say that the world has no beginning is to say that the past is infinite. But Kant thinks that to say the past is infinite is to say that it would be possible to begin a 'counting of moments' procedure (somehow), reach the present moment, and pronounce 'infinity!' Of course one cannot count *to* infinity in this sense. However, Kant sees no difficulty in assuming the future is infinite. One can simply assert that if I were now to begin counting moments, there would be no end to it; it would be an incompletable synthesis.

Disentangling all that has gone wrong in the Thesis argument is not our purpose here.[18] What is significant is that Nietzsche became aware of this argument, either directly, or indirectly, by reading Eugen Dühring. Nietzsche may have had direct acquaintance with the first *Critique* as early as 1872–3. Dühring, however, reproduces the argument of the Thesis to the First Antinomy as to time without modification, in his *Cursus der Philosophie* (Leipzig, 1875). In the summer of 1875, Nietzsche placed this work, which can be found in Nietzsche's personal library, on a 'to read' list (*KGW* iv.1. 204–5 (1875)) along

---

mind, all was undifferentiated? (Matters are further confused by the fact that for Schopenhauer, there could be no temporality unless mind existed first.) It is unclear from Kant's text whether he regards a reference to causality as essential to the argument. One way to construe the argument without such a reference is as follows. If the world began at t_1, then before t_1 there would have been an infinite number of moments empty of all events. A moment empty of any events is qualitatively identical to any other moment empty of any events. Moments do not have labels. Therefore the statement 'W began at t_1' has the same verification conditions as 'W began at t_{1-1}' 'W began at t_{1-2}' . . . , 'W began at t_{1-n}'. It makes no sense to suppose that two statements could have identical verification conditions, but different truth conditions. Therefore there can be no fact about when the world began. If there is no fact about when the world began, the world did not begin. Therefore the world is of infinite past duration.

[18] In essence, I concur with Bennett, who claims that Kant confuses the notion of actual infinity with the notion of a highest number. Kant's arguments hinge on the slide from interpreting the cardinality of the upshot of an iterative procedure as the last term produced by an iterative procedure. The idea of a procedure makes sense, but the idea of a completed totality, generated by said procedure, does not. If we refuse to identify the completed totality with the last term (identifying infinity as the highest natural number), then the paradoxes dissolve. If instead we think of cardinality as arrived at by pairing off, then the infinity or finitude of that procedure is immaterial. See Jonathan Bennett, *Kant's Dialectic* (Cambridge: Cambridge University Press, 1974), 114–42.

with Dühring's *Der Werth des Lebens* (Breslau, 1865). Quotes from the latter appear throughout manuscript UIII1, dated summer of 1875 (*KGW* iv.1. 207–61 (1875)). Though Nietzsche does not quote from *Cursus* until 1883 (*KGW* vii.1. 278 (1883)), it is quite possible that he was reading both texts concurrently, which would place his first reading of *Cursus* sometime between 1875 and 1883. Sometime between the beginning of 1881 and the autumn of 1881, we have the first mention of the doctrine of the eternal recurrence (*KGW* v.2. 392 (1881)).

We know that Nietzsche associated the doctrine of recurrence with Dühring; if Dühring's reuse of the First Antinomy Thesis were successful, a crucial premiss (the infinity of time) in one of Nietzsche's arguments for recurrence would be unavailable. Nietzsche himself saw this, as he reports early in 1888:

Lately one has sought several times to find a contradiction in the concept 'temporal infinity of the world in the past' (*regressus in infinitum*): one has even found it, although at the cost of confusing the head with the tail. Nothing can prevent me from reckoning backward from this moment into the infinite. Only if I made the mistake—I shall guard against it—of equating this correct concept of a *regressus in infinitum* with an utterly unrealizable concept of a finite *progressus* up to the present, only if I suppose that the direction (forward or backward) is logically a matter of indifference, would I take the head—this moment—for the tail: I shall leave that to you, my dear Herr Dühring! (*KGW* viii.3. 166 (1888)/ *WP* 1066)

In this passage, Nietzsche then goes on to give the 'combinatorial' argument for the eternal recurrence: if there are a finite number of possible world-states and an infinite amount of time, then the history of the world must necessarily recur eternally.[19] Nietzsche's encounter with the argument of the Thesis to the First Antinomy (as reformulated by Dühring in his *Cursus*) and Nietzsche's own rejection of this argument may have inspired the arguments[20] for eternal recurrence. They may even have suggested the doctrine to him. The eternal recurrence is often thought of as a normative doctrine rather than as a cosmological doctrine; one ought to live in such a way that one can affirm the eternal recurrence. Though the eternal recurrence may be best understood this way, one must formulate the cosmological doctrine before one can formulate the normative doctrine.

[19] The argument fails. Even if there were a finite number of 'power-centres' or a finite amount of force, this would not establish that such a Boscovichian world would have only a finite number of world-states. Given infinitely divisible space, this makes possible an infinite number of possible positions for any one power-centre, and therefore an infinite number of possible world-states.

[20] If this line of thinking is correct, then all of the arguments Nietzsche offers in the *Nachlaß* for the eternal recurrence are indebted to his rejection of the Thesis to the First Antinomy, since all of them take at least the infinity of time as a premiss, and some of them specifically require the infinity of the past as a premiss.

The Second Reading

Nietzsche's metaphysical commitment to the reality and infinity of time is also central to his 'genealogical' critique of Kant. First, rejection of a beginning to time is of a piece with Nietzsche's rejection of the Judaeo-Christian tradition, with its conception of a creator God. Second, Nietzsche's concern to vindicate the reality of time is not only of a piece with (though not strictly required by) the historicist aspect of genealogical critique; Nietzsche sees Kant's rejection of the reality of time as symptomatic of a more general failing of philosophers since Parmenides. By making time transcendentally ideal, Kant can distinguish between an apparent world, in which there is destruction, and a real world, in which there is no destruction. This contrast, in turn, allows Kant to associate that which he values (noumenal agency) with a domain distinct from the world of experience and immune to decay. Such a line of thought is symptomatic, Nietzsche thinks, of an inability to cope with, and subsequently a hatred for, life itself.

You ask me which of the philosophers' traits are really idiosyncrasies? For example, their lack of historical sense, their hatred of the very idea of becoming, their Egypticism. They think that they show their *respect* for a subject when they de-historicize it *sub specie aeterni*—when they have turned it into a mummy. All that philosophers have handled for thousands of years have been concept mummies; nothing real escaped their grasp alive. When these honourable idolaters of concepts worship something, they kill it and stuff it; they threaten the life of everything they worship. Death, change, old age, as well as procreation and growth, are to their minds objections—even refutations. Whatever has being does not become; whatever becomes does not have being. But since they never grasp it, they seek for reasons why it is kept from them. 'There must be mere appearance, there must be some deception which prevents us from perceiving that which has being: where is the deceiver?' 'We have found him,' they cry ecstatically; 'it is the senses! These senses, which are so immoral in other ways too, deceive us concerning the *true* world . . .' (*TI* III. 1)

The above described line of thinking is hardly the official basis for Kant's doctrine of the phenomenality of time. It would also do a great injustice to the subtleties of Kant's epistemology to claim that he regarded the empirical world as a deception. However, it is surely fair to say that Kant is happy to exploit the phenomenal/noumenal contrast. It is crucial to his arguments licensing faith in such transcendent goods as free will, immortality, and God, as we shall see in our discussion of the second *Critique*. Nietzsche's assessment of such a metaphysics is that 'Any distinction between a "true" and an "apparent" world—whether in the Christian manner or in the manner of Kant (in the end, an underhanded Christian)—is only a suggestion of decadence, a symptom of the *decline of life*' (*TI* III. 6)

We have seen that Nietzsche's interest in the metaphysics and physics of space and time was a feature of his thought emerging at the very beginning of his philosophical career and continuing to engage him to the end. His evolving views, however, were at each stage developed against the backdrop of Kantian assumptions, problems, and solutions. Nietzsche felt driven to reject Kant's placement of the transcendental subject outside nature. However, he never rejected Kant's insistence that the space and time with which we are directly acquainted are the products of the mind. This tension motivated much of his theoretical thinking, as he sought to make sense of the relations among the self, perception, nature, science, and things-in-themselves.

There is some irony here. Nietzsche's project began by refusing to identify phenomenal with physical space, thus removing Kant's first unquestioned case of synthetic *a priori* knowledge (geometry). It concluded with an argument (the eternal recurrence proof) Kant would have rejected as a clear example of dogmatic metaphysics. Striving to be more 'postmetaphysical' than Kant is not as easy as it seems.

Kant on Metaphysics 5

Nietzsche's debt

In Chapter 6, I will argue that Nietzsche's critique of metaphysics is crucially dependent on the transcendental psychological theory Kant sketches in the Transcendental Deduction and the use he puts it to in the Paralogism's attack on rationalist arguments for the existence of mental substance. This claim is central to my interpretative hypothesis that Nietzsche's debt to Kant cannot be accounted for by reference to Schopenhauer (who displays limited understanding of the Deduction and the Paralogisms and makes no positive use of this aspect of Kant's transcendental psychology in his own account of the 'world as representation').[1] Unfortunately, the Transcendental Deduction is the most difficult of Kant's texts to interpret, and arguably one of the most difficult texts in the history of Western philosophy. So before we can see what Nietzsche appropriated and to what extent he may have misappropriated Kant, we must pass through the valley of the shadow of some thorny Kant exegesis.

The Deduction introduced

Kant began his career committed to Leibnizian/Wolffian metaphysics and Newtonian physics. By the time he had written his Inaugural Dissertation, he had arrived at the view of space and time presented in Chapter 4. This allowed Kant to claim that Newtonian physics was correct as a characterization of the world of appearances; Leibnizian argument can independently establish the character of things-in-themselves.

This resolution was unstable. First, we need some intellectual resources beyond sensibility to be able to construct Newtonian theory, in particular, the

---

[1] *WWR*, 'Criticism of the Kantian Philosophy', 438–91.

concepts of substance and causality, and seemingly *a priori* principles concerning them; reason thus leaks into appearances. Second, there is a question about the status of these principles themselves. They are clearly *a priori*, but are they analytic or synthetic? If they were analytic, there would be no problem about their application to either appearances or reality.[2] All attempts to show that they are analytic have failed. Furthermore, it is difficult to explain why historically there have been competing conclusions from reason about the nature of reality, if the deliverances of reason are analytic. It looks as though these principles must be synthetic. Now synthetic *a posteriori* truths are easy to come by, given empirical intuition. How are we to account for synthetic *a priori* truths? We lack any intuitive connection to things-in-themselves. If we are not directly aware of things-in-themselves, there is something inexplicable about the mind and reality being in harmony in this fashion. Descartes had ascribed the assurance we have that our *a priori* beliefs correspond to reality to the non-deceiving God. Kant was not having any of that.

There is a solution: what if the mind imposed order on its experience at an intellectual and an intuitive level? Transcendental idealism resolved the problem of synthetic *a priori* knowledge for geometry; perhaps the same approach would work for metaphysics? Lacking the consensus we have over geometry, we need some sort of argument that will justify the synthetic *a priori* principles of metaphysics that we need to do Newtonian theory. There is the answer: we can do Newtonian theory, but we need these principles to do it, so these principles must be true. Could a sceptic not reply that perhaps we are mistaken in thinking we can do Newtonian theory?

However that may be, we can be sure that we have experience. Understand by experience the capacity to encounter nature-for-us and to make assertions about it at all. That is something the sceptic cannot deny. If we can show that there are 'quasi-Newtonian' concepts and principles presupposed in any assertion-making about appearances at all, then it will follow that since we can 'have experience', the world of experience must be quasi-Newtonian.[3]

---

[2] Kant's view of analytic truths is that they are instances of logical laws; that is why they are *a priori*. Thus 'All bachelors are unmarried' is *a priori* because 'For all x, if x is U and x is M, then x is U' is a law of logic. Kant's metaphor of concept containment is clear: 'U' is notationally contained in 'x is U and x is M' (*CPR* A 7/B 11–A 10/B 14). Quine's objection, at least at this juncture, hinges not on any denial of the *a priority* of logical law, but on the claim that 'x is U and x is M' is synonymous with 'bachelor' is *a priori* knowledge. See W. V. O. Quine, 'Two Dogmas of Empiricism', in *From a Logical Point of View* (Cambridge, MA: Harvard University Press, 1953), 20–46.

[3] Suppose that we could survey all possible worlds. In some of them, Newton's laws would prevail. Assume the truth of Newtonian theory. To say that something is physically possible is to say that it happens in one of these worlds. Now imagine that we could introduce variations on these laws: in some worlds, gravity is stronger, in others, light behaves somewhat differently, etc. Worlds that are

The Second Reading

Thus we have an argument establishing that certain synthetic *a priori* principles must be true of the experienced world if we are to have experience, which we do. The explanation for this remarkable harmony is that we impose this structure in the act of generating experience, just as geometrical truths' *a priority* was explained. We cannot impose order on what we cannot experience. Therefore the application of these synthetic *a priori* principles must be limited to experience, and cannot be applied beyond it. The residual reality remains unknowable: a safe haven for God, immortality, freedom, and morality.

The project of isolating and justifying those *a priori* contributions of the mind to experience which are intellectual rather than intuitional will take place in two stages. First, the legitimacy of the concepts deployed in synthetic *a priori* truths must be vindicated in the face of Humean objections. Locke had argued vigorously against the thesis that certain of our ideas are innate and not acquired from experience, as part of a larger empiricist attack on rationalist claims to *a priori* knowledge. If Locke could show that a concept could not be acquired from experience at all, and that the innateness hypothesis was implausible, then the use of such a concept to establish a metaphysical claim must be rejected. Hume repeated this strategy with devastating results. For Locke had always assumed that 'good' concepts could be acquired from experience, even if this took some showing. With the Lockean toolkit in Hume's hands, we find that many 'good' concepts cannot be generated from experience and thus must be rejected on empiricist scruples. Kant's argument in the Deduction provides an alternative mechanism of acquisition for such concepts. Without tracing them to experience directly, Kant displayed their connection to experience so that an empiricist would have to accept them. Intellectual representation of empirical objects requires acts of rule-governed synthesis; the rules needed for synthesis turn out to be the categories themselves. Thus if an empiricist is to accept that we can think about empirical objects at all, he must concede that we have at least some concepts that do not have an empirical origin. Second, the Analytic of Principles vindicates a body of metaphysical claims, 'quasi-Newtonian' principles that make substantive claims about

---

either Newtonian or near-Newtonian are 'quasi-Newtonian'. Now take the worlds in which there are experiencers sufficiently similar to ourselves in some sense (at the least, sharing the same forms of intuition). Call these the 'experiential' worlds. Kant's claim would be that the set of quasi-Newtonian worlds and the set of experiential worlds are coextensive. This interpretation is made more plausible once we consider that for Kant Euclidean space and time are our forms of intuition, and that every Newtonian world is also a Euclidean world. So at least the Newtonian–Euclidean spatiotemporal worlds are coextensive with the Kantian–Euclidean intuitional worlds. An experiential world has to be at least an intuitional world too.

nature. Though these claims are implicit in Newtonian theory, they are nonetheless not verified by direct appeal to experience.

The Deduction is usually divided by Kant scholars into two distinct discussions, the Metaphysical Deduction (*CPR* A 65/B 90–A 83/B 116) and the Transcendental Deduction (*CPR* A 84/B 116–A 130/B 169). The Metaphysical Deduction is titled 'On the Guide (*Lauterkeit*) for the Discovery of All Pure Concepts of Understanding', though Kant refers to this discussion as 'the metaphysical deduction' (*CPR* B 159). The Transcendental Deduction is in the text 'On the Deduction of the Pure Concept of Understanding'. These two texts are chapters 1 and 2 respectively of the Analytic of Concepts, as contrasted with the Analytic of Principles that follows.

The functions of the Metaphysical Deduction and the Transcendental Deduction are distinct. Both are concerned with non-empirical (or, as Kant calls them, 'pure') concepts. The Metaphysical Deduction offers us a theory of what a non-empirical concept is which departs from both the rationalist notion of an innate idea and the empiricist notion of an idea of reflection. The Metaphysical Deduction suggests that our own cognitive processing imposes syntactic forms on our thoughts, and that these forms can be exhaustively specified. For each syntactic form, there is a corresponding 'category'. These categories are concepts representing forms that empirical facts must have which parallel the forms judgements must have.

The Transcendental Deduction shows that using such concepts is inescapable if we are to possess even the most rudimentary kinds of empirical knowledge, thus justifying their use in the face of empiricist objections. It does this by establishing that we must employ the categories if our would-be-representations are to have objective references or content (i.e. if our mental states are to be representational) at all. While doing this, Kant establishes that unity of the experiential field, unity of the cognitive self, and use of the categories, all go together. Finally, a cognitive processing model is proposed in which not only are thoughts given quasi-linguistic form, but in which sensory states are as well, thus allowing thought to mirror what is perceived. The 'module' which effects these tasks, thus generating enipirical knowledge, along with the physical world, out of the data of sense, is the *imagination*.

Categories

Kant wants to show that certain concepts have legitimate employment in the sphere of experience, though these principles are not arrived at via abstraction from experience. The strategy exploits the formal properties of a judgement; in what follows, we will find it helpful to reinterpret 'judgement' to mean 'sentence in the language of thought'. Though Kant seems to be classifying judgements into kinds much as Aristotle seemed to classify terms into kinds,[4] many judgements will simultaneously belong to several kinds. Since the basis for the classification is formal, it is plausible to suppose that the forms of judgement are syntactical forms. Kant associates each form of judgement with a non-empirical concept. Yet Kant repeatedly characterizes concepts as rules. What sorts of rules, then, would constitute the formal properties of a judgement? Presumably formal rules, and what else could these be but syntactical rules? This explains how an individual judgement can possess many different forms simultaneously. For example, 'If the rain falls, then the pavement is soaked', contains both the features of two categorical judgements and one hypothetical judgement, though it is properly classified as the latter. One way to characterize this is to say that by following one generative rule, the rule for categorical judgements, we yield 'The rain falls' and 'The pavement is soaked'. Using these judgements as input, we can apply the rule for the construction of hypothetical judgements to yield 'If the rain falls, then the pavement is soaked'. Since Kant refers to these rules also as 'functions of judgement' I suggest that we read him as identifying the forms of judgement with rules or functions for generating well-formed formulas. Notice here that whether 'the rain falls' is regarded as a categorical judgement or as an antecedent is a function of where it falls in a larger context by virtue of the rules that have been applied in generating it.

[4] Aristotle argued in the *Categories* that reality presents itself to us and is spoken of as structured in certain fundamental ways. For example, when a ball is blue, a quality is attributed to a substance. To say that there are substances and qualities, these being but two of the many categories Aristotle canvases, means that reality contains these as metaphysical kinds. However, one could also easily read his text as concerned with enumerating a list of basic concepts necessary for representing reality, or even as merely concerned with what minimal linguistic resources are needed for speaking of it, as when he writes, 'Of things said without any combination, each signifies either substance or qualification or a relative or where or when or being-in-a-position or having or doing or being-affected' (*Cat.* 1ᵇ25). The sentence is about what is *said*, about our linguistic resources, and yet they are characterized by way of what they signify, which concerns the character of the world. Rather than say that Aristotle is ambiguous, it is fairer to say that he is simultaneously doing ontology and linguistics, connecting the two domains with 'signifies'.

One can easily imagine that Aristotle arrived at his list of categories by examining the parts of speech and extracting the basic kinds of words. The kinds of words served as a clue to the basic metaphysical types: nouns correspond to substances, verbs to actions, adjectives to attributes, etc. Kant takes the same tack, but appeals to types of sentences rather than words. Again, Kant no more writes explicitly of language than Aristotle does, but grammatical considerations do seem to have served as the clue to basic metaphysical types. Aristotle, *Categories*, in *The Complete Works of Aristotle*, trans. J. L. Ackrill and ed. Jonathan Barnes (Princeton: Princeton University Press, 1984).

The fact that Kant starts his analysis at the level of the judgement, rather than at the level of the concept, suggests that he distinguishes one concept from another by the functional roles mental tokens play in the context of a larger whole, the context of the judgement. This holism enables Kant to escape from the false alternative: either categories are abstractions from experience, or else they are innate ideas.

Kant closely associates the forms of judgement, and the categories that flow from them, with a faculty he calls the understanding. We should take this as saying nothing more than that the mind has the capacity to generate judgements by the application of syntactical rules to information. If it helps to picture the fact that these functions are performed by imagining a module labelled 'The Understanding' into which mental tokens flow and out of which emerge syntactically correct sentences in the language of thought, then there is little harm in speaking this way.[5] Kant claims that the understanding is a unity, and that from the unity of the understanding we can derive twelve forms of judgement. He means nothing more dramatic by this than that a cognitive system that represents sententially (in the language of thought) must possess an interconnectedness of its syntactical forms as the forms of one language.

The idea of associating the categories with the table of the forms of judgement avoids one of Hume's problems with the concept of causality. Hume can find no distinct impression from which we receive the concept of causality. Kant's response is that claims are more than just bundles of information; they are *structured* bundles of information. The concept of causality lies not in any component of the judgement (the concept of this billiard ball, of that billiard ball, of motion, etc.) but in the structure of the judgement as a whole, in how those components are arranged. If Kant can show that a non-empirical concept can be identified with a syntactical structure indispensable for language, then such a concept is vindicated, impression or no impression.

The Metaphysical Deduction, then, is just the idea that one can discover the short list of basic categories by way of examining the short list of basic syntactical

---

[5] We should not think of the various faculties as box-like; rather, they are functional systems that may very well penetrate each other. One mental activity may, in one context, be seen to be a component of one function, and therefore 'in' that faculty, while in another context the same activity may serve a different function, and therefore be 'in' that faculty. This explains how Kant can be both quite serious about his faculty talk, while being free in his assignment of activities to faculties at different points of his writing. The 'module' metaphor is a ladder to be thrown away once the relationships between the various activities are made clear.

forms or 'forms of judgement'.[6] Now the notion of a form of judgement is reasonably clear: it is just the notion of a rule for the well-formedness of sentences in the language of thought. For example, the Form of Negative Judgement could be paraphrased this way: 'If "P" is a sentence, then "It is not the case that P" is also a sentence'. The list of the forms of judgement should be the minimum of such basic rules necessary to characterize the syntax of the language of thought.

Now the question is: what is the difference between a form of judgement and its corresponding category? A category is the form of the experienced fact; it is the rule for the structure experiences must have for a syntactic form to be used in a statement to represent that experience correctly. For example, one of the twelve forms of judgement is the Hypothetical; in reconstruction, the rule: 'If "P" is a sentence and "Q" is a sentence, then "If P then Q" is a sentence'. To say that P causes Q is to say that the sentences 'P' and 'Q' can be truthfully concatenated into a conditional statement. For each of the twelve judgement types, there is supposed to be a category. But it doesn't work as neatly in each case as it does for causality and substance.[7]

---

[6] Kant has been criticized for the arbitrariness of the categories, but one can make too much of this. In our post-Fregean terminology, Kant is trying to express the minimal syntactical resources for a language that includes quantification, classes, truth-functions, and modality. If we were to translate Kant's table into resources more familiar to a post-Fregean audience, we would need: sentences (which would yield 'Affirmative' judgements); some basic truth-function like Scheffer's stroke (which would yield 'Negative', 'Hypothetical', and 'Disjunctive' judgements); quantifiers, names, and predicates (which would yield 'Categorical', 'Universal', 'Particular', and 'Singular' judgements); and one modal operator, either possibility or necessity (whose absence would leave us with 'Assertoric' judgements, 'Problematic' and 'Apodeictic' judgements being interdefinable given one modal operator and negation). Beyond quantified modal logic, I mention class membership only because Kant is explicitly committed to it as a distinct function by positing that Negative and Infinite judgements are distinct, that there is something being said by 'Apples are non-animals' not said by 'Apples are not animals'. If there is a difference, it must be that the former posits a complement class and the latter does not.

What matters about members of the table is not that they are irreducible, but that they are syntactical. Kant himself claims that we could, using the table as a basis, construct further concepts; it seems to matter little if we could reduce the list. The problem with the Metaphysical Deduction is not the table. Rather, it is that the individual categories make little sense in relation to their form of judgement. Though substance, causality and the modal categories make sense, it is utterly unclear what is intended by the association of the remaining forms with the categories of unity, plurality, totality, limitation, and community, or what they have to do with their associated forms of judgement. The most sense one can make of them is simply to identify them with their associated forms, whereas with causality, we have independent notions of the form and the category. Since none of the categories do any work except the relational and modal ones, it may not matter.

[7] Clearly this cannot be the whole story, as there are true conditionals which do not express causal claims. Kant recognizes this; the obscure theory of schematism may be meant to address this problem.

The Transcendental Deduction

The Metaphysical Deduction proposes that the twelve categories are syntactical rules, necessary if we are to have complete thoughts at all. The Transcendental Deduction shows that categories have legitimate employment, but only in empirical claims, despite their being neither empirical concepts nor innate ideas.

Kant claims that the categories are conditions of empirical consciousness analogous to the forms of intuition, space and time. Unfortunately, this analogy has generated more confusion than clarity in Kant's readers, who read 'empirical consciousness' to mean 'sensation' or 'perception'. Though Kant writes of perception, 'empirical consciousness' is better read to mean '*thoughts with empirical content*'. For there to be thoughts with empirical content, we must have sensations that lend empirical content to these thoughts. Simultaneously, we must have the syntactical forms that make a mental state a thought at all. How are these two processes linked?

At the sensory level, the mind takes in the data as the data of one, unified mental apparatus (this operation Kant calls 'synopsis', without which there would be nothing to judge about: *CPR* B 127, n. 48) and then assigns spatiotemporal relations to it, for example, assigning a particular red datum to a particular spatiotemporal location in the phenomenological field. The formal structure that guides the mind in this assigning activity is isomorphic with that of Euclidean geometry (and the related temporal structure). For an analogy, consider the assignment of a particular colour value to a pixel by software generating a virtual reality environment. This formal structure cannot be identified with phenomenological or physical space, any more than the virtual space produced by a particular piece of software can be identified with the structural features of the software responsible for the space having the character that it does.[8]

[8] If I were a brain in a vat, being stimulated in precisely the same way that I would be stimulated if I were looking at the Mona Lisa, there would still be a question about whether anything I said regarding the Mona Lisa was correct. Depending upon what theory of reference one adopted, my expression (or thought) 'Mona Lisa' might refer to the real Mona Lisa (in which case many of my thoughts about Mona Lisa would be incorrect), the Virtual Mona Lisa (in which case some of these very thoughts might be correct, e.g. 'I see the Mona Lisa'), or it might refer to the proximate causes of the brain state associated with the thought 'I see the Mona Lisa', that is, the states in the computer that generated the stimulation.

Space for Kant, like the Mona Lisa in my example, is an intuition, although a 'pure' and not 'empirical' intuition. I suspect that some confusions in Kant literature concerning whether space can be identified problematically with some feature of noumena (the famous 'neglected alternative') or with some feature of the mind by virtue of which we intuit under the form of space, or with a 'pure intuition', are problems that would become more tractable if we were to clarify the various accounts of reference each interpretation tacitly involved. Though this remark obviously owes something to Putnam, I am especially indebted to Hugh Chandler for suggesting it to me.

Nonetheless, the two are very closely related to each other. This explains why Kant refers to space and time as 'forms of intuition', though it may be more appropriate to reserve this term for those structural features of the mind by virtue of which space and time come to have the structure that they do.

The product of the operations of the sensibility is animal consciousness.[9] For though we can now be conscious of spatiotemporal regions as qualified by perceptible attributes, thus yielding something akin to objects and something akin to consciousness of them, we could not characterize this as *human* consciousness. What human beings possess beyond sensibility is the capacity to produce quasi-linguistic representations of phenomena, to 'think' about them or 'judge' about them. We can without too much distortion characterize this as uttering sentences in a language of thought. Kant believes that to make meaningful, well-formed assertions in the language of thought, further operations on the phenomena are necessary. Once we see what those operations are, we are compelled to adopt a much richer account of the structure of conscious experience.

This structure is *object-structure*, something that is missing from an awareness of a spatiotemporal field qualified by attributes at locations. For though region R_1 at t_1 may be red, region R_2 at t_1 may also be red, and both regions may be red at t_2, none of this adds up to observing an apple endure over time.[10] For that, we need to organize the data further so that these qualified regions become seen as unified into an object. The Kantian notion of object is the notion of a referent.

What is striking in Kant's account of this process of 'objectification' is that he seems to have held something anticipating Frege's context principle. Suppose that the concept of a Kantian object is the same as that of a referent. A referent is to be understood in relation to a referring expression (a name). If an expression acquires the function of being a referring expression only in the context of a sentence (or judgement), then neither objects nor thoughts about objects can stand alone. For something to be an object, it must be referred to by a referring expression. For something to be a referring expression, it must be so in the context of a sentence. For a sentence to serve as a representation of the object, other

---

[9] Kant never claimed in the Transcendental Aesthetic that the resources of the sensibility were sufficient for geometrical knowledge, only that they were necessary. Presumably a geometer needs to be able to think as well to form geometrical concepts.

[10] We must not confuse Kant's problem with the Ship of Theseus problem. Kant is not asking what principles we ought to follow to unify correctly several distinct parts together into a single whole, or what principles enable us to identify correctly two seemingly diverse entities as the same entity. Rather, Kant is interested in what conceptual resources are necessary for us to be able at any given moment to be able to regard a ship as an entity at all. Despite the reference to time in my example, and Kant's frequent mention of temporal disparateness being unified in the first-edition ('A') Deduction, identity over time is not Kant's concern here.

expressions in the sentence (predicates) must also represent. This means that objects must present themselves to us as embedded in facts or states of affairs. But just as there must be rules for concatenating expressions into sentences, lest a sentence be just a mish-mash of expressions, there must be isomorphic rules for organizing phenomena into states of affairs so that these sentences might map or represent them. This operation is executed by the imagination, but it performs it under the direction of a system of rules that impose syntactical order both on thoughts and on phenomena. The module where this system of rules can be found Kant calls 'the understanding'. With syntactic order imposed both on the phenomenon and the sentential representation of it, a lexicon can then be drawn on for making claims about the object—that it is an apple, that it is red, etc.

At this point it is important to head off a possible misunderstanding that talk of 'organizing phenomena' might induce. One might think that before phenomena get organized into facts, the mind is presented with a mere chaos of impressions. Such a picture fails to take sufficient account of the prior role the forms of intuition play in organizing the data of sense into a spatiotemporal framework. The visual presentation of an apple sitting on a table is the same for a consciousness that possesses sensibility but no understanding, and a consciousness that possesses both sensibility and understanding. The understanding does not lift us out of some sort of Jamesian 'blooming, buzzing confusion' into orderly, stable perceptual experience. Nor does the understanding lift us out of blind unconsciousness into the light of sheer sensory awareness. Rather, what it does is lift us out of brute, mute awareness of the apple on the table, and into a state in which we interpret (or imagine) the apple as an object. Kant is not vulnerable to the charge that he has a too intellectualistic account of sensation, because the Deduction properly understood does not provide us with an account of sensation at all.

To see why this must be so, consider the case of animal consciousness. How one locates animal consciousness within Kant's philosophy is crucial to interpreting correctly his account of the relationship between sensation and thought. It is clear from the organization of the text into a 'Transcendental Aesthetic' and a 'Transcendental Logic' that Kant draws a sharp contrast between sensation and conception; this is his point of departure from the rationalist and empiricist tendency to run these together under the ambiguous term 'ideas'. The argument of the Deduction concerns the role the categories play in enabling intuition. If Kant is claiming that conceptual resources are necessary to sensation, this leaves him on the horns of a dilemma concerning animal consciousness: either they have conceptual resources they almost certainly do not possess, since animals would have to synthesize their experiences by way of the categories, or else they do not sense at all. Kant could not have accepted either conclusion. Therefore 'experience' must mean for Kant something more than animal consciousness, but something distinct from pure thought.[11]

The only way out of this dilemma is to regard experience as something more than sensation, involving conceptual resources not available to animals. Interpreting 'experience', awareness of empirical objects, as 'thought with empirical content' satisfies this condition.

If this is correct, it follows that the premiss of the transcendental argument (i.e. that we have experience) designed to rebut the empiricist sceptic is stronger than it seems, and the argument is thus weaker. On the rejected interpretation, the empiricist has to contend with the objection that the categories are the condition of the possibility of sensory awareness, something the empiricist obviously cannot deny the existence of while still being an empiricist. On my interpretation, we have a more plausible argument that may leave the empiricist unmoved. For an empiricist to reject Kant's argument now would involve not denying that we have sensation, but that we are aware of empirical objects *qua* objects. This is conceivable, for this is precisely what animal consciousness is.

Matters are complicated by the fact that Kant calls experience 'empirical intuition'. Did Kant intend the term 'empirical intuition' to carry with it the presumption of objecthood and thus the application of the categories? In the preceding chapter, I characterized intuition as 'awareness of an individual'. Does this mean the same thing as 'awareness of an object as an object'? Since empirical intuitions play a prominent role in the Transcendental Aesthetic, it might seem that Kant is claiming that the account of the sensibility there is incomplete, pending a discussion of the role the understanding plays in contributing objecthood to the construction of an intuition. Conversely, we might take the absence of the discussion of objecthood in the Transcendental Aesthetic to imply that an intuition is a purely sensory affair, not involving any contribution from the understanding.

Consider the following passage that seems to suppose the view that intuitions require the categories. 'The manifold given in a sensible intuition is

---

[11] The same point applies if one considers perception instead of sensation. Kant cannot suppose that animals cannot perceive items in their environment. He cannot suppose that they are presented with a blooming, buzzing confusion. Nor can he claim that animals require intellectual resources associated with the capacity to think and have language to do so. If we use the term 'perception' to refer to what animals do, Kant cannot be concerned with perception in the Deduction. Though he does use the term to refer to what the Deduction describes, it is a term best avoided in exegesis.

subject necessarily to the original, synthetic unity of apperception; for solely through this unity is unity of intuitions possible' (*CPR* B 143). We might read this passage as saying that *in us* intuition is subject to apperception (object-awareness). For the second clause does not say that it is solely through this unity that intuition is possible. It says that solely through this unity is the unity of intuition possible. This interpretation seems supported elsewhere. In the following passage, Kant seems to include animal consciousness under the heading of 'intuition' as in

the uncombined manifold of presentations can be given in an intuition that is merely sensible, i.e. nothing but receptivity; and the form of this intuition can lie *a priori* in our power of presentation without being anything but the way in which the subject is affected. But a manifold's *combination* (*conjunctio*) as such can never come to us through the senses; nor, therefore, can it already be part of what is contained in the pure form of sensible intuition; and the power must be called understanding . . . (*CPR* B 129–30)

What I wish to suggest here is that we have merely a terminological difficulty, rather than a difficulty in the structure of Kant's thought. If we take 'intuition' to mean sensation without objecthood, then the understanding contributes objecthood, thus transforming an intuition into an intuition of an object. If we take intuition to mean awareness of an object, then the understanding contributes the elements necessary to make a sensation into an intuition.

What is clear is that Kant associates 'experience' and therefore objecthood with what he calls perception. Thus he says at B 161: 'all synthesis, the synthesis through which even perception becomes possible, is subject to the categories.' It is not clear that the contrast to perception is total blindness. Rather, I suggest we deflate the notion of perception in Kant to what I have been characterizing as awareness of empirical objects *qua* objects, or, interpretation of the empirical field in terms of the objecthood.

Later, Kant tries to explain that the pure intuitions of space and time also involve conceptual resources, but that this only means our capacity to relate to space and time as objects, which I take to mean objects of possible judgement (*CPR* B 161, n. 305). Again, it is not clear whether Kant wishes to distinguish between pre-conceptualized intuitions and post-conceptualized intuitions, or to use the term 'intuition' to designate that which is already conceptualized.

In summary, animals have a kind of awareness of individuals through their senses that enables them to respond to them. This is to be distinguished from awareness of an object as an object, a fine distinction but a crucial one. Whereas a dog *sees* an apple on a table, a human being sees *that* an apple is on a table. To see that an apple is on the table goes hand in hand with judging in the light of experience that an apple is on the table. Expressed in our Fregean argot, we can see that, and therefore can judge that, there is an x, such that x is an apple and x is on the table. The 'x' is our introduction of referentiality into our awareness, something that the dog cannot do. But for us to do it, we need syntax, the rules of syntax, and thus the categories. Since the categories are equivalent to certain important non-empirical concepts, this shows that the use of these concepts is legitimate, despite the failure of an attempted empiricist reduction of them to raw sensations.

The preceding discussion may puzzle the reader well-versed in the Kantian corpus as focusing exclusively on the unity of an object or the unity of an intuition. What happened to the unity of the self, the mysteriously named 'transcendental unity of apperception'? It is often thought that there is some more powerful argument lurking in Kant's discussion of the transcendental unity of the apperception, based on some transparent, immediately evident quasi-Cartesian premiss about the self as object of introspection. Such a premiss seems more evident than any claim to the effect that we are aware of objects or have perceptions. However, it is misleading to think that there is some distinct argument here. Rather, there is the same argument with a different focus.

Kant claims that I am at least aware of my thinking. Kant agrees with Descartes that this claim is indubitable, and therefore something from which one can safely infer. Kant's use of this claim in the Deduction is peculiar, however. For he begins by observing that in any thought, there will be a plurality (or 'manifold') of content brought together in the thought. While the plural content can be, in some sense, derived from the data of sense, the unity of the thought containing the content cannot be simply read off the data of sense. This unity must, then, be produced by an act of rule-governed synthesis. Thus, the sheer awareness of thinking reveals the inescapable role of the categories. For there to be one thought with empirical content, there must be, beyond the data furnished by the sensibility, a synthesis of this data into the form of a unified thought. Once this synthesis has been accomplished, *ipso facto*, a thinker exists, since a thinker is just that which has a thought. The conditions of this synthesis imply the legitimacy of the categories.

Suppose that the data of redness was presented in one mind, call it M_1, while the data of apple-ish shape was presented in another mind, call it M_2. In no way could we say that either M_1 or M_2 are thinking the thought 'the apple is red' or (if this is all the data there is) any thought at all. Nor would we say, if M_1 and M_2 are not in communication with each other, that there is some larger system, M_1+M_2, that collectively has the thought that the apple is red. For in either alternative, there has not been the requisite act of synthesis that combines the two elements, together with the rule that governs categorical judgements, to form the unified judgement 'the apple is red'.

Now in a way, our example is a ladder that must be kicked away, for it trades on the notion that M_1 and M_2 are already, just intrinsically, minds in their own right. Because a mind is something that thinks a thought, M_1 and M_2 are not yet minds at all, for absent the necessary synthesis and the rule to govern it, there is no thought, and therefore no thinkers. Conversely, should there be, somehow, the requisite act of communication between M_1 and M_2 such that rule-governed synthesis did occur, and the thought 'the apple is red' transpired, then M_1+M_2 would constitute a mind. This shows that, for Kant, the notion of a mind is a purely functionalist one: a mind just is the occurrence of one or more connected or connectible judgements. Thus whenever there are appropriately combined contents and therefore judgement(s), 'mind happens'. The mind that happens is nothing above and beyond the fact that judgement happened. This is what Kant means when he says that 'the I think must be capable of accompanying all my presentations' (*CPR* B 131).

When we are aware of an object (in the sense of a referent) it has unity by virtue of its necessary embedding in a fact or state of affairs, and a fact must have sentence-like structure. When Kant writes of the unity of apperception, his focus is instead on the judgement, rather than the truth conditions of the judgement. To apperceive is simply to be in a state of intellectual awareness, be aware of something in a judging way. To be aware in a judging way is to have a certain complexity to one's cognitive state. This complexity must possess the form necessary for the state to be an assertion of anything, to wit, syntactical form. If I were not in a state which exemplified the form of judging, the components of my state could not come together into anything like a judgement. Therefore I would not be in a state of *intellectual* awareness. We should not confuse Kant's concern here with some Lockean or Parfittian concern over the conditions of continued identity over time. The topic is what lends a state unity as an intellectual act, not what binds together many such acts over time.

If that is correct, then there should not be any question of an 'Objective Deduction' versus a 'Subjective Deduction' or the advantages of one over the other. That said, there is a passage of the 'A' Deduction that seems to lend priority to the unity of the self over the unity of the object. Kant says that

since we have to deal only with the manifold of our representations, and since that x (the object) which corresponds to them is nothing to us—being, as it is, something that has to be distinct from all our representations—the unity which the object makes necessary can be nothing else than the formal unity of consciousness in the synthesis of the manifold of representations.   (*CPR* A 135)

This passage (the entire section from p. 133 to p. 138 is relevant) not only establishes a link between the unity of the object and the unity of the subject. It suggests that the unity of the object is derived from the unity of the subject. In a sense, this is true: the unity of the object is the product of the operations of the mind. But on the interpretation we have been offering, there is an exact parity between what the mind does to create empirical facts, and what the mind does to create empirical judgements. The unity of the judgement and the unity of the judged are both products of the same transcendental 'act'. This passage suggests that the unity of the object is somehow projected into our sensory information after we discovered the unity of the subject.

This idea is the result of Kant's over-hasty characterization of what his view really is. On the object pole, what is in question is not the unity of an object, but the unity of a fact within which an object is embedded. Only in this way can we make sense of the idea that objecthood presupposes the categories, for there is nothing about the common-sense notion of an object that demands them. Facts possess the sentence-like structure that makes the involvement of the categories, themselves sentence-like structures, plausible. The necessary embedding of objects in facts leads us from objects to categories. By contrast, the unity of the self (in a cognitive act) is the unity of an act of judging. Thus the notion of the unified self cannot be literally understood as a model for the notion of an object. If we are to think in terms of a 'projection hypothesis', the best we can do is think of a fact being a projection of an act of judgement. Why then does Kant speak of objects instead of facts?

This slip is not too difficult to explain. If we take the simplest kind of empirical judgement, we are likely to be thinking of a categorical judgement, a claim that a substance is qualified by an attribute. Since the concept of substance is nothing but the concept of an object minus its attributes, it is easy to confuse the fact in which the object is embedded with the object itself. In your mind's eye, visualize the fact that a particular apple is red. Do you visualize anything beyond a red apple? Probably not.

Even so, the 'projection hypothesis', *if* it is present in *CPR* A 133–8, is probably incoherent. We could not (1) judge that the apple is red, (2) notice the unity of our cognitive state, (3) acquire the notion of a thing with unity, (4) project that notion into our sensory field, and (5) thereby arrive at the experience of a unified apple, (6) which we then notice is red, (7) thus leading us to judge that the apple is red. It is more helpful to think of the upsurge of cognitive unity, factual unity, the forms of judgement, and the categories as coeval; this was Kant's considered view of the matter as well.[12] We shall see below whether Nietzsche's use of a projection hypothesis, probably derived either from a reading or misreading of *CPR* A 133–8, is vitiated by a similar incoherence.

The Paralogisms

For Descartes, sheer awareness of thinking revealed something more than synthetic unity: the existence of a substance.[13] By the end of the *Meditations*, Descartes hoped to have proved a great deal about the mind: that it was non-composite, that it was a property-bearer in which thoughts inhere, that it is radically distinct from matter, and so on. Though Descartes himself never succeeded in showing that the mind was immortal, clearly it was his hope to make the idea of immortality more plausible by his account. The prospects for immortality are bleak if the mind is composite, adjectival on another substance, or identical to some physical system such as the body. Kant's first target in the *Critique of Pure Reason* is what he calls 'rational psychology'—the attempt to spin substantive metaphysical conclusions about the self from the mere fact of my thinking. Accordingly, Kant begins with the model of the mind established in the Deduction. Because the mind is this way, Descartes is irresistibly tempted to argue from certain features of first-person awareness to metaphysical conclusions that support the belief in immortality. Kant shows that by an equivocation of terms, the rational psychologist takes the characteristics of the thinking self to be more than they are. Kant is not averse to the idea that human beings are immortal. But this is supposed to be an object of faith, not demonstration.[14]

---

[12] The passage presenting these difficulties only occurs in the 'A' Deduction.

[13] For Descartes, 'thinking' includes many 'mental' states that we would not think of as involving the entertaining of something with propositional content—the sensation of pain, for example. But in the specific instance of thinking Descartes appeals to in the *cogito* argument, doubting my own existence, we are concerned with a purely intellectual act. For Kant, awareness of thinking means only awareness of states involving propositional content—awareness of pain, for example, would be excluded.

[14] The Paralogisms occur in distinct versions in the first and second editions. I focus on the first edition because it helpfully disentangles four distinct threads of paralogistic reasoning that are combined into one discussion in the second edition. Also, I set aside the fourth Paralogism, which concerns Cartesian scepticism (and replies to it with a variety of phenomenalism) as not relevant to my main concerns here. Kant's motive in rewriting the Paralogisms chapter is that the fourth Paralogism, which stresses the 'transcendental idealist' aspect of Kant's solution to the problem of the external world, is replaced by the 'Refutation of Idealism', which stresses the 'empirical realist' dimension of Kant's thought.

161

The Second Reading

The first three paralogisms argue (1) that the self is a substance (as opposed to a property of another substance), (2) that the self is simple or atomic (as opposed to an aggregate), and (3) that the self is the enduring substratum of change.[15] All the rational psychologist needs is a reason to think that the self is a genuine substance. According to Kant, this move comes about by virtue of a misunderstanding of the conditions of the possibility of empirical thought. The necessary unification of contents leads to a transcendental illusion of a substantial self.

As Hume pointed out, when we introspect during an act of judgement, we find no substantial self amid the objects of introspection. What we do find, Kant claims, is the peculiarly empty fact that 'all these contents are *mine*'. This further judgement reflects nothing more than the potential unity a plurality of contents must possess if I am to join them together in a judgement. Yet this further judgement, 'and it is I who am thinking this thought!' does not represent an empirical fact the way that 'this apple is red' does. It is utterly empty of all but formal content.

---

[15] These discussions all hearken back to Aristotle's account of the concept of primary substance in the *Categories*, and his analysis of change in the *Physics*. In the *Categories*, Aristotle had seen significance in the fact that we speak in topics and comments, from which he concluded that the world comes in things and properties. The concept of substance is the concept of a property-bearer. When we say that man is a rational animal, we are predicating rationality and animality to man. Man is a substance. When we say that Socrates is a man, we are predicating man to Socrates. Aristotle calls substances that can inhere in substances 'secondary substances'. Those substances that are only subjects of predication and never in turn predicated of something else, Aristotle calls primary substances.

In the *Physics*, Aristotle gives an account of change that exploits these distinctions, while disposing of the ancient Greek controversy over permanence and change. For Aristotle, change is the replacement of properties inhering in a substance with other properties. One day my face is pale. The next day it is sunburned. The face persists, but paleness is removed and replaced with redness. As an analysis of change, this raises a problem for understanding origination and destruction. In the *Physics* analysis, for change to occur, there must be an enduring something that undergoes the change. If the change were from existing to no longer existing, what could be said to undergo this? What is it that at one time has the 'property' of existing, only to have that property removed and replaced by the property of not existing? There are two possible responses. One is to come up with a special account of origination and destruction that differs from the changes an enduring thing undergoes. This was Aristotle's approach, and it has the merit of keeping the concept of substance firmly yoked to the notion of an ordinary, medium-sized object. Aristotle, *Physics*, in *The Complete Works of Aristotle*, trans. J. L. Ackrill and ed. Jonathan Barnes (Princeton: Princeton University Press, 1984).

The other is to take this difficulty as the discovery that substances cannot be originated or destroyed. Therefore, ordinary medium-sized objects, which are subject to origination and destruction, are not genuine substances. The subsequent history of Western philosophy was shaped by this notion of indestructible substance. It is this notion that Descartes and Leibniz made use of to support the belief in immortality. Furthermore, we can also see that an aggregate of parts could in principle be disaggregated; such a thing could undergo origination and destruction too, although not by 'property swap'. So if a genuine substance is to be indestructible, it also must not be an aggregate.

162

According to Kant, this purely formal content gets misinterpreted by the rational psychologist as an extraordinary introspectible fact about the self. For any given judgement P, I can always further judge that I judge that P. This further judgement takes the 'I' as a logical subject. Aristotle had claimed that one of the marks of primary substance is that it is a subject of predication without being predicated of anything else in turn. The 'I' as logical subject also never appears as the logical predicate of some further judgement. We appear to have hit metaphysical bedrock. The rational psychologist takes the purely formal fact that we know we can always construct a first-person propositional attitude judgement from any judgement we make, to be the introspection of the self as primary substance. Having made that identification, the rational psychologist goes on to argue that since primary substances cannot undergo destruction, neither can the self. The relevance to the hope for immortality is clear.

Kant's initial concern in the Transcendental Logic was to reply to an empiricist concern: concepts crucial to empirical science, substance and causality, could not be shown to have an empirical genesis. Kant's reply was to shift ground from ideas to judgements and show that thoughts with empirical content require structure that cannot have an empirical genesis anyway. The empiricist does not have the option of paring away bogus innate ideas to reveal a solid core of empirical thought, for without the structure the categories makes available, there is no thought at all. Just as the empiricist tried to recreate the genesis of empirical concepts, Kant was obliged to provide a parallel account of how the mind generates the structures necessary for thoughts about empirical fact. This account showed that facthood itself is imposed on the sensory field much as space and time are.

But it showed more. The very unity of awareness that constitutes our introspective selves is itself imposed on the conceptual field: the self is also a product of synthesis. This paradox provided Kant with a tool for attacking inflated notions of selfhood prevalent in the rationalist tradition. Nietzsche's encounter with Kant's thought decisively shaped his own account of self as synthesis and his critique of metaphysics. But thinking that the synthetic falsifies, that facts are the product of synthesis, and truth a mapping from thoughts to facts, he concluded that the truth is not truth. He inspired a vertigo which today lures us to an abyss into which deconstruction has already fallen.

Appendix: textual issues concerning the Transcendental Deduction

Since the chief purpose of this chapter has been to give an exposition of Kant's claims in the Transcendental Deduction and the Paralogisms with an eye to how this material influenced Nietzsche, I have spared the reader the narrower issues of textual exegesis that exercise Kant scholars. However, rather than dogmatically present my exegesis without at least some mention of the interpretative choices I have made and what motivates them, I thought it best to consign this material to an appendix. Kant scholars will find some of what they want here, while others may safely skip this material and go on to Chapter 6.

There are three textual issues: (1) The first-edition Deduction versus second-edition Deduction, (2) the long Deduction versus short Deduction, and (3) the precise location of the crucial argument that deduces the categories.

The Transcendental Deduction was significantly revised for the second edition. There is the question of the relationship between the first-edition Deduction chapter (*CPR* A 84–A 130) and the extensively rewritten second-edition Deduction chapter (*CPR* B 116–B 169). The first edition is filled with psychological claims about how it is that consciousness can become unified and by what means awareness of unified objects is possible. If we wish to understand Kant's transcendental psychology fully, this material, largely absent in the second edition, cannot be dismissed. However, the very absence of this material from the second edition shows that while Kant's discovery of the argument of the Deduction may have resulted from reflection on these psychological processes, an adequate exposition of the central argument did not strictly require them. This is not to endorse Strawson's anti-psychologistic approach. For Kant, philosophical and psychological theorizing cannot be separated. Rather, it is a matter of *how much* psychology is needed to accomplish the goal of the Deduction. Suppose that I were to present a text introducing decision theory as a piece of explanatory psychology, and I included a lengthy discussion of the psychological causes of the desires. In a revision of such a text, I might choose to delete this discussion as unnecessary for understanding decision theory. One might claim that whereas the first text was psychology, the second was concerned with 'the logic of action concepts' or somesuch. To reply that I am still concerned with psychology, pared of superfluous issues, is a perfectly straightforward reply; the burden would be on the other to show that there *is* a clear contrast that can be made out between an empirical theory and the 'logic' of the concepts it employs. Kant came to feel that much less was needed than had been offered in the first edition, and that this excess of detail had obscured the main contours of his argument. I propose we take him at his word and largely set aside the first-edition Deduction in favour of the second.

There is a further question about when the Transcendental Deduction can be said to end; Kant scholars divide into advocates of the 'short Deduction' reading, who restrict the Deduction to the Analytic of Concepts, and advocates of the 'long Deduction' reading, who regard the Deduction as a long argumentative strategy not completed until the end of the Transcendental Analytic as a whole. The difficulty that commentators have had in locating the Deduction rests on uncertainty about what Kant is even attempting to accomplish with his argument. Since causality is a category, and the Deduction is supposed to vindicate the categories in some sense, there is some confusion about the function of the Second Analogy later in the Analytic, which also concerns causality. If the Second Analogy is essential for accomplishing Kant's goals concerning causality, then it is tempting to conclude that the work of the Deduction is not done when the Deduction chapter ends. This is generally called the 'long Deduction' interpretation, which claims that the Deduction chapter is only a fragment of a larger argument encompassing the Analytic as a whole. Now in one sense this is innocuous enough; surely Kant is not finished with his tasks, whatever they may be, at the end of the Deduction chapter, or else the book would have ended right there. But it obscures his intentions to refer to the arguments of the Analytic collectively as a Deduction of the Categories. To count as a 'long Deduction' interpretation, one must claim something stronger than that Kant's task in the Analytic is not complete until the Analytic is complete, for this is trivial. Rather, the claim is that the express task the Deduction chapter announces is not completed there. Such an interpretation requires us to believe that Kant seriously misunderstood the character of his own enterprise, even after revising the text substantially in the second edition.

Kant himself provides us with ample clues about what the differing tasks of the Deduction and later parts of the Analytic (such as the Second Analogy) are. In his architectonic, he calls the Deduction the heart of an 'Analytic of Concepts' whereas the Analogies and other Principles are part of an 'Analytic of Principles'. Kant was acutely sensitive to the difference between elements of thought that have sentential form and those that have subsentential form. He must make this distinction to make the surprising claim that categorical concepts, which one would think are subsentential elements of thought, are really syntactical rules, and are thus implicated in the structure of completed sentential thoughts. The contrast between an Analytic of Concepts and an Analytic of

Principles ought to signal to us that in the former, Kant is concerned to vindicate the legitimacy of each of the categorical concepts, thus preventing us from dismissing every claim in which they appear. If the concept of causality is illegitimate, then every causal claim must be dismissed. The Principles, however, are plainly concerned with vindicating specific claims employing the categories. Kant wished to prove (1) that not all causal claims are illegitimate and (2) that everything we can experience has a cause. Clearly, if some argument showed that the concept of causality had no sense or proper employment, every claim that contains reference to causality will be impugned, including the claim that everything we can experience has a cause. However, simply showing that the concept of causality is not illegitimate is compatible with holding that not everything we can experience has a cause. It is even compatible with holding that nothing has a cause. After all, once we have contented ourselves that the concept of redness is legitimate, and that claims using it are not to be impugned simply for containing reference to redness, it hardly follows that everything is red.

Restricting ourselves to the second-edition Deduction chapter, where precisely do we find this argument? This too is a matter for contention. We find section 20 ending with: 'the manifold in a given intuition is subject necessarily to the categories' (*CPR* B 143), which certainly sounds as if Kant's mission had been accomplished (this is in fact the case). But in section 21 we read: 'hence in the above proposition I have made a *beginning* of a deduction of the pure concepts of the understanding' (*CPR* B 144, emphasis mine), thus seeming to imply that section 20 did not complete the task. To compound the confusion, in section 26, whose very title 'Transcendental Deduction of the Universally Possible Use in Experience of the Pure Concepts of Understanding' suggests that it is only here that we find what we seek, we learn that 'in the transcendental deduction we exhibited the possibility of [the categories] as *a priori* cognitions of objects of an intuition as such (§§ 20, 21)' (*CPR* B 159).

There is less confusion here than meets the eye. First, the sentence 'hence in the above proposition I have made a beginning of a deduction of the pure concepts of the understanding' does not tell us to which proposition it refers. If it referred to the passage in section 20, 'the manifold in a given intuition is subject necessarily to the categories', then this would suggest that Kant had not yet deduced the categories. But Kant does not tell us that. For all we know, he may be referring to one of the premisses of the section 20 argument, not to its conclusion. This would be compatible with regarding the task as complete by the end of section 20. But the most natural reading of the reference to 'a beginning' is the immediately preceding proposition, 'the empirical consciousness of a given manifold of one intuition is just as subject to a pure *a priori* self-consciousness' (*CPR* B 144). This is not the *conclusion* to the argument of section 20; it is the first *premiss* of section 20: 'The manifold given in a sensible intuition is subject necessarily to the original synthetic unity of apperception' (*CPR* B 143). It is a further question to ask what makes apperception possible. The answer to that question is *judgement*. And judgement is already clearly and intimately connected with the categories, entailing that sensible intuition requires the categories.

On this reading, section 20 is the Deduction proper; section 21 is a gloss on it. This squares with Kant referring in section 26 to an already completed Deduction said to have taken place in sections 20 and 21. The only remaining question is: what is going on in section *26*? Why is it even there? Here I think Kant has made a tactical error. Section 26, while furnishing us with a new argument, both presupposes section 20 and concludes with nothing stronger than what section 20 has already shown. Kant knew that section 26 presupposed section 20. He failed to see that it does not establish anything new.

What section 20 shows is that we cannot encounter an empirical fact without employing the categories, because every fact is complex, or 'manifold'. To experience this complexity as *one* fact (a prerequisite of encountering anything within the fact-structure as an object) this complexity must be unified: some form must be imposed on it. This 'form of fact' is isomorphic with the 'form of thought'. It is this that enables us to think about the fact. A form of thought is a syntactical form in the language of thought. This, in turn, is associated with a category. Thus in every empirical object we encounter, the empirical fact it is embedded in exemplifies some categorical concept or other.

In section 26, Kant reminds us that space and time as forms of intuition are also pure intuitions. A pure intuition is non-empirical awareness of a non-empirical individual. Thus we can be aware of space as an individual though it has no sensible properties. Similarly, a circumscribed region of space can be the target of a pure intuition. The fact that space and time are both forms of intuition and pure intuitions leads Kant to a further conclusion. Since space and time are pure intuitions, whatever has been said in the Deduction about empirical intuitions ought to apply to them too. The argument of section 20 can be restated, with the intuitions of space and time replacing the arbitrarily selected empirical intuition. This would license the conclusion that we must employ the categories to be aware of space and time as objects. Since space and time are also forms of intuition, the intuiting of space and time should accompany any empirical intuition at all. Therefore, all the empirical intuitions of objects occupying space and time will also be subject to the categories.

The Second Reading

The first part of this argument is interesting. It seems to imply that to be aware of space and time as objects, the manifold regions of space that comprise them must be synthesized into a unity according to a rule. On the face of it, this conflicts with the claim in the Transcendental Aesthetic that: 'we can present only one space; and when we speak of many spaces, we mean by that only parts of the same unique space. Nor can these parts precede the one all-encompassing space, as its constituents, as it were (from which it can be assembled); rather, they can be thought only as *in it*' (*CPR* A 25/B 39, emphasis Kant's). If Kant is concerned with synthesis into an object of judgement, and that taking space as an object is different from having spatialized presentations, then no trouble need arise. However that may be, there is the further question of how it is that empirical objects inherit the relevant feature of space by virtue of occupying positions within it. After all, space is odourless, and all socks occupy space, but it does not follow that all socks are odourless.

The argument concerning space and time as pure intuitions does no work for Kant other than to show the application of the categories to empirical objects in so far as they occupy space and time. It appears that the difference between sections 20 and 26 comes down to the claim that *each* empirical object requires the categories (20) as opposed to the claim that *all* empirical objects require the categories (26). The vanishing difference between these two claims, combined with Kant's impression that they were somehow distinct, is what accounts for his tactical error and confusing remarks regarding where exactly the Deduction is supposed to have taken place. The argument happens twice, one time too many. But the argument of section 20 is superior in clarity, and less roundabout in execution, than section 26. Both conclude that the categories pervade all of nature. The latter *seems* more impressive in its claim that the categories pervade all of nature because nature is coextensive with space and time. But if each empirical fact is informed by at least one category, then all of nature is covered this way too, for there are no supernatural empirical facts.

Nietzsche on Metaphysics

Kant's and Nietzsche's critiques compared

Though Nietzsche is most widely known as a critic of morality, he is also a critic of metaphysics. In both areas, our best mode of access to Nietzsche's thought must take us through Kant first. However, there are problems with the idea that Nietzsche's critique of metaphysics is a further development of Kant's.

Kant's critique of metaphysics is found in three discussions of the first *Critique*'s 'Transcendental Dialectic': the Paralogisms, the Antinomies, and the Ideal of Pure Reason. The Ideal chapter criticizes proofs for the existence of God. Though the 'death of God' is as crucial to Nietzsche's thought as the critique of rational theology is to Kant's, their goals and methods are too divergent to make a comparison particularly helpful. Nietzsche explicitly rejected Kant's arguments on the pragmatic ground that they play a very modest role in combating theism. This is a goal better pursued by his own 'genealogical' strategy of diagnosing the motives people have for religious belief.

In former times, one sought to prove that there is no God—today one indicates how the belief that there is a God could arise and how this belief acquired its weight and importance: a counter-proof that there is no God thereby becomes superfluous.—When in former times one had refuted the 'proofs of the existence of God' put forward, there always remained the doubt whether better proofs might not be adduced than those just refuted: in those days atheists did not know how to make a clean sweep. (*D* 95)

The Antinomy chapter criticizes arguments using the concept of infinite or infinitesimal magnitudes to establish the magnitude of the world or its fundamental constituents. It also grapples with the problem of free will versus determinism. Nietzsche's unpublished arguments concerning the eternal recurrence show that he rejects (or does not consider) Kant's objections to this use of the concept of infinity. This may be because Schopenhauer explicitly rejected the

Antinomies, arguing that there is nothing wrong with postulating an infinite past, a universe of infinite spatial extent, or an infinite regress of causal conditions. The Paralogism chapter criticizes Cartesian arguments that the self is an immaterial substance. Nietzsche did take Kant's arguments there as a first step towards overturning 'the soul hypothesis'. However, there is a deeper Kantian source for Nietzsche's own critique of metaphysics, a source upon which the Paralogisms depend: the Transcendental Deduction.

For Kant, the critique of metaphysics is not restricted to attacking rationalist claims. Because natural science demands the use of concepts not susceptible to direct empirical justification, Kant needed to vindicate them while restricting their use to natural science. The Transcendental Deduction is meant to solve this problem. Kant argued that just as the mind imposes Euclidean form on its experiences, thus vindicating the use of geometry in physics while explaining the possibility of *a priori* knowledge of physical space, it also imposes conceptual form on its experiences. The mind-imposition thesis explains the otherwise inexplicable harmony between our non-empirical concepts and principles, on the one hand, and the structure of nature on the other. Not only does the mind-imposition thesis parallel Kant's views about space and geometry, it also presupposes them. Because nature is the product of the sensibility's imposition of geometrical form on experience, it makes sense to imagine that the mind also imposes conceptual form on experience.

Clearly, there are costs to Kant's solution to the problem of explaining the non-empirical elements of physical theory. For if nature is mind-dependent, and its structure is due to mind-imposition, then the mind itself cannot also be a natural phenomenon. Ironically, though Kant is concerned to rule out arguments that take us from non-empirical concepts and principles to metaphysical claims about a realm outside nature, the transcendental subject required to complete Kant's project proves to be an entity whose existence outside nature must be accepted.

Nietzsche rejects the idea that the space and time of nature are forms of intuition; consequently, he cannot follow Kant in his account of nature as assembled from the data of sense formed geometrically and then further formed according to the categories. However, it is open to Nietzsche to extend his own version of the mind-imposition thesis in a way that parallels Kant. Recall that while Nietzsche rejected Kant's identification of phenomenal with physical space, he did not reject the idea that phenomenal space is the product of mind-imposition. This was what led to the falsification thesis: because of the constitution of the human mind, we are systematically misled about the space of nature.

170

This is the key to understanding Nietzsche's critique of metaphysics. The wedge that Nietzsche drives between the phenomenal and the natural allows him to attack our projection of metaphysical structure onto our experience, using the account of projection Kant had employed to vindicate synthetic *a priori* knowledge. Just because we must experience under the direction of the categories does not mean that nature must be structured by them.

By denying the identity of the phenomenal and the natural, Nietzsche escapes from the requirement that the transcendental subject be located outside nature. The position occupied in Kant's thought by things-in-themselves (including the self-in-itself) gets taken over by a nature open to human knowledge. This allows Nietzsche to naturalize the subject and eliminate one aspect of metaphysical excess in Kant's system. The unknowable thing-in-itself drops out of Nietzsche's thought. It is no longer needed as the domain in which one finds the subject or from which one gets the data of sense. We are left with the gratifying post-Kantian result that there is no domain of reality from which we are necessarily excluded.

But there are costs as well. Since the mind-imposition thesis serves in Kant's thought to underwrite the claims of *a priori* knowledge of nature, Nietzsche is compelled to abandon Kant's justificatory project for geometry and the metaphysics of experience. Having reduced transcendental psychology to empirical psychology, Nietzsche not only loses rationalist metaphysics, but *a priori* knowledge altogether. The result is an inevitable strategic retreat to empiricism. It is no coincidence that Nietzsche's mature thought shows the marks of a continuing affinity with scepticism as a result.

The presence of Kant in *Truth and Lie*

Nietzsche's first extended discussion of the Kantian account of the mind occurs in the 1873 essay *Truth and Lie*. His purpose in the essay is to develop further his critical contrast in *Birth of Tragedy* between the artistic culture of ancient Greece and its antagonist, Socratism. However, his strategy in *Truth and Lie* is to show the psychological and epistemological bases for these competing stances to undercut the assumption that the Socratic person prefers truth to the artist's illusions. By showing that both stances are rooted in the creation of illusion, he undermines the preference for Socratism. Rejecting Socratism (now simply referred to as 'the rational man') involves two parallel criticisms. First, the rational man's high evaluation of the pursuit of truth can be genealogically traced to social-utilitarian considerations—the desire to avoid the disadvantages of being lied to. Second, given Kantian assumptions about the nature of the intellect, we are unable to produce truths in any case. Our concern is with Nietzsche's argument that truth is inaccessible, for it is here that Nietzsche employs a Neo-Kantian model of the intellect.

The first stage of the intellect's construction of empirical knowledge is, unsurprisingly, 'the mathematical strictness and inviolability of our representations of time and space' which 'we produce . . . in and from ourselves with the same necessity with which a spider spins' (*KGW* iii.2. 379 (1873)/ *TL* 1). 'The process . . . with which every sensation begins in us already presupposes these forms and thus occurs within them' (ibid., 380). Sensation itself is 'a nerve stimulus . . . transferred into an image . . . a complete overleaping of one sphere, right into the middle of an entirely new and different one' (ibid., 373). We cannot infer anything about the character of the object, because 'the further inference from the nerve stimulus to a cause outside of us is already the result of a false and unjustifiable application of the principle of sufficient reason' (ibid., 372). Generally, a person does not even recognize the need to infer from the one to the other, because 'he again proceeds from the error of believing that he has these things immediately before him as mere objects. He forgets that the original intuitional metaphors (*die originalen Anschauungsmetaphern*) are metaphors and takes them to be the things themselves' (ibid., 377). The senses provide only partial access to our bodily states, and 'lock [us] within a proud, deceptive consciousness, aloof from the coils of the bowels, the rapid flow of the blood stream, and the intricate quivering of the fibres!' (ibid., 371). Human senses are but one possible sensory apparatus. 'The insect or the bird perceives an entirely different world from the one that man does . . . The question of which of these perceptions of the world is the correct one is quite meaningless' (ibid., 378). 'If we could only perceive things now as a bird, now as a worm, now as a plant, or if one of us saw a stimulus as red, another as blue, while a third even heard the same stimulus as a sound—then . . . nature would be grasped only as a creation which is subjective in the highest degree' (ibid., 379). Consequently, '(the) senses nowhere lead to truth; on the contrary, they are content to receive stimuli and, as it were, to engage in a groping game on the backs of things' (ibid., 370).

The second stage is the construction of language. 'The image, in turn, is imitated in a sound' (ibid., 373). The image in question is a 'unique and entirely individual original experience' (ibid., 373). Nietzsche says very little about this relationship; it is unclear whether he sees this primary association of word and image as denotative, since he characterizes it as pre-conceptual. We then compare similar images and, 'overlooking what is individual and actual' (ibid.,

374), let the word 'simultaneously . . . fit countless more or less similar cases' whereby 'a word becomes a concept' (ibid., 373).

Though Nietzsche never discusses the point, it is implicit that once many people possess these capacities, spoken words come to be used as part of a system of communication. This is presupposed in his claim that 'insofar as the individual wants to maintain himself against other individuals, he will under natural circumstances employ the intellect mainly for dissimulation' (ibid., 371) and that the way out of this social problem is something like a social contract that mandates semantic conventions and truth-telling. Clearly, there cannot be a rule against lying if there is no language in which lies can be couched first or the negotiation for the 'peace treaty' (ibid.) to stop endemic lying can be expressed. At this stage we have a population of individuals with convergent idiolects. There is enough of a *disposition* to use similar expressions under similar circumstances for communication and miscommunication to occur, but no agreement to cooperate by fixing rules governing the use of expressions.

Finally, social advantages accrue to groups that can implement binding semantic conventions with sanctions for 'liars' (ibid., 371–2). Nietzsche then goes on to explain that the moralization of this agreement accounts for the 'drive for truth' (ibid., 375). Correct speech now involves using the conventionally agreed upon designations in response to similar stimuli.

Two points should be raised at this juncture. First, though many readers are quite struck by the way Nietzsche uses the concepts of metaphor and convention in the essay, they really play a very modest role. 'Metaphor' and its cognates are used extensively in the essay, but always in the context of describing the relationship, not between words and other words, but between words and objects; the weight of Nietzsche's attempt to show that words cannot express how things really are rests on the inaccessibility of the real things we mistakenly take the images to be. In short, the concept of metaphor in the essay is merely a 'metaphorical' way of expressing Cartesian scepticism. Second, conventionality cannot be constitutive of language as a system of communication as Nietzsche describes it, any more than a French language minister constitutes French by issuing edicts against the use of foreign terms. Nietzsche may be right in thinking that the valorization of truth takes place against the backdrop of sanctions against lying. But whether the semantic concept of truth can be constituted by sanctions against lying is much more doubtful; lying would have to be initially reduced to mere miscommunication between idiolects, and this may involve circularity if we suppose that the idiolects are languages with meaningful expressions in the first place. Given the tight relationship between truth and meaning, it would appear that conventions constituting the one would constitute the other. But to characterize the idiolects as meaningless renders characterizing their use as dissimulative problematic.

More important for our purposes, the use of Kantian materials in the essay is extremely limited. Nietzsche's concerns about sensation could be articulated within almost any classical modern framework. The sceptical comments are closer to what Kant calls empirical idealism than transcendental idealism. The only reason one might guess that Kant was behind the essay is the reference to the transcendental ideality of space, time, and causality. To be sure, Nietzsche is not simply reiterating Schopenhauer even here; he carefully eschews any suggestion that one can identify the thing-in-itself with the will. But his attempt to be more Kantian than Schopenhauerian seems to involve merely taking over Schopenhauer's epistemology, 'the world as representation' and refusing to step beyond it to 'the world as will'. Even Nietzsche's concern over the falsifying role of concepts depends upon an account of concepts that is more Lockean than Kantian, and Schopenhauer's own theory of concepts in *The World as Will and Representation* is Lockean in essence. This suggests that in Nietzsche's earlier phase, the first *Critique* meant little more to him than the Transcendental Aesthetic.

Mistaking the early Nietzsche for the late Nietzsche in this respect explains the common suspicion that Nietzsche owes little to Kant and perhaps understands him badly as well. However, when we turn to the late Nietzsche, several themes emerge that suggest otherwise. The key to seeing this lies in the differing ways Nietzsche talks critically about language. In *Truth and Lie*, language is blamed for misleading us into thinking that empirical assertions can be true, given the subjectivity of sensations and the conventionality of referring expressions associated with them. In short, what troubles early Nietzsche about language is exclusively associated with reference and denotation. Syntax is scarcely mentioned.

By contrast, the late Nietzsche's critical discussions of language recur almost obsessively to the role that syntax plays in shaping our thought, 'the unconscious domination and guidance by similar grammatical functions' (*BGE* 20). This feature of Nietzsche's thought has become so familiar that it is worth pointing out that there is simply no source for this preoccupation in Schopenhauer. And yet Nietzsche's critique of the role that subject–predicate structure plays in shaping our thought and experience is fundamental to his late critique of metaphysics.

The contours of Nietzsche's argument are familiar. Once the mind conceives of the distinction between subject and predicate, it then projects this syntactical structure into sensations, coming to interpret the empirical world as composed of stable substances and changeable properties. This leads to expectations about how nature should be structured that come to grief on closer empirical inquiry. Rather than rejecting the concepts of stable substances in response to the discovery that nothing in the empirical world quite corresponds with our conceptions, we speculate that the empirical world is not altogether real, and that there is some other domain in which our concepts find a home.

Before proceeding to a closer comparison between this line of thought and Kant's, it is important to note two typical themes in Nietzsche's discussions of this process that find no counterpart in Kant. First, Nietzsche has an hypothesis about where the distinction between subject and predicate comes from that apparently concerns mental processes *preceding* the emergence of judgement. Kant is silent on this issue. Second, Nietzsche is tireless in insisting that psychological motives reinforce the conceptual concerns that lead to positing another world beyond the empirical. It is here that Nietzsche's discussions of decadence and the ascetic ideal have their place. Though I believe that there is a Kantian provenance for these speculations as well, their origin lies in the second *Critique*. I shall reserve discussion of them for the following chapter.

The argument of *Twilight of the Idols*: 'Reason' in Philosophy

Though there is a profusion of material in Nietzsche on the critique of metaphysics, both published and unpublished, much of it is repetitive and opaque. Fortunately, he crafted what appears to be a synopsis of his final view in *Twilight of the Idols*, which has the advantage of being clear, concise, very late (1888), and published.

Nietzsche's purpose is in the section of *Twilight* subtitled '"Reason" in Philosophy' (*TI* III) is to provide his own critique of rationalist metaphysics. His first point is that rationalist metaphysicians distinguish between *being* and *becoming*, and valorize the former at the expense of the latter. The motive for doing so is that 'Death, change, old age, as well as procreation and growth, are to their minds objections' (*TI* III. 1). Second, *becoming* is aligned with appearance, that which is presented to the senses. The rationalist downgrades the senses so that the unsavoury world of becoming is regarded as an illusion. In opposition to this, Nietzsche insists that 'the senses . . . do not lie at all. What we make of their testimony, that alone introduces lies . . . In so far as the senses show becoming, passing away, and change, they do not lie . . . Being is an empty fiction. The "apparent" world is the only one: the "true" world is merely added by a lie' (*TI* III. 2).

The Second Reading

Despite Nietzsche's claim that 'we possess science precisely to the extent to which we have decided to accept the testimony of the senses' (*TI* III. 3), Nietzsche's empiricist credentials at this juncture are rendered problematic by comments such as 'the antithesis of this phenomenal world is not "the true world", but the formless unformulable world of the chaos of sensations—another kind of phenomenal world, a kind "unknowable" for us' (*KGW* vii.2. 59–60 (1887)/*WP* 569). However, recall that in the discussion of the Transcendental Deduction two different interpretations of what synthesis is supposed to accomplish were contrasted. On one popular interpretation, sensations require moulding by the categories before perception is possible. This view was rejected in favour of an interpretation that assigns to the categories the task not of transforming sensations into perceptions, but of creating thoughts with empirical content. The grounds for this are that animals perceive, but that the categories, given their close connection to the forms of judgement, involve intellectual resources animals do not possess. On this interpretation, animal consciousness, lacking the categories, would not be a chaos of sensations, but rather a mute, pre-conceptual awareness of spatiotemporal regions qualified by sensible properties, devoid of object- and fact-structure. One possible explanation of Nietzsche's shift from regarding the senses as furnishing us with unknowable 'chaos' to regarding them as reliable is that he has rejected the standard interpretation of the Deduction in favour of an interpretation more like the one offered in Chapter 5 above.

What precisely is it that the intellect adds to the data the senses provide that introduces what Nietzsche calls 'lies'? 'The lie of unity, the lie of thinghood, of substance, of permanence' (*TI* III. 2); 'The prejudice of reason forces us to posit unity, identity, permanence, substance, cause, thinghood, being . . . This is where the error lies' (*TI* III. 5). This positing is associated with language.

In its origin language belongs in the age of the most rudimentary form of psychology. We enter a realm of crude fetishism when we summon before consciousness the basic presuppositions of the metaphysics of language, in plain talk, the presuppositions of reason . . . 'Reason' in language—oh, what an old deceptive female she is! I am afraid we are not rid of God because we still have faith in grammar. (*TI* III. 5)

Nietzsche's picture here accords quite closely to Kant's. For Kant, the operation of synthesis involves taking the syntactical forms of the language of thought and projecting them into our sensations so that sensations appear to us as possessing fact-structure, a structure isomorphic with the structure of judgement. This allows judgements to map onto empirical facts making representations of empirical fact possible. As a result, terms in the language of thought come to have references; the sensory field comes to be populated with objects to which these terms refer. It was precisely this interconnectedness of object, reference, and syntax that enabled Kant to argue that syntactical structure must be presupposed if there is to be empirical awareness of objects *qua* objects. It is difficult to see what connection Nietzsche might have seen between 'the lie of thinghood' and 'faith in grammar' unless he held a similar view.

At this point, however, it is important to clear up a possible confusion. It is common enough to read Nietzsche's reflections on language as suggesting that what ensnares thought in metaphysics is its tendency to internalize the grammatical norms of language. Such a view differs from Kant's. Instead of seeing the inner syntax of the language of thought shaping both judgement and empirical fact, a shaping expressed in a derivative way in spoken and written natural language, as Kant has it, Nietzsche would be locating the original shaping in external, natural language, which then works its way inward, so to speak, shaping thought and fact. Such a view would still bear interesting relations to the Kantian source, but would involve a radical recasting: the ultimate agent of transcendental structuring would not be the self, but the linguistic community the self is embedded in.

However, that does not appear to have been Nietzsche's view. 'The judgement does not produce the appearance of the identical case. Rather it believes it perceives one: it works under the presupposition that identical cases exist. Now, what is that function that must be much older and must have been at work much earlier, that makes cases identical and similar which are in themselves dissimilar?' (*KGW* vii.3. 366–7 (1885)/ *WP* 532). While he continues to talk about the role the linguistic community plays in determining what we will talk about (*GS* 354), the discussion in *Twilight* III. 5 concerns the individual psychological origin of syntax.

Everywhere it sees a doer and doing; it believes in will as the cause; it believes in the ego, in the ego as being, in the ego as substance, and it projects this faith in the ego-substance upon all things—only thereby does it first create the concept of 'thing'. Everywhere 'being' is projected by thought, pushed underneath, as the cause; the concept of being follows, and is derivative of, the concept of ego. In the beginning there is that great calamity of an error that the will is something which is effective, that the will is a capacity. Today we know that it is only a word. (*TI* III. 5)

Nietzsche's hypothesis begins with the phenomenon of action as a complex of psychological processes connected to bodily movement producing changes in the environment. The psychological processes have three aspects: sensory, cognitive, and affective. The sensory aspect involves 'the sensation of the state "away from which", the sensation of the state "towards which", the sensations of this "from" and "towards" themselves, and then also an accompanying muscular sensation' (*BGE* 19). That is, there are sensations which we are attracted to (say, the visual impression of a slab of steak) and the sensation of the attraction itself; at the same time there are sensations which we are repelled by (say, the kinaesthetic impression of gnawing in the stomach) and the sensation of the repulsion itself.

The cognitive aspect or 'ruling thought' (ibid.) is left unexplained. Since the purpose in bringing *Beyond Good and Evil* 19 to bear on *Twilight* III. 5 is to clarify Nietzsche's account of the origin of predication, which must be presupposed if there is to be thought at all, Nietzsche must be thinking of some sort of pre-predicative animal cognition. There is no fundamental difficulty in invoking such a notion here; higher animals may lack language, and thus the capacity to represent propositionally, but that does not prevent a cat from 'believing' on the basis of the sound of a can opener that he is about to be fed. 'Animal belief' does not involve propositional representation, whatever its underlying nature is.

The affective aspect is the most complex. Nietzsche imagines that the inner world is not only composite, but that the 'parts' of the inner world are arranged in a hierarchical structure much like a social organization. 'The way is open for new versions and refinements of the soul-hypothesis; and such conceptions as "mortal soul", and "soul as subjective multiplicity", and "soul as social structure of the drives and affects", want henceforth to have citizens' rights in science' (*BGE* 12). Given such a conception, Nietzsche suggests that during action, there is an 'affect of command' in which the dominant coalition of soul-parts experiences its preponderance over subordinate coalitions, an experience of 'command(ing) something within him that renders obedience' (*BGE* 19). At the same time there are 'the feelings of delight of his successful executive instruments, the useful "under-wills" or under-souls' (*BGE* 19).

There is nothing in the total system which is the executive entity or Cartesian agent as distinguished from the choices made. Nonetheless, the affective experience of efficacy and unity, given the hierarchical structure of the system, leads to the impression that there is an executive entity. If this is what action is like, then every action will have an executive aspect, just as at any given moment in the history of a parliament, there is a ruling coalition. Each act of the nation may be produced by different governments, and each government is merely a temporary ruling party composed of a flux of party members. There is no one individual who *is* the United Kingdom engaging in a succession of distinct acts. There are only the products of successive ruling coalitions. But we might treat the United Kingdom as a *nation*, ascribing beliefs and desires to it. As long as we realize that this is a kind of fiction, no harm is done. If, however, we reify the fiction, we might imagine that the nation is a special kind of individual, hidden within Westminster, from which the edicts of the state emanate mysteriously.

For Nietzsche, this is just what happens to the experience of our own agency, with the qualification that the special kind of individual is our will. To borrow a felicitous image from Daniel Dennett, wills are *abstracta*, analogous to centres of gravity; a centre of gravity is not a separable *entity* embedded in the middle of an object like a peach pit, but there is a geometrical point which is the real centre of gravity, given the distribution of mass in the object. Correlative with viewing the will as a separable entity is viewing choices and actions flowing from them as distinct from it. Since choices appear to flow from the will, we imagine that the will *causes* choices. This bifurcation of the continuum of action gives us the distinction between 'doer and doing' with the doer 'as the cause', as 'something which is effective', as 'a capacity' (*TI* III. 5). Nietzsche calls this imaginary doer 'the ego' (cf. *GS* 112).

This bifurcation of the continuum of action into the ego and its activities is the prototype for the distinction in thought between subject and predicate; this is the origin of primitive mental syntax. Mental syntax then becomes embodied in the syntax of natural languages. 'In its origin language belongs in the age of the most rudimentary form of psychology. We enter a realm of crude fetishism when we summon before consciousness the basic presuppositions of the meta-physics of language' (*TI* III. 5).

In the first edition of the *Critique of Pure Reason*, Kant said:

since we have to deal only with the manifold of our representations, and since that *x* (the object) which corresponds to them is nothing to us—being, as it is, something that has to be distinct from all our representations—the unity which the object makes necessary can be nothing else than the formal unity of consciousness in the synthesis of the mani-fold of representations. (*CPR* A 135)

Like Kant, Nietzsche also entertains a 'projection hypothesis' linking the con-cept of an object to syntactical structure when he says that

(language) believes in the ego, in the ego as being, in the ego as substance, and it projects this faith in the ego-substance upon all things—only thereby does it first create the con-cept of 'thing'. Everywhere 'being' is projected by thought, pushed underneath, as the cause; the concept of being follows, and is derivative of, the concept of ego. (*TI* III. 5)

However, if the preceding analysis is correct, Nietzsche's analysis of how the mind produces empirical facts has one deeper layer absent from Kant's analy-sis. Kant offers no explanation of where mental syntax comes from. Once he has the concept of mental syntax, he is able to argue that syntactical rules govern acts of synthesis to generate judgements and empirical facts. In this way the mind produces empirical objects as the correlates of referring expressions in the language of thought. Nietzsche's analysis is similar. However, he offers a prior analysis of where subject–predicate structure (the core of syntax) comes from in the first place. The account of how the experience of action leads to reifying the will or ego as an entity separable from its acts provides us with a prototype of subject–predicate structure and a template from which mental syntax and fact-structure alike will be derived.

Is Nietzsche's account coherent? Two difficulties must be addressed. The first is Nietzsche's apparent debt to Kant's Paralogisms as a source of the idea that the ego is a product of synthesis and reification. The second is the peculiar role the concept of causality plays in the account.

Nietzsche's reading of the Deduction and Paralogisms

Does Nietzsche show any awareness of or sympathy for the idea that the unity we experience as conscious beings is merely a synthetic unity of apperception? Indeed he does, both in published and unpublished texts.

If our 'ego' is for us the sole being, after the model of which we fashion and understand all being: very well! Then there would be very much room to doubt whether what we have here is not *a perspective illusion—an apparent unity that encloses everything like a horizon*. The evidence of the body reveals a tremendous multiplicity; it is allowable, for purposes of method, to employ the more easily studied, richer phenomena as evidence for the understanding of the poorer. Finally: supposing everything is becoming, then knowledge is possible only on the basis of belief in being.   (*KGW* viii.1. 104 (1886)/ *WP* 518, emphasis mine)

In this passage, we can discern three claims: (1) the 'projection hypothesis'; (2) the claim that 'knowledge', depending upon a belief in being, involves falsification, because the known is always becoming; and (3) Nietzsche's naturalistic suggestion that the multiplicity of the body is a better guide to the nature of the mind than introspective evidence. There is a promising sign of the Kantian roots of Nietzsche's conception of 'our "ego"': it is only 'an apparent unity that encloses everything like a horizon'. To see the Kantian ancestry of this idea, turn to the following passage.

Since Descartes (and more in defiance of him than because of his example) all philosophers have attempted to assassinate the old concept of the soul, under the guise of criticizing the subject–predicate concept. . . . In earlier times people believed in the soul just as they believed in grammar and the grammatical subject. They said 'I' is a condition, that 'think' is a predicate and thus conditioned: thinking is an activity for which a causal subject *must* be thought. And then, with admirable tenacity and cunning, people tried to see whether they might not be able to get out of this trap, whether perhaps the reverse was true: that 'think' was the condition, and 'I' the conditioned; 'I' would be a synthesis, which was *made* through the thinking itself. Basically, Kant wanted to prove that the subject could not be proved by means of the subject, nor could the object be proved either. Perhaps he was already familiar with the possibility of an *apparent existence* of the subject . . .   (*BGE* 54)

This passage makes little sense unless viewed as a gloss on the Deduction and Paralogisms. First we have a conflict being between people in 'earlier times' and Descartes, on the one hand, and 'all philosophers' since Descartes (ibid.). These post-Cartesians are ascribed the view that ' "I" [is] a synthesis, which was *made* through the thinking itself' (ibid.). The next figure mentioned, as if to gloss this notion, is Kant. And yet who besides Kant and post-Kantians idealists ever claimed that the self is a product of *synthesis*? However, the final remark is puzzling. For surely it is clear in Kant's text that the self of apperception is only an apparent unity. So why the hedge? Why say that 'perhaps' Kant was familiar with this idea? The most plausible explanation is that despite Kant's view of the self of apperception, the noumenal self remains. It is this which performs acts of synthesis, and in which inheres the sensory material upon which the syntheses are performed. Nietzsche is signalling his difference with Kant: whereas Kant believes that behind the merely synthetic unity of the apperceiving self, there is a noumenal self, Nietzsche claims that there is no such thing. There is only the body. A genuine substance must not be adjectival on any other substance or attribute and it must not be composed of parts. The body is composed of parts. Thus there is no substantial self, either 'here' or 'elsewhere'. This, Nietzsche takes it, represents a critical advance beyond Kant's position, and depends crucially upon his rejection of things-in-themselves.

Thus it would appear that Nietzsche accepts some variant on Kant's account of the idea of the substantial self, since he invokes both the notions of grammar (i.e. the categories as syntactical rules) and synthesis to explain the production of the false appearance of an introspectible mental substance, much as Kant does, in an aphorism which explicitly names Descartes and Kant in this connection.

But there is more. As we saw in the posthumous note quoted above, Nietzsche seems to have also borrowed from Kant the 'projection hypothesis' that appeared briefly in the 'A' version of the Transcendental Deduction, where Kant claimed that the very idea of the unity of the transcendental object is in some sense derived from the unity of the transcendental subject. This notion, which seems not to be crucial to the development of Kant's views, is probably incoherent. Nor does Nietzsche need to avail himself of it, if he is willing to endorse the idea that our thought is shaped by 'grammar'. Nonetheless, Nietzsche does avail himself of it, suggesting, not only that physical objects are products of synthesis, but that they are fictitious projections of an already fictitious notion of mental substance.

When one has grasped that the 'subject' is not something that creates effects, but only a fiction, much follows. It is only after the model of the subject that we have invented the reality of things and projected them into the medley of sensations. If we no longer believe in the effective subject, then belief also disappears in effective things, in reciprocation, cause, and effect between those phenomena that we call things. There also disappears, of course, the world of effective atoms: the assumption of which always depended on the supposition that one needed subjects. At last, the 'thing-in-itself' also disappears, because this is fundamentally the conception of a 'subject-in-itself'. But we have grasped that the subject is a fiction. The antithesis 'thing-in-itself' and 'appearance' is untenable; with that, however, the concept of appearance also disappears.   (*KGW* viii.2. 47–8 (1887)/ *WP* 552, emphases omitted)

This passage shows us how thoroughly Nietzsche is enmeshed in Kantian patterns of thought, even as he seeks to overturn them. The argument against Kant's notion of a thing-in-itself depends on a succession of Kantian claims. First, the Paralogisms inspire the claim that the self as mental substance is a merely apparent unity. Second, the Deduction inspires the claims that empirical objects are the product of acts of synthesis following syntactical rules and that the unity of the transcendental object is a projection of the unity of the transcendental subject.

However, there is a crucial difficulty here, once we recall how the Paralogism argument works. Recall that for Kant, the mind gathers together mental elements to form judgements; this gathering or 'synthesis' occurs under the direction of syntactical forms as rules governing the synthesis. Prior to the synthesis, there is no thought and no thinker. After the synthesis, there is thought. The existence of a complete thought with propositional content is what it is for there to be a thinker. Thinkers are produced by acts of synthesis. Every thought so produced can be further transformed into a propositional attitude thought about the thought. Once I can produce 'P' I can produce 'I think that P'. Thus the possibility of synthesis is the ongoing possibility of producing self-referential thoughts. This ongoing possibility is then mistaken for a substance in which thoughts inhere. Since there cannot be *any* thought without this ongoing possibility, we have the cognitive illusion of the 'I' as an indestructible logical subject: the Cartesian self. For suppose that we could judge that there had been an 'I' and now there no longer was. That could only occur if it was no longer possible to form the judgement 'I think that P' from 'P'. And that could only occur if judgement itself could no longer occur. Thus the destruction of the 'I' is not an event about which we could judge.

This is the Kantian source for Nietzsche's remarks about the reification of the self; it is what 'reification of the self' means in a Kantian context. However, Nietzsche cannot take over Kant's account wholesale without falling into incoherence. For Kant's account of reification appeals to the role that syntax plays in constructing propositional attitude statements. Nietzsche's account of the reification of the self is clearly meant to explain the origin of the concept of object, subject–predicate syntax in the language of thought, and its subsequent use in structuring experience and natural language. Nietzsche cannot use an account of reification which depends on the notion of syntax to explain the emergence of syntax without circularity. One possibility is that Nietzsche did not understand how the Paralogism argument is supposed to work. Another possibility is that he was inspired by the notion of the self as a product of synthesis by reading the Paralogism argument, but wishing to use a similar notion to explain syntax in the first place, was compelled to provide a rival hypothesis which does not rely on the notion of syntax as Kant's hypothesis does. The texts can support either reading.

However, this leaves Nietzsche in an unfortunate position, for Kant's hypothesis is far more plausible than Nietzsche's. The idea that once we can form judgements we can form judgements about judgements is straightforward. That propositional attitude judgements suggest the illusion of indestructible selfhood is a purely formal claim, and it connects Kant's transcendental psychology nicely with the traditional discussions of substance in rationalist metaphysics. The referent of 'I' will naturally seem to share the characteristics of non-compositeness and non-attributiveness the Scholastic and rationalist traditions impute to genuine substance. By contrast, Nietzsche's hypothesis is a purely empirical one. Worse, at the crucial juncture of the argument, where Nietzsche has us bifurcate the continuum of action into agent and act, there seems to be no compelling reason to see why we would do this. To be sure, Nietzsche argues persuasively that *after* we deploy predication and objecthood to interpret external events, we gain pragmatic advantages (a world of objects is simpler, more computationally tractable, can be responded to more quickly, etc.). But none of these considerations will help to explain why we do the same thing to inner events.

Nietzsche's argument remains puzzling in another sense. Kant's transcendental-psychological theorizing is meant to show that the legitimate use of the concept of substance ought to be restricted to phenomenal objects of the outer

183

sense. Nietzsche seems to think that the very fact that something is a product of synthesis delegitimizes it. One is apt to be reminded at this juncture of Nietzsche's 'genealogical' method; an idea, belief, practice, or institution is delegitimized by revealing its unsavoury origins. But one is just as apt to be reminded here of the rebuttal: it smacks of genetic fallacy. What difference does it make where we get our idea of substance from, as long as it permits us to formulate testable empirical claims? And if it does this, does that not serve as the best possible evidence that there *are* substances?

We see a similar tendency in Nietzsche's treatment of causality. For Kant, causal facts are the products of imposing the syntactical rule of hypothetical form on a pair of already synthesized facts, with the proviso that the logically antecedent fact temporally precede the logically subsequent fact. For Kant, this conception of causality is a step toward the conclusion (shown by separate argument in the Second Analogy) that the only tenable form of the principle of sufficient reason restricts the scope of its application to efficient causality connecting empirical facts, thus barring its use in transcendent metaphysics. Nietzsche agrees with this account of causality, from which he seems to infer that there is no such thing as causality.

'Changes' are only appearances. . . . But appearances cannot be 'causes'!   (*KGW* vii.3. 285–6 (1885)/ *WP* 545).

We have absolutely no experience of a cause. . . . There is no such thing as 'cause'. . . . (*KGW* viii.3. 66 (1888)/ *WP* 551)

Kant no longer has a right to his distinction 'appearance' and 'thing-in-itself'—he had deprived himself of the right to go on distinguishing in this old familiar way, in so far as he rejected as impermissible making inferences from phenomena to cause of phenomena—in accordance with his conception of causality and its purely intraphenomenal validity—which conception, on the other hand, already anticipates this distinction, as if the 'thing-in-itself' were not only inferred but given. (*KGW* viii.1. 189–90 (1886–7)/ *WP* 553)

It is obvious that things-in-themselves cannot be related to one another as cause and effect, nor can appearance be so related to appearance; from which it follows that in a philosophy that believes in things-in-themselves and appearances the concept 'cause and effect' *cannot be applied.*   (*KGW* viii.1. 133 (1886)/ *WP* 554)

As in the case of substance, Nietzsche's psychology of causal inference employs a Kant-inspired notion of projection. What is interesting about these passages is that they seem to conclude that because causality as we understand and experience it is a product of synthesis according to a rule, it follows that there is no such thing as causality.

It is crucial to get clear on what Nietzsche is up to here, because on the simplest interpretation, Nietzsche is incoherent. If Nietzsche wants to borrow a Kantian analysis of causality and use it to impugn the concept of causality as a falsifying projection, he owes us an explanation of why causal concepts permeate his explanation of synthesis in the first place. Not only does Nietzsche implicitly appeal to causal notions in the very explanation of why causality is a fiction; he also seems explicitly to contradict himself. For example, in *Twilight* he says: 'In the beginning there is that great calamity of an error that the will is something which is effective, that the will is a capacity. Today we know that it is only a word' (*TI* III. 5). In *Beyond Good and Evil* he says: 'The question is in the end whether we really recognize the will as *efficient*, whether we believe in the causality of the will: if we do—and at bottom our faith in this is nothing less than our faith in causality itself—then we have to make the experiment of positing the causality of the will hypothetically as the only one' (*BGE* 36).

These two passages are so close together in theme and date of composition that it is not plausible to suppose that the contradiction is an oversight. However, in the history of discussions of causality there are two different types of theories that compete for the mantle of being the correct analysis of causality: 'influx' theories (like Aquinas') and necessary succession theories (like Spinoza's). The influx theory holds that when one object or event causes another, something is transferred from the cause to the effect. The necessary succession theory posits some sort of relationship between cause and effect that is akin to (or an instance of) logical entailment. Hume, for example, criticizes both notions separately. Though Nietzsche would not agree to everything that has been said by proponents of the influx theory, he is clearly tacitly committed to it by virtue of his commitment to Boscovich. For in Boscovich, a force complex attracts another force complex in just the way that Newtonian masses attract gravitationally. It is no abuse of usage to say that one force complex causes the other to move towards it. Kant's analysis of causality, by contrast, is a descendant of the necessary succession theories. What makes one event the cause of another is nothing other than the fact that the two states succeed one another according to a rule. Kant differs from his rationalist predecessors in limiting the operations of causality so conceived to the phenomenal sphere, and in explaining causality in terms of his mind-imposition thesis. With this foundation, we can see that Nietzsche can accept a broad notion of causality as the operation of force in nature, while rejecting the necessary succession notion as a fiction. However, Nietzsche can still employ Kant's transcendental-psychological account of how we impose necessary succession on appearances as an account of causality as a fiction.

185

Truth

An important aspect of Nietzsche's critique of metaphysics involves negative comments about truth. Yet Nietzsche's remarks on truth have the distinct air of paradox. Rather than survey everything Nietzsche says here, consider a few representative remarks.

What are man's truths ultimately? Merely his *irrefutable* errors.   (*GS* 256)

Without accepting the fictions of logic, without measuring reality against the purely invented world of the unconditional and self-identical, without a constant falsification of the world by means of numbers, man could not live . . . Renouncing false judgements would mean renouncing life and a denial of life . . . Untruth [is] a condition of life . . . (*BGE* 4)

An isolated judgement is never 'true', never knowledge; only in the connection and relation of many judgements is there any surety.   (*KGW* viii.1. 273 (1887)/ *WP* 530)

Let us be on guard against the dangerous old conceptual fiction that posited 'a pure, will-less, painless, timeless knowing subject'; let us guard against the snares of such contradictory concepts as 'pure reason', 'absolute spirituality', 'knowledge in itself': these always demand that we should think of an eye that is completely unthinkable, an eye turned in no particular direction, in which the active and interpreting forces, through which alone seeing becomes seeing *something*, are supposed to be lacking; these always demand of the eye an absurdity and a nonsense. There is *only* a perspective seeing, *only* a perspective 'knowing'; and the *more* affects we allow to speak about one thing, the *more* eyes, different eyes, we can use to observe one thing, the more complete will our 'concept' of this thing, our 'objectivity', be.   (*GM* III. 12)

Indeed, it might be a basic characteristic of existence that those who would know it completely would perish, in which case the strength of a spirit should be measured according to how much of the 'truth' one could still barely endure—or to put it more clearly, to what degree one would require it to be thinned down, shrouded, sweetened, blunted, falsified.   (*BGE* 39)

Many claim that Nietzsche is not writing incoherently about truth, but discussing different theories of truth. If truth is correspondence, then there is no truth; if truth is what works, there is. This interpretative move, first made by Danto,[1] introduces the further interpretative question: what is Nietzsche's theory of truth?

---

[1] Arthur Danto, *Nietzsche as Philosopher* (New York: Macmillan, 1965).

One must distinguish clearly between what truth *is*, what psychological processes cause us to value it, what value its possession has, and how one obtains it. The answers to these questions do not collectively make up a theory of truth in any accepted sense of the phrase. A theory of truth tells us what truth, a semantic property, is. Psychology, value theory, and epistemology are other enterprises. Furthermore, attempts to produce a theory of truth in the narrow sense are not always directed at the same set of philosophical difficulties. As Kirkham[2] makes clear, even within this restricted compass, theories of truth are directed at a variety of problems, including: explaining the metaphysical nature of representation, vindicating physicalism in the face of the threat of non-physical semantic properties, solving semantic paradoxes (e.g. 'I am lying'), avoiding scepticism by collapsing truth into idealized justification, and analysing the function of truth ascription in ordinary language.

The most sophisticated of attempts to impute a theory of truth to Nietzsche can be found in Schacht.[3] Schacht claims that for Nietzsche, to give a theory of truth is to give a theory of the meaning of the predicate 'is true' and related expressions. If meaning is closely related to actual use, in something like Wittgenstein's sense, then our theory must follow the actual use of our truth talk.

Schacht outlines a three-tiered theory of truth he ascribes to Nietzsche. At the first level, there are the beliefs and assumptions that participants in a particular cognitive practice have about what they are doing. For example, many working mathematicians believe that they are exploring a mind-independent domain of Platonic objects. One can say that these mathematicians are at least tacitly committed to a correspondence theory of truth. Suppose, however, that there are no Platonic objects. Instead, mathematical claims are substantiated by proof procedures which can be made intelligible without the hypothesis of Platonic objects and the associated theory of truth. Whatever is really going on (in this example, adherence to certain proof con-structing conventions) is described in an account of the nature of mathematical truth at the second level. Finally, there is the question of the truth of Nietzsche's own utterances, in asserting the claims about mathematics at the lower levels; an account of this gives us the third level of Nietzsche's theory of truth.

Despite the considerable amount of material to be classified under these three headings, the question remains: is any of this a theory of *truth*? In the case of mathematics, we have (1) what people believe about mathematics, (2) why they are wrong to believe it, and what they ought to believe about it, and

[2] Richard L. Kirkham, *Theories of Truth: A Critical Introduction* (Cambridge MA: MIT Press, 1992), 1–40.

[3] Richard Schacht, *Nietzsche* (London: Routledge and Kegan Paul, 1983), 52–117.

(3) what it is to predicate 'is true' of an assertion, for example, about (1) or (2). Only third-level analyses could be regarded as theories of truth properly speaking. Only third-level analyses concern what it is that makes a true assertion true, rather than why it is that people make false assertions in various domains. Thus, it would be more natural to speak directly of Nietzsche's views on mathematics, rather than to speak of Nietzsche's theory of truth in the mathematical domain.

Thus our attention is led to what, on Schacht's view, Nietzsche's theory of truth on the third level is. Only this would be, properly speaking, a theory of truth. According to Schacht, the answer is that Nietzsche accepts a correspondence account of truth at the third level; therefore Nietzsche regards truth itself as correspondence. This certainly resonates with *Beyond Good and Evil* 36. But the evidence for imputing a correspondence theory to Nietzsche is at best evidence that Nietzsche's usage on certain matters accords with common usage (e.g. that if Nietzsche believes that P, then Nietzsche believes that 'P' is true) and that he takes his own assertions seriously. Worse, one would not turn to Nietzsche for an account of what correspondence is, let alone a critique of competing theories of truth. This suggests that in one sense of the phrase, Nietzsche has no theory of truth at all.

However, bearing in mind Kirkham's observation that theories of truth are a mixed bag, often addressed to fundamentally different questions, more progress can be made by determining what Nietzsche's questions about the nature of truth are before we examine his answers. That way we will not be misled into trying to identify his doctrine with theories formulated by others, addressed to fundamentally alien concerns.

In Kant, we also see a commitment to a conception of truth as correspondence, but without any sign of concern over the kinds of issues that typically motivate theories of truth. 'Truth is the agreement of cognition with its object' (*CPR* A 58/B 82). However, if we narrow the question to 'what is empirical truth?' more can be said. Though one could simply say that empirical truth is the agreement of empirical cognition with empirical object, we know that Kant has quite an elaborate theory of what transcendental mechanisms make this possible. These mechanisms involve the imposition of categorial form on sensations to yield empirical facts to which similarly formed judgements can correspond. So while Kant has no answer to the kinds of questions most theories of truth are meant to solve, he does have a great deal to say concerning the conditions of the possibility of empirical truth.

What Nietzsche says about truth can be illuminated by seeing him as taking over Kant's theory of empirical truth in this sense. Nietzsche's sceptical remarks on truth can be seen as expressing the view that if this is all empirical truth comes to, it is not worthy of the name. What exactly does Nietzsche find disreputable about empirical truth conceived along Kantian lines? The key seems to be that the mind is active in producing the very facts to which our judgements should correspond. 'When someone hides something behind a bush and looks for it again in the same place and finds it there as well, there is not much to praise in such seeking and finding. Yet this is how matters stand regarding seeking and finding "truth" . . .' (*KGW* iii.2. 377/ *TL* 1). In short, the early Nietzsche hesitates to call use the word 'truth' to characterize judgements that map onto mind-dependent items.[4]

If this is correct, then we can see why the early Nietzsche links the concept of truth to things-in-themselves. If truth worthy of the name cannot be a mapping of judgements onto mind-dependent items, then it would be a mapping of judgements onto mind-independent items. Things-in-themselves are mind-independent. Thus truth worthy of the name is a mapping of judgements onto things-in-themselves. These considerations are the basis for the Wilcox–Clark view. According to Wilcox, when Nietzsche believed that there were things-in-themselves, he regarded truth as an adequate representation of them. But since Kant has shown that we cannot represent things-in-themselves, it follows that there cannot be any truth. Once Nietzsche realized that there are no things-in-themselves because thinghood itself is mind-dependent, he rejected the alignment between truth and things-in-themselves. Thus in his late phase, he writes without ambivalence about truth and its value, claiming truth for his own utterances. Accordingly, we would expect late Nietzsche to abandon the sceptical claims he makes in *Truth and Lie*.[5]

This expectation comes to grief in light of the following passage:

This is the essence of phenomenalism and perspectivism as I understand them: owing to the nature of animal consciousness, the world of which we can become conscious is only a surface- and sign-world, a world made common and meaner . . . all becoming conscious involves a great and thorough corruption, falsification, reduction to superficialities, and generalization . . . You will guess that it is not the opposition of subject and object that concerns me here . . . It is even less the opposition of the 'thing-in-itself' and appearance; for we do not 'know' nearly enough to be entitled to any such distinction.

---

[4] One must be cautious to not read too much into the term 'mind-dependent' given its extensive use by analytic philosophers in discussions of realism and anti-realism. As used here, it does not mean 'truth conditions for claims that in principle transcend all possible evidence for them'. It merely means 'items which would not exist if there were no minds'.

[5] John Wilcox, *Truth and Value in Nietzsche* (Ann Arbor: University of Michigan Press, 1974), 98–126.

The Second Reading

We simply lack any organ for knowledge, for 'truth': we 'know' (or believe or imagine) just as much as may be useful in the interests of the human herd, the species; and even what is here called 'utility' is ultimately also a mere belief, something imaginary, and perhaps precisely that most calamitous stupidity of which we shall perish some day. (*GS* v. 354 (1887)).

This passage is curious for many reasons. First, it is preceded by a lengthy speculation about the historical origins of consciousness. This willingness to speculate seems puzzling if we take seriously the claim that 'all becoming conscious involves . . . falsification'. Are Nietzsche's own claims about the distant past exempt? Second, he distinguishes between correct and incorrect claims in a particularly vivid way at the end, suggesting that we may be significantly mistaken about the world. It is difficult to read that many of our claims may be 'calamitous stupidity of which we shall perish some day' without imagining that it is *reality* that takes its revenge. Most important, he claims that 'it is even less the opposition of the "thing-in-itself" and appearance'. Since sceptical rhetoric is prominent throughout Nietzsche's writings, the source of the mature Nietzsche's scepticism must be something other than this opposition. Nietzsche's later contrast between our cognitive powers and the world in which they find themselves is a contrast to be drawn within the realm of 'appearances' because 'the reasons for which "this" world has been characterized as "apparent" are the very reasons which indicate its reality; any other kind of reality is absolutely indemonstrable' (*TI* III. 6).

So if mind-imposition yields fictions, what are these fictions contrasted with? If Nietzsche were to align the notion of truth with things-in-themselves, as he did in *Truth and Lie*, then phenomenality in Kant's sense would entail fictitiousness. But this course is unavailable to the late Nietzsche, for he has no things-in-themselves with which to contrast Kantian phenomenality. Nietzsche seems to be attacking anything which is a product of synthesis by virtue of an implied contrast with what is really the case; operating within a Kantian framework, a natural candidate for what is really the case, if the products of synthesis are meant to be in contrast with it, is the thing-in-itself. But Nietzsche rejects the idea of the thing-in-itself, and with it, a contrast in light of which the synthetic could be condemned.

The only way out of this difficulty is to substitute a contrast between the phenomenal world (= nature) and the noumenal world with a contrast between ordinary illusions generated by our evolved transcendental-psychological mechanisms and how nature is described in our best empirical theory. As we saw in Chapter 4, Nietzsche appropriated Kant's transcendental psychology in the following fashion. Rather than view nature as a product of transcendental syntheses performed by a subject outside of nature, he instead naturalized the Kantian subject, allowing that such syntheses were real psychological processes taking place *in* nature, yielding experience, to be sure, but an experience which not only does not coincide with the character of the natural world but which falsifies it. We saw how Nietzsche's views on geometry deviated from Kant's. Whereas Kant claims that the subject imposes Euclidean form on experience, thus yielding a nature which is guaranteed *a priori* to obey Euclidean laws, Nietzsche claims that the naturalized Kantian subject imposes Euclidean form on experience, thus misleading us about the real geometrical character of nature, which, for all we know, might be non-Euclidean. (The explanation for this imposition of form, in turn, is a Darwinian one.) The discovery of the correct geometry for nature thus falls on natural science, which can yield only *a posteriori* knowledge.

Nietzsche's approach to the categories and principles is essentially the same. Kant had claimed that the categories are to be derived from forms of thought, which he correlates with forms of judgement. Nietzsche retains the Kantian account of how categories are generated from forms of judgement, and how categories inform and structure experience, with the proviso that such transcendental processes are to be understood naturalistically.

As in Nietzsche's use of Kant's account of geometry, Nietzsche claims only that we are so constituted as to organize our experience in terms of the categories. Rejecting the Kantian identification of nature with the phenomenal world (the world we experience as we do by virtue of the mind's form-imposing activities), Nietzsche claims that experiencing the world as composed of observable facts whose formal structure mirrors the structure of thought may be of great practical value while distorting the actual character of nature. The character of nature, in turn, must be discovered by natural science. Though it is possible that it will prove to have the structure implicit in our ordinary, pre-theoretical experience of it, this need not be the case.

A simple example showing the parallel between categorical form and geometrical form may be helpful here. If Nietzsche is right, we are predisposed to encounter the world as composed of objects embedded in states of affairs. If we reflect on the sentence-like structure that the experienced world presents us with, we are likely to produce theories about nature that privilege these implicit assumptions of our categorical scheme. For example, Aristotle's account of change in the *Physics* supposes that the world consists of substances which are both formally objects in our sense (referents), but also the familiar topics of discussion in ordinary life. He then goes on to characterize change as what one might call 'attribute swapping' by the primary substance. An apple rotting can be seen as consisting of an enduring substance, the apple, its possession of an attribute at t_1 (ripeness) and the replacement of that attribute with another at t_2 (rottenness). This little piece of folk physics is coloured by how we report change in language and represent it in thought. One name is used in two claims. Two predicates are used, one of which replaces the other from the first to the second claim. Though it may be useful to talk of familiar topics in this manner, we are at some remove from an adequate scientific account of rotting. Though the scientific account is also couched in language and thought, it may require us to abandon talk of the apple as the object undergoing attribute swap and talk instead of a region through which a chemical or biological process is spreading. We cannot stop talking in language any more than we can stop sensing in a Euclidean manner. But we can resist allowing these features of ourselves as cognitive beings from biasing our scientific theorizing. We need not assume that physical space is Euclidean simply because it looks that way. We need not assume that familiar objects should be the primary referents in an adequate explanatory theory just because they are what we have always talked about. We cannot eliminate this bias by removing these features of ourselves as cognitive beings. We do not become aware of space more clearly by somehow not experiencing it as Euclidean, by eliminating our contribution; rather we draw on our resources as cognitive beings who experience in a Euclidean fashion in order to envision how the physical world might not be Euclidean. We use Euclidean analogies to express non-Euclidean truths, e.g. that three-dimensional space is 'curved' even though it seems 'flat' in the same way that a two-dimensional being might exist on the surface of a large sphere believing it is a plane. Similarly, when a physicist explains the behaviour of a familiar object in terms of chemical processes, and then explains the chemical processes in terms of electrons, she is using our pre-theoretic notion of a familiar object to help us understand imperceptible occurrences involving posits (the electrons) that resemble our notion of the familiar object up to a point. We do not grasp the change of an apple from ripe to rotten by turning off our tendency to think in terms of facts, objects and properties, but by redeploying the tendency in novel ways. Our physical knowledge of the apple is not complete once it has been characterized in Aristotelian terms; the influence of the formal features of language and thought prevent us from seeing this. Yet we can undo this error without ceasing to think or speak; the historical fact of the New Science of Descartes, Galileo, and Newton shows this. It is an error correctable within our experience of nature. We need not appeal to things-in-themselves in this context. We had better not, for we either have no access to them (Kant) or else they do not exist (Nietzsche).

Once Nietzsche saw that the phenomenal/noumenal contrast could not be drawn, but that Kant's insight into the mind-dependence of the world of ordinary experience could be preserved, he rejected his earlier commitment to the idea that mind-dependence alone casts doubt on the veracity of our judgements. This is the point behind such late dicta as 'there is *only* a perspective seeing, *only* a perspective "knowing"; and the *more* affects we allow to speak about one thing, the *more* eyes, different eyes, we can use to observe one thing, the more complete will our "concept" of this thing, our "objectivity", be' (*GM* III. 12). This passage is often read as a commitment to some sort of postmodern pluralism: if there is no unitary reality onto which our judgements must map, then anything goes. But while Nietzsche does believe that there are multiple ways of gaining epistemic access to reality, his target here is not the concept of reality itself. Nietzsche has a rich conception of reality as the totality of Boscovichian force-complexes and their relations. Rather, he is retracting his earlier commitment to the idea that mind-dependence means epistemic taint. If mind-dependence is pervasive and inescapable, any theory of knowledge that requires mind-independence of objects as a condition of our judgements about them being true will leave us with no knowledge at all. Such scepticism sweeps too broadly. But to embrace knowledge reconceived as situated and dependent on constructive mental processes is not to endorse automatically the construction that first comes naturally to us as 'phenomenal truth'. Room remains for criticism of our folk theories, and explanation of their genesis can play a role in such criticism. However, such criticism must take place within the sphere of an expanded empirical inquiry.

This renewed commitment to empiricism means that Nietzsche must abandon Kant's epistemology of synthetic *a priori* knowledge. Not only do synthetic *a priori* judgements become regulative fictions; Kant's whole strategy of rational reconstruction falls apart.

The legitimacy of belief in knowledge is always presupposed: just as the legitimacy of the feelings of conscience-judgements is presupposed. Here moral ontology is the dominant prejudice.

The conclusion is therefore:

1. there are assertions that we consider universally valid and necessary;
2. necessity and universal validity cannot be derived from experience;
3. consequently they must be founded, not upon experience, but upon something else, and derive from another source of knowledge! . . .

But the origin of a belief, of a strong conviction, is a psychological problem: and a very narrow and limited experience often produces such a belief! It already presupposes that there is not (just) '*data a posteriori*' but also *data a priori*, 'preceding experience'. Necessity and universal validity could never be given to us by experience: why does that mean that they are present without any experience at all? . . . These are not forms of knowledge at all! They are only regulative articles of belief . . . Hume had declared: 'There are no synthetic *a priori* judgements'. Kant says: But there are! Those of mathematics! And if there are such judgements, perhaps there is also metaphysics . . . (But) mathematics is possible under conditions under which metaphysics is never possible. All human knowledge is either experience or mathematics.   (*KGW* viii.1. 273–4 (1887)/ *WP* 530)

Synthesis and struggle

The preceding interpretation places a great weight on Nietzsche's naturalization of Kant's transcendental psychology, and takes, one might think, an easy way out in dealing with the problem of falsification by simply substituting nature where Kant had things-in-themselves, thus deflating what appears to be some sort of global philosophical scepticism to a more humdrum cognitive caution akin to not trusting your senses when it comes to reporting bent sticks in water. To be sure, the extent of our errors would be far greater, according to Nietzsche, than the errors Descartes mentions in the first *Meditation*. Beyond thinking that sides of roads meet at the horizon and that far away objects appear smaller than they are, we have to worry about pervasive biases in thought that only fairly sophisticated natural science can uncover (as the example of Euclidean geometry suggests). But this humble naturalism seems a far cry from the grander themes of Nietzsche's world-interpretation: perspectivism, will to power.

Nonetheless, they are rooted in it. What makes Hegel distinctively post-Kantian is his attempt to transform Kant's critique of the subject into a metaphysics. In a different way, the same can be said of Nietzsche. Recall our discussion of Nietzsche's panpsychism in Chapter 4. There we saw that reality outside of us is best understood as many loci of dispositions to affect our experience, in something like the way that Berkeley understood God. Our awareness of the world is, in part, a product of the world's efforts to impress itself on us. But whereas for Berkeley, finite minds are purely passive, for Nietzsche, as for Kant, our minds are independent sources of activity, striving to subjugate and reduce to order the sensory states that arise in us. Though it may sound strange to our ears, for Nietzsche the concept of the will to power serves to unify elegantly his post-Kantian account of experience as synthesized by the subject.

The material of the senses adapted by the understanding, reduced to rough outlines, made similar, subsumed under related matters. Thus the fuzziness and chaos of sense impressions are, as it were, logicized;

2. the world of 'phenomena' is the adapted world which we feel to be real. The 'reality' lies in the continual recurrence of identical, familiar, related things in their logicized character, in the belief that here we are able to reckon and calculate;

3. the antithesis of this phenomenal world is not 'the true world', but the formless unformulable world of the chaos of sensations—another kind of phenomenal world, a kind 'unknowable' for us;

4. questions, what things 'in-themselves' may be like, apart from our sense receptivity and the activity of our understanding, must be rebutted with the question: how could we know that things exist? 'Thingness' was first created by us. The question is whether there could not be many other ways of creating such an apparent world—and *whether this creating, logicizing, adapting, falsifying is not itself the best-guaranteed reality; in short, whether that which 'posits things' is not the sole reality*; and whether the 'effect of the external world upon us' is not also only the result of such active subjects— The other 'entities' act upon us; our adapted apparent world is an adaptation and overpowering of their actions; a kind of defensive measure. The subject alone is demonstrable; hypothesis that only subjects exist—that 'object' is only a kind of effect produced by a subject upon a subject—a modus of the subject.   (*KGW* viii.2. 59–60 (1887)/ *WP* 569, emphasis mine)

For Nietzsche, as for Kant, imagination (or what Nietzsche calls 'interpretation') is essential to the constitution of experience. However, given that we are partly passive in relation to experience, both Kant and Nietzsche write of a prime matter of sensation that the mind works up into experience. This 'chaos', as Nietzsche calls it, enters into an *agon* with the subject, who seeks to master it by interpretation (synthesis). Nietzsche identifies both the source of the chaos and the organizing system we are with the will to power. Having rejected the intelligibility of a thing-in-itself, Nietzsche could only conclude that 'this world is will to power, and nothing else besides' (*KGW* vii.3. 339 (1885)/ *WP* 1067). Kant could scarcely have imagined that his concept of synthesis would prove the seed of such florid growth.

The Critique of Morality 7

The three pillars of Kantian ethics

Kant's moral philosophy involves three projects: rational reconstruction, justification and metaphysical explanation. The rational reconstruction of morality takes the data of moral intuitions as authoritative and tests Kant's moral theory against them. The justification of morality shows that moral action is a species of rational action by proposing a new model of agency: the voice of conscience proves to be the voice of reason. Metaphysical explanation shows how action can be morally accountable despite the determinism of nature by exploiting the phenomenal/noumenal contrast and locating the will outside of nature. This metaphysical setting then paves the way for a 'practical' commitment to the existence of God as guarantor of a moral order outside nature.

Each of these three pillars of Kant's moral philosophy finds echoes in Nietzsche's three essays of the *Genealogy of Morals*. The first essay traces the moral intuitions Kant relies on to slave morality and its social and psychological conditions, thus undermining their legitimacy as unquestioned data in the project of rational reconstruction. The second essay appropriates key aspects of Kant's model of agency to explain away rather than to justify the dictates of conscience. Nietzsche severs the link between practical reason and the categorical imperative, thus allowing a new, post-Kantian conception of autonomy and its value. The third essay traces the phenomenal/noumenal contrast to the ascetic ideal, which is shown to have its roots in incoherent and destructive attitudes towards life.

Kant's first project rationally reconstructs our moral intuitions in terms of a unifying principle. Like Rawls, Kant assumes that our moral intuitions have *prima facie* authority. The purpose of moral philosophy is simply to articulate their underlying structure. Moral intuitions test moral theory just as empirical data test empirical theory. For Rawls, the process of regimenting our intuitions into a simpler form need not be entirely subservient to our intuitions. If a model of moral reasoning possesses theoretical desiderata without conforming to some of our intuitions, then these intuitions ought to be revised. Thus the process of modelling is a kind of back and forth movement between intuition and model. In the end, we arrive at a stable result: reflective equilibrium. Rawls's conception of reflective equilibrium is reminiscent of certain features of Quine's account of empirical theory. According to Quine, no class of sentences in an empirical theory possesses a special 'foundational' status immunizing them from revision, including observation sentences; in the interest of preserving an otherwise attractive theory, we may wish to explain away or dismiss observation reports incompatible with the theory.

Though Kant shares Rawls's project of rationally reconstructing our moral intuitions, his confidence in the authority of our intuitions is too high to accept the notion of reflective equilibrium. While Rawls's methodology for moral theory resembles Quine's, Kant's resembles Popper's. A theory that does not square with the observed is falsified. It is part of the virtue of a theory that it not be easily patched up by *ad hoc* modifications. Similarly, for Kant there is no freedom to dismiss intuitions that conflict with an otherwise compelling theory. Kant's confidence in the moral competence of the untutored moral agent is exceptionally high. Far from regarding moral theory as likely to lead to new moral truths, he is more concerned with the sophistical temptations theorizing may lead to. For example, everyone knows that breaking a promise for the greater good of society is immoral. Only reading utilitarian ethicists leads us to ignore the clear dictates of conscience. In this respect, Kant follows the path laid out in the first *Critique*: the untutored do not need rationalist metaphysics to shore up their religious commitments. The only likely result of opening theological questions to rational discussion and adjudication is to lead us into confusion and irreligion.

Rational reconstruction, however, is but one pillar of Kant's ethical thought. The second pillar is justificatory. The first project at most could show the structure of the commitments we already possess, but it would leave the question of their correctness untouched. Kant was concerned with Glaucon's challenge: that morality and rationality can diverge, that it is only rational to be moral when being moral serves our self-interest.

The third project responds to the threat Newtonian mechanism poses to free will and moral accountability. Showing that accountable action is possible involves the use of the phenomenal/noumenal contrast, which is then put to further use in Kant's philosophy of religion. Though it is sometimes difficult to determine which challenge a particular point of doctrine is intended to address, it is important both to distinguish these three projects and to show how they are interdependent. Recent appropriators of Kant, typically concerned with at most one or two of these projects, tend to miss both the distinctions and the connections.

The project of rational reconstruction is perhaps that which current readers of Kant are most familiar with, since it is the project that dominates Kant's most widely read ethical text, the *Grounding for the Metaphysics of Morals*. Kant concludes that we regard an action as moral because it is caused by the appropriate intention. Intentions are rule-like or procedural items (Kant calls them 'maxims', though 'policies' might be a more idiomatic translation) which generate behaviour. The procedure that embodies morally praiseworthy intentions is the categorical imperative, which he characterizes in three different, allegedly synonymous, ways, e.g. acting so that one's choice should become a universal law. Much of the literature on Kant concerns whether the categorical imperative could serve as a reliable algorithm for moral action, there being immoral actions authorized by it and moral actions prohibited by it.[1]

The justification problem is best understood in light of Glaucon's challenge in Book II of Plato's *Republic*. Given a plausible identification of rational action with enlightened self-interest, it would appear that morality, as Kant's rational reconstruction has it, is impossible. Not only can enlightened self-interest diverge from morality. Glaucon's argument suggests that we perform moral acts when we do only because they are recommended by self-interest. If so, then one requirement for moral action on Kant's account, that it stem from the

---

[1] Kant would not have been much moved by these sorts of objections. There is now an extensive literature on Wittgenstein that calls into question whether *any* behaviour can be determined by a rule. If the classical arguments against Kant are really only instances of rule-scepticism, then they may have more bark than bite. No one thinks rule-sceptical arguments compel us to reject the possibility of following some particular rule. Rather than reject the categorical imperative, Kant's position might be strengthened if it were revised to allow for post-Wittgensteinian insights into the conditions of the possibility of rule-following. Whether such a strategy could succeed would take some showing. It is possible that in describing a rule-governed system one may mischaracterize a rule, sceptical issues aside—saying '4' in response to '2,2' might show adding or multiplying, depending upon responses to other mathematical requests. Kant's ethics might fail in the same way that one might misidentify what a mathematician is up to in this sort of case.

There are difficulties in Kant's ethics, but I am inclined to locate them in his doctrine of virtue. The very idea of a distinction between perfect and imperfect duty is questionable. The idea of a duty to oneself is an attractive one (and does much to counter the impression of servility that constant harping on 'duty' has made on Kant's readers). However, Kant's specific examples of it all fail by depending on unjustified assumptions about Nature's intentions. This notion really has no place in a Kantian ethic given Kant's deepest assumptions and commitments about nature, agency, and value.

appropriate disinterested intention, requires that moral action be action done in defiance of practical reason. This would introduce incoherence into the norms governing action. What one 'ought to do' in certain cases is follow the incompatible dictates of rational self-interest and irrational morality. Kant concludes that the conception of practical reason presupposed by Glaucon must be mistaken.

In constructing an empirical theory, we seek theories that make predictions or retrodictions supported by observations. Not just any theory that does this is acceptable. There are many formal desiderata that enable us to rank theories that are otherwise equally empirically adequate. Similarly, for Kant, the rationality of a plan of action is constrained by formal desiderata independent of the efficacy of the plan at achieving its goals. It is from these formal constraints that Kant hopes to derive the constraints on self-interested action we regard as moral obligations. If such a project were successful, then one could argue that immoral actions, even when responsive to empirical facts and effective at achieving self-interested goals, are nonetheless irrational.

It is well known that the formal constraint is the categorical imperative, the requirement that action flow from a maxim that could be willed as a universal law. However, the secondary literature misses why Kant thinks this formal constraint has merit in an account of practical reason apart from its value in reconstructing morality. The underlying source of the categorical imperative is that rationality requires a cognitive or practical being to treat relevantly similar things in relevantly similar ways. It is irrational to appeal to a piece of evidence to shore up a favoured belief on the one hand, and then reject relevantly similar evidence when it undermines another cherished belief. Similarly, it is irrational to pay a much higher price than elsewhere available for identical merchandise. Both forms of irrationality involve treating relevantly similar items differently.

Kant believes that each agent is committed to a principle of self-respect. One's own preferences are worthy of satisfaction because one's self has worth. Otherwise self-interest would not be pursued. By making this commitment to self-worth explicit, a commitment most philosophers of action take for granted, he sees a way to use the 'treat relevantly similar things in relevantly similar ways' principle to show that moral action is rational. When an agent uses another as a means without respecting her own preferences, this involves a contradiction. The satisfaction of my preferences is worthy of pursuit because I am an agent, and as an agent, I have value. The satisfaction of the other's preferences is not worthy of pursuit, because the other is not *me*. Yet the other is relevantly similar, being an agent, and therefore, possesses value too if I do. So the use of another involves a distinction without a difference, and that is what makes it irrational.

The universalization 'test' is not intended to provide a decision procedure for distinguishing morally right actions from morally wrong ones. Rather, it is meant to illustrate the implications of a fully systematized rational plan of action for an individual. We should not expect that a decision procedure would be available here any more than that one would be available in producing an empirically adequate, fully systematized physics. Kant does not suppose that the categories can provide us with a decision procedure for laws of physics; one goal of the Introductions of the third *Critique* is to argue that the categories and principles of the understanding are insufficient for fully determining a complete natural science, even if the empirical data are given. Rather, we also need to exercise judgement in the construction of theory, allowing ourselves to be guided by cognitive desiderata such as 'elegance' when systematizing laws hierarchically, and when constructing an adequate taxonomy of empirical objects.

The process of systematizing my desires makes explicit that there is nothing special about my desires that demands their realization to the exclusion of the desires of others. Similarly the systematization of our empirical knowledge leads to the realization that there are no such things as 'natural places' or privileged inertial frames of reference. The central result of systematizing my desires is the grounding of the value of equality on the norm of consistency.

Grounding ethical demands on a purely formal norm enables Kant to achieve ethical objectivity while retaining the virtues of a subjectivist conception of practical reason of the sort that Hume advanced. Any conception of practical reason will involve the following of practical syllogisms, the efficient adjustment of means to ends, etc. However, there is a perennial debate in the philosophy of action about whether the ultimate ends of action can themselves be evaluated. If there are certain ends that are objectively valuable as such, we could evaluate agents' preferences independent of whether their reasoning or behaviour reflects a rational course of action for the realization of the preferences they do possess. The notion of objectively valuable ends cuts across the distinction between egoistic ends and altruistic ends. For example, Spinoza defends a version of rational egoism while insisting on a distinction between an agent's preferences and an agent's objective interests. Spinoza can judge an agent irrational even if she efficiently realizes her preferences, if satisfying them does not secure her objective interests. Similarly, Aquinas would judge an agent irrational for preferring not to promote the objective good, though that good would not be understood in terms of objective self-interest. By contrast,

Hume insists that the notion of objectively valuable ends independent of the agent's preferences makes no sense. We can evaluate the rationality of an agent in terms of their ability to conform to practical syllogisms, etc., but what goals the agent seeks to realize are not open to rational discussion.[2]

Kant agrees with Hume; Kant's account of practical reason begins with the subjectivist assumption that one cannot evaluate preferences for their objective value. It may appear that Kant's claim that there is no intrinsic value other than a 'good will' contravenes this interpretative claim. Actually, it illustrates it. For the value of an agent is what bestows value on the satisfaction of preferences. There is nothing in the notion of an agent as the source of value that could, all else being equal, single out some subset of preferences as more worthy of realization than others. Kant's commitment to this notion, though implicit in his ethical thought, is of a piece with his anthropocentrism, and the value he places on human autonomy. If there were objectively valuable preferences, there would be something outside the human will to which the will ought to be subject. In that sense, we would not be purely self-determining and free. Though Kant dismisses the preferences of the wicked as having no value when realized, this is not because some preferences are intrinsically good or bad. Kant's conception of a good will is that of an agent moved by intentions the appropriateness of which is not fixed by their content, but by their formal properties. The formal property the set of intentions must possess is their consistency with universalization, which is simply an instance of the 'treat relevantly similar cases in relevantly similar ways' principle. Rather than assigning determinate content for the will to realize 'from outside' as both theological and naturalistic theories do, Kant claims the good for human beings must be purely self-defined and self-determined, subject to unavoidable formal constraints. Morality for Kant is analogous to a liberal democratic state: a neutral framework within which all citizens can pursue the good as they see it without prejudice to others' diverging attempts to do the same. There is tight linkage between Kant's subjectivism (which assures freedom from heteronomous values), his demand for consistency (the satisfaction of my preferences should not trump the satisfaction of yours), and his commitment to equality (agents are equal in value and deserve equal respect). These interlocking components of Kant's thought make him the advocate of political modernity *par excellence*.

---

[2] Hume's own solution to Glaucon's problem is to insist that there can be basic altruistic preferences. If preference satisfaction is all that practical reason requires, acting to satisfy altruistic preferences is no less reasonable than acting to satisfy egoistic ones.

The Second *Critique* and the *Genealogy of Morals*

Nietzsche's close reading of the second *Critique* is at the heart of his mature thought. Though one finds a growing preoccupation with Kant's ethics throughout the 1880s, it is significant that Nietzsche's *Genealogy of Morals* appears in 1887, the year for which we have documentary proof of Nietzsche's close reading of the second *Critique*.[3] What Nietzsche calls 'morality' in the *Genealogy* is precisely the phenomenon that Kant was striving to reconstruct rationally and vindicate. Nietzsche took Kant to have provided an exemplary account of what needed to be attacked. This implies that there is a significant body of agreement between Nietzsche and Kant. Nietzsche regards Kant's ethical thought as much closer to the heart of Western morality than, say, Mill's. Attacking Western morality involves attacking Kant essentially. Conversely, if Kant's ethical thought collapses, Western morality itself stands indicted.[4]

Because Nietzsche accepts so much of Kant's moral thought as an accurate analysis of Western morality, the three pillars of Kant's ethics will turn out to correspond with surprising neatness to the three essays attacking morality in Nietzsche's *Genealogy*. That said, Nietzsche's positive ethical views, often understood in Aristotelian virtue-ethical terms, can be interpreted as nonetheless sharing important normative elements in common with Kant's, beyond their agreements concerning Kant's analysis of morality.

---

[3] Nietzsche quotes Kant once in the *Genealogy*, from the second *Critique* (*CPrR*, Ak.v. 162) and paraphrases him once from the third *Critique* (*CJ*, Ak. v. 211 at *GM* III. 6). There are five other references to Kant in the *Genealogy*: that Kant had a low regard for sympathy (a point Nietzsche could have extracted from reading the second *Critique*, see *CPrR*, Ak. v. 34, 82, 84–5, 118, 156) (*GM*, Preface 5); that 'the categorical imperative smells of cruelty' (*GM* II. 6); that his bachelorhood reveals his affinity with the ascetic ideal (*GM* III. 7); that his critique of rationalist metaphysics reveals his affinity with the ascetic ideal (*GM* III. 12); that his critique of theology, far from damaging religious speculation, has promoted it (*GM* III. 25).

Nietzsche copied out two passages from the second *Critique* in May/June of 1887; according to Hayman, Nietzsche began working on the *Genealogy* in June. The finished work was published in November 1887. Though this confirms the priority of a reading of the second *Critique*, I believe that Nietzsche's interest in it dates as far back as 1881, when he read Romundt's book on it. A reference to the practical postulates occurs as early as 1882 (*GS* 335) (Ronald Hayman, *Nietzsche: A Critical Life* (London: Weidenfeld & Nicolson, 1980)).

[4] This suggestion has been made previously, for example, in Lester Hunt's *Nietzsche and the Origin of Virtue* (London: Routledge, 1991), 22–3. My claim is stronger than Hunt's, however. Not only is Nietzsche committed to the correctness of an analysis of morality much like Kant's. I also claim that he accepts Kant's analysis *in detail* because he actually *derived* his conception of the moral in the *Genealogy* from reading the second *Critique*.

Genealogy

While some claim that genealogy is a new method for investigating history, others have maintained that genealogy is simply historical investigation itself, and nothing new. Neither of these claims captures what is distinctive about Nietzsche's enterprise. Rather, genealogy is a new method of applying historical investigation to philosophical concerns.

In Book I of the *Republic*, Plato portrays Socrates as seeking substantive philosophical knowledge of justice by discussing proposed definitions of 'justice'. The *elenchus* is the method for testing proposed definitions. In *Genealogy* II: 13 Nietzsche claims that 'only that which has no history is definable'. If the expressions which concern us have a history, then Socrates' project fails. We better clarify the sense behind such expressions as 'justice' by examining the history of the practices that have shaped our disposition to classify some acts as just. Plato maintains that the *basis* for our acts of classification guarantees their objectivity. We apprehend an unchanging, independently real *eidos* of justice, and it is our capacity to intuit the presence of justice in an act that accounts for our linguistic dispositions. Consequently, the history of our linguistic dispositions can only be the history of our clear vision of what is always already there; such a history cannot possess much philosophical interest.

On Nietzsche's view, however, there is no such *eidos*. Therefore, it cannot be responsible for our semantic intuitions or our consensus about them. History itself moulds and shapes our practices and intuitions over time; in an account of what moulds the history, we will find nothing but competing and cooperating forces, interpretations, interests. Thrasymachus was right: justice is the benefit of the stronger, not because this is what we mean by 'justice' but because others have subjugated us. Nietzsche's interest is directed at normative practices whose dominance requires that their participants do not understand how the practice came to be.

As Nietzsche views it, genealogy supersedes earlier forms of philosophy. The sweeping character of this methodological claim rests on his confidence that traditional philosophical strategies fail on their own terms. (This point is crucial for escaping the common complaint that the genealogist commits the genetic fallacy.) Traditional strategies falsely presuppose that our intuitions are reliable. If, for example, our moral intuitions were broadly unreliable, traditional moral theory would collapse, given the moral theorist's reliance on these intuitions for data by which to judge the moral theories under discussion.

The Second Reading

If our conceptual or semantic intuitions are unreliable, similar considerations will apply to conceptual or linguistic analysis.[5]

History, according to the Nietzsche, is not teleological (as it is for Hegel). We cannot identify a *goal* of a historical process, and then go on to show how it gradually emerged from its embryonic beginnings. Rather, we must chart the processes that, by contingent confluence, produce a contemporary result. Hence the metaphor: no individual is the goal of a family history. A family is a vast fabric of relationships, and any one individual represents only one among many confluences of past lines of descent.

To avoid the temptation of projecting current norms into the past, which would promote a teleological picture, genealogy adopts the German historicist view. Each cross-section of history has its own autonomous structures, meanings, and values, which the historian must work to recover hermeneutically. However, unlike the hermeneutic historian, the genealogist allows that the alien culture's self-understanding is not the end but the beginning of investigation. Since the function of genealogy is to undermine our own hermeneutical self-understanding, we cannot grant self-understanding final authority elsewhere either.

[5] The question of the genetic fallacy is helpfully viewed by an analogy with empirical theory, with observations playing the same role as moral intuitions. Suppose I observe what appears to be a UFO near Roswell, New Mexico. I develop a theory that includes reference to extraterrestrials, their interests, the character of their spacecrafts, the government's knowledge and interest in concealing it from the public, etc. Now there are good reasons for supposing that there was no UFO near Roswell. The planets in our solar system do not appear capable of supporting human-like life, and special relativity rules out the possibility of faster-than-light travel. ETs are not in New Mexico because they have no way of getting there according to our best physical theory.

The observer might retort: yes, but I saw it with my own eyes. This claim cannot be left unaddressed, for empirical evidence is all our other claims regarding the viability of ETs in our solar system or faster-than-light travel rest on. In response, the critic can claim that there is empirical evidence supporting explanations for faulty observations: it turns out that the government is secretly testing military aircraft in New Mexico. Now none of this entails that it is necessarily not the case that there are alien spacecraft in New Mexico; to infer that would be to commit a genetic fallacy. If the UFO observer now rests her claim on the fact that it seemed to her that there was an alien spacecraft, and that it is logically possible that there had been one, and that it is logically possible that the competing explanation is mistaken, we would be ill-advised to concur on such slim grounds. Genealogical debunking occurs in the larger context of theory evaluation; it attacks the supportive role of an observation or intuition statement by offering an explanation for the genesis of the statement that better satisfies the desiderata of good theory than the positing of the statement's truth (here, the claim that alien spacecraft caused me to say that I had observed alien spacecraft).

If this analogy is apt, then we might suggest that Nietzsche is in no way committed to rejecting normative intuitions out of hand, any more than the UFO debunker is committed to rejecting empiricism. In Nietzsche's own practice, he does not simply offer sceptical arguments that demolish, e.g., slave morality along with all other normative systems and practices. Instead, he attempts to awaken, along with his explanation for slave-moral intuitions, another, rival intuition: that slave morality is contemptibly cowardly and dishonest.

What determines the content of such a self-understanding is, ultimately, multiple conflicting interests and interested interpretations. Genealogy characterizes the underlying historical processes as a 'power struggle'. Just as an account of a war will differ depending upon which combatant pens it, aspects of these historical processes will appear differently to different viewers. Attention to this plurality of 'perspectives' leads Nietzsche to claim that there is no absolute fact as to the significance or value of a particular historical event or process. If we add the claim that experienced fact is largely constituted by the interpretations of those experiencing it, a question arises: does it make sense to speak of historical fact at all? This feature of genealogy raises familiar epistemological problems, and sits uncomfortably with its intended critical function. However that may be, the Nietzsche does *not* claim that one perspective is as good as another, either normatively or cognitively. Genealogy serves a critical function, undermining the myths and mystifications a particular contemporary perspective may have about itself. To the extent that the perspective depends upon mystification, participants' understanding of the processes that constructed the perspective will lead to its disintegration.

The critical nature of genealogy can be understood as follows. The genealogist is concerned to undermine ahistorical and inflationary interpretations of mundane facts about human life. These interpretations typically appeal to structures, norms, entities, etc. which stand above both nature and history. The genealogist is also apt to undermine the propensity to regard what is artificial (and therefore mutable) as naturally, rationally, or metaphysically necessary (and therefore immutable). Norms may appear to possess a greater degree of legitimacy if they are associated with such necessities as opposed to artifice. If norms are artificial, produced by struggle and veiled by mystification, they will be an expression of someone's pragmatic interests. Inflationary interpretations conceal these interests and the ways that the practice in question promotes them.

First essay: slave morality as a source of moral intuitions

The first pillar of Kantian ethics is the idea that moral theory rationally reconstructs our moral intuitions; if we act on the advice of the theory, our actions will tally with the advice of our moral intuitions. Moral intuitions thus become the data by which the correctness of the moral theory is tested. Nietzsche's purpose in the first essay of the *Genealogy* is to argue that our moral intuitions are shaped by history in such a way as to render them unattractive and unsuitable for playing this role in moral theorizing. Therefore, the fact that Kant's moral theory tallies with his intuitions does not provide him with the evidentiary support he needs for his theory. Since Kant's theory also tallies with widely shared intuitions, our own morality is called into question.

Nietzsche argues that 'English psychologists'[6] err in regarding the original sense of 'good' as 'useful'. The sense of 'good' varied, depending upon which class perceived it. For the dominant class, or 'masters', the primary sense of what is good is the self and that which resembles the self. By contrast, the socially subordinated, the 'slaves', behave in very different ways, which the master designates as 'bad', ignoble, or base. However, from the slave perspective, what the master calls 'good' causes the slave's suffering and subordination. Thus, he designates the master as 'evil' or wicked. The slave then invents the fiction of free will. The master is free not to behave in a wicked way, and the slave is equally free to begin to do so. The slave then constructs a moral scheme according to which his own passivity makes him morally superior to the master and therefore 'good'. Here many characteristic themes of genealogy are sounded: pragmatic interests, perspectivality, demystification. The relevance of Nietzsche's critique to Christianity is clear. Beyond that, he broadens his analysis by claiming that modern liberal institutions, norms, and intuitions are so much secularized Christianity. Thus liberalism inherits much of Christianity's unappetizing 'slavishness' without the religious rationale which legitimated it.

Nietzsche's distinction between master morality and slave morality precedes by several years the writing of the *Genealogy*, and thus does not directly confirm the hypothesis that a reading of the second *Critique* inspired it. In particular, as Nietzsche himself points out, the distinction is spelled out quite clearly in *Human, All-too-human* (§ 45), which appeared in 1878. What is more, this passage comes after what I have called the 'first reading', a period dominated by Nietzsche's interest in the third *Critique*, during which there is scarcely any discussion of Kant's ethics. It also precedes the 'second reading', which began with a reading in 1881 of Romundt's book on the practical postulates in the second *Critique*. That said, Nietzsche's reading of Kant had a significant impact on the master/slave distinction in Nietzsche's thought. In the 1878 discussion, Nietzsche claims that *our* morality descends from that of the *masters*. Nietzsche's reversal on this point first appears in *Beyond Good and Evil* in 1886, after the reading of Romundt and the second *Critique*.

---

[6] Nietzsche singles out Paul Rée, though his remarks apply to many others, notably Hume. As Clark points out, the term 'English' should be taken loosely to mean something like 'utilitarian'.

The relevance of the concept of slave morality to Kant should also be clear.[7] For Kant, our moral intuitions serve as the initial data for the rational reconstruction of morality. The purpose of the first essay of the *Genealogy* is to question the authority of these intuitions by showing that they can be adequately explained without appeal to any characteristics that might underwrite their objectivity. If moral intuitions vary from social class to social class, it is difficult to see what grounds there might be for choosing between master morality and slave morality. This consideration is not decisive, lest Nietzsche fall foul of the genetic fallacy. If a defender of slave morality could show that, questions of social origin aside, there are independent grounds for accepting it, grounds lacking for master morality, then the discussion of masters and slaves will be irrelevant.[8]

For Kant, the independent grounds are the formal constraints of rationality, the norm 'treat relevantly similar things in relevantly similar ways'. This norm is not only broader than the moral realm, but broader than the practical realm. For Nietzsche's genealogical case to succeed he must adduce independent grounds against reading the categorical imperative as licensed by reason alone, lest he fall foul of the genetic fallacy. He had already done this in *Gay Science*, where he argued that each action is too idiosyncratic for us to be able to formulate universalizing rules that might determine its deontic status.

And now do not cite the categorical imperative, my friend! . . . Anyone who still judges 'in this case everybody would have to act like this' has not taken five steps towards self-knowledge. Otherwise he would know that there neither are nor can be actions that are the same; that every action that has ever been done was done in an altogether unique and irretrievable way, and that this will be equally true of every future action; that all

[7] The crucial connection between slave morality and Kant is egalitarianism. Nietzsche also stresses in the first essay the slave origin of the concept of free will, but I defer discussion of this until my account of the second essay, which deals with Kant's conception of agency. A more detailed consideration of the specific virtues Kant recommends in, e.g., the *Tugendlehre* in *Metaphysics of Morals*, would betray many differences from the unappetizing details of Nietzsche's account of slave morality. In particular, Kant makes a duty out of self-respect (because the self is as much an end as others are) and rejects servile attitudes (see Kant, Ak. vi. 435–7). If there were a distinctive class origin for Kant's intuitions in all their particularity, it would more likely be the middle class. Despite important differences from slave morality like the duty of self-respect, even these differences lend support to Nietzsche's case. Presumably one need not caution masters against the temptation to servility. The self-respect Kant urges us to is one independent of station, non-moral qualities, or achievements. In this respect, it shares levelling traits in common with slave morality.

[8] The question of independent grounds is important. Though Nietzsche is very effective at painting an unattractive picture of slave moral attitudes and interests, their existence and relation to Christian and modern values is scarcely news. The irony of the alleged fact that the dispossessed, downtrodden, and ignorant are in possession of religious truth and moral superiority is never far from view in the Pauline letters, nor is this something that we moderns have entirely forgotten.

regulations about actions relate only to their coarse exterior (even the most inward and subtle regulations of all moralities so far); that these regulations may lead to some semblance of sameness, but really only to some semblance; that as one contemplates or looks back upon any action at all, it is and remains impenetrable. (*GS* 335)[9]

As Nietzsche is at such pains to emphasize elsewhere, this norm can only be applied if a prior condition is met: that there are relevantly similar things. Nietzsche does not think that things lack any characteristics independent of our interpretation, that we are perfectly free to view them as we wish. Rather, he claims that the character of the world is so overwhelmingly rich and diverse that there are indefinitely many ways an interpreter can classify phenomena. Which scheme of classification we adopt will determine what counts as equal to what. Only then does applying the norm of equal treatment lead to a specific result. Nietzsche might have claimed that if we classify people as masters and slaves, then the norm would yield 'treat masters like masters; treat slaves like slaves' and would not generate any egalitarian content at all. Nietzsche's distaste for slave morality derives in part from a judgement that it is unfair to the masters to insist that they receive the same treatment as slaves. This would be to treat what is different as if it were relevantly similar.[10] Slave morality denies that the value of the satisfaction of preferences can be objectively ranked. Once that is conceded, the content of one's preferences drops out of the evaluative picture, leaving only agency and preferences, characteristics the masters and slaves share. The underlying subjectivism that leads to egalitarian results has not itself been adequately justified. If master preferences had common characteristics linking them to objective values that slave preferences lacked, then the egalitarian case could not get started. Worse, the denial of objective value may be motivated by nothing more than the need to generate the desired egalitarian result.

Considerations such as these lead Lester Hunt to argue that Nietzsche has some conception of objective value, which the cultivation of virtuous traits of character promotes. This would give him an ethics not unlike Aristotle's.[11]

[9] Interestingly, after rejecting 'sitting in moral judgement' Nietzsche urges that we should instead become 'human beings . . . who give themselves laws'. I discuss Nietzsche's debt to Kant in his concept of autonomy below.

[10] As I suggested above, the unfairness would hinge on there being something valuable in the first place that the masters display and the slaves do not, which warrants approval. We might begin such an evaluation by noting the masters' courage, honesty, and cheerfulness.

[11] I argued for such a view myself in 'MacIntyre's Nietzsche: A Critique', *International Studies in Philosophy*, 24/2 (1992), 135–44. I now believe that MacIntyre's account was closer to Nietzsche's view than I had then thought. The difficulty in interpreting Nietzsche is to make sense of the competing strands of objectivism and subjectivism in his thought; the temptation is to take sides and downplay the aspect one has ignored in the interests of a more unitary interpretation.

Such an interpretation ignores textual evidence for subjectivist commitments in Nietzsche to make sense of his clear distaste for slave morality, and his apparent preference for master morality. By contrast, MacIntyre sees Nietzsche's attack as directed against the presupposition that there can be sufficient similarities in the world to ground egalitarian claims. On this interpretation, Nietzsche can be granted a subjectivism like Hume's or Kant's. However, in the absence of any rule like the categorical imperative, there can be no constraint on what counts as a permissible preference or action. The masters, to their credit, do not restrain themselves, while the slaves do. Nietzsche, far from leading us back to antique nobility, is actually the final stage in liberalism's gradual shedding of objective standards.

Nietzsche's own view actually straddles these two rival interpretations. Indirect evidence for this claim can be found in the fact that Nietzsche ascribes some favourable characteristics to slave morality (its interest in freedom) and some unfavourable characteristics to master morality (its interest in conformity and tradition). Furthermore, Nietzsche characterizes modernity in terms of a dangerous yet promising fusion of master and slave characteristics, a fusion which could lead to bourgeois mediocrity or to over-humanity.

The key to resolving this difficulty lies in a closer examination of the concept of the will as it passed from Kant to Schopenhauer and subsequently to Nietzsche. In Kant, the will is the faculty of desire, i.e. preference-satisfaction. Kant believed that he must locate the will in the noumenal realm to secure moral accountability and escape from the pervasive determinism of phenomenal nature. It is this very noumenal will, however, that Schopenhauer reinterprets as a kind of life force underlying nature, expressing itself in the biological phenomena of growth, reproduction, competition, etc., and in the psychological phenomena of egoism and malice. In Schopenhauer's hands, the will acquires quasi-teleological characteristics. Though the early Nietzsche dismissed Schopenhauer's arguments for such claims (they cross epistemic bounds laid down by Kant), he did allow that the claims might be true nonetheless.

The mature Nietzsche did not endorse the grand metaphysical claims of Schopenhauer, the *Birth of Tragedy*, or the early Nietzsche *Nachlaß*. He cannot speak of a noumenal will at all once the concept of noumenon becomes unavailable to him. However, this does not bar him from claiming that nature immanently displays the characteristics Schopenhauer ascribed to it. Something of the sort is afoot when Nietzsche claims that 'this world is will to power and nothing else besides' (*KGW* vii.3. 339 (1885)/ *WP* 1067).

Nietzsche's argument for this claim in *Beyond Good and Evil* superficially resembles Schopenhauer's argument for identifying the will with the thing-in-itself.

Suppose nothing else were 'given' as real except our own world of desires and passions
. . . is it not permitted to make the experiment and ask the question whether this 'given'
would not be sufficient for also understanding on the basis of this kind of thing the so-
called mechanistic (or 'material') world? I mean, not as a deception, as 'mere appearance', an 'idea' in the sense of Berkeley and Schopenhauer) but as holding the same rank
of reality as our affect . . . In the end not only is it permitted to make this experiment; the
conscience of *method* demands it. Not to assume several kinds of causality until the
experiment of making do with a single one has been pushed to its utmost limit . . . that is
a moral of method which one may not shirk today . . . The question is in the end whether
we really recognize the will as *efficient*, whether we believe in the causality of the will: if
we do—and at bottom our faith in this is nothing less than our faith in causality itself—
then we have to make the experiment of positing the causality of the will hypothetically
as the only one . . . [O]ne has to risk the hypothesis whether will does not affect will
wherever 'effects' are recognized—and whether all mechanical occurrences are not, in
so far as a force is active in them, will force, effects of will.

Suppose, finally, we succeeded in explaining our entire instinctual life as the development and ramification of *one* basic form of the will—namely, of the will to power . . .
then one would have gained the right to determine *all* efficient force univocally as—*will
to power.*   (*BGE* 36, ellipses mine)

Schopenhauer's argument takes one premiss over from Kant: that the will as
moral agent is a noumenon. To this he adds that what it is like to be a will as
moral agent is directly present to consciousness. Finally, space and time are the
only basis for plurality. From these premisses he infers that there is only one
noumenon underlying all phenomena, and that we know its character by introspection. Nietzsche's argument appears superficially similar. However,
Nietzsche not only rejects the concept of the noumenon. He also rejects elsewhere the concept of the will and the claim that there are incorrigible data of
consciousness knowable by introspection. This leads to difficulties in knowing
how to take his argument.

However, Nietzsche warns us not to read the argument as a variant of
Schopenhauer's when he says that 'the . . . mechanistic . . . world . . . [is not]
. . . a deception, [a] "mere appearance," an "idea" in the sense of Berkeley and
Schopenhauer, but . . . [holds] the same rank of reality as our affect.' This
should serve as a signal that 'given' is not being used in the first sentence to refer
to an incorrigible epistemic datum on one side of the veil of perception, with
reality on the other. 'Given' should instead be read as the antecedent in a conditional: given that there are desires, what follows? Similarly, Nietzsche's criticisms of the concept of the will elsewhere are directed against the notion that
we are introspectively aware of 'atomic' acts of choice undetermined by prior
psychological processes, and that it is this which causes action. However, the

German word '*Wille*' and its cognates does not necessarily suggest a *chooser*, a selector from a range of options. It can also refer to wants and desires. For Nietzsche to say that the will is efficacious in this context means merely that desires can produce changes in the world. Viewed this way, the argument is simply a generalization: we know that our own desires produce changes in the world. It is more parsimonious to suppose that something like desire is involved in every mechanical force than to suppose that there is a fundamental difference between psychological forces and mechanical forces. Put that way, the argument merely presupposes that there are desires and mechanical forces. These presuppositions, in turn, require no further epistemological or metaphysical assumptions beyond those required for empirical knowledge more generally.[12]

Why, however, does Nietzsche say will to *power*, rather than will to live, as Schopenhauer had? For Schopenhauer, restricting ourselves now to the human sphere, all desires must be in one form or another, expressions of a desire for

---

[12] Note that the argument from parsimony could have led to a reduction of psychological 'forces' (desires) to mechanical forces, with metaphysical materialism or physicalism as its conclusion. So there appears to be an implied premiss: desires cannot be reduced to mechanical forces. This may be why Nietzsche says that 'we could not get down, or up, to any other "reality" besides the reality of our drives' (*BGE* 36).

He offers three reasons for rejecting metaphysical materialism in *Beyond Good and Evil*. First, it requires a distinction between force and matter, but Boscovich's dynamist reduction of matter to repulsive force shows that there is only force (*BGE* 12). Second, the concept of matter is derived from making too much of visual and tactile evidence (*BGE* 14). I take it that Nietzsche's point here, given his dynamism, is that visual and tactile evidence suggest that physical objects have brute space-occupying being (which explains, for example, their impenetrability), but that phenomena like impenetrability are better explained in terms of Boscovich's repulsive force. Third, the concept of natural law is a projection of democratic political preferences. However, he qualifies this objection by making clear that he does not reject the concept of natural necessity itself (*BGE* 22).

None of these objections are germane to the question: in which direction should the reduction parsimony recommends go? Once we accept Boscovichian dynamism as our account of non-human nature, there is still the question of whether psychological forces should be reduced to physical forces or vice versa. Rejecting a *materialist* version of physicalism leaves this question open. The deeper reason why Nietzsche thinks that 'Beings will have to be thought of as sensations that are no longer based on something devoid of sensation' is that otherwise 'physics must construe the world of feeling consistently as lacking feeling and aim—right up to the highest human being' (*KGW* vii.1. 692 (1883–4)/ *WP* 562). That is, a reduction of the psychological to the mechanical implies that human beings do not have feelings (sensations, desires) and this is manifestly not so.

Notice that this argument presupposes that psychological properties are not emergent. The further stage of the argument, that because the will to power explains biological phenomena, it explains all phenomena, also depends upon the presupposition that there are no emergent properties. Since all biological systems are composed of physical systems, the will to power must be found below the biological level. If it wasn't, then the will to power would be an emergent biological property. But there are no emergent biological properties. Therefore the will to power is found at the physical level, that is, everywhere.

self-preservation, as means to that end. This places Schopenhauer closer to Spinoza than to Kant or Hume, for self-preservation is an objective state of affairs. Hume and Kant would be quick to point out that we may and often do have preferences that cannot be interpreted in terms of a desire for self-preservation; for both of them, the very possibility of morality depends upon being able to have self-sacrificing preferences.[13] Nietzsche explicitly rejects the idea of a self-preservation *conatus*, and chooses the expression 'will to power' to signal his modification of Schopenhauer's view.

But what is power? According to Clark, the concept of power is the concept of the capacity to satisfy one's preferences. Clark argues that Nietzsche's psychological claim that all desires are in some sense an expression of a more fundamental desire for power is incoherent, because it presupposes that one have non-power-directed desires in the first place, in order for the concept of seeking the capacity to satisfy them to make any sense. Yet this would seem to make the 'first-order' desires more fundamental. But then it seems that the first-order desires could not themselves be desires for power, on pain of infinite regress or circularity.

However, Clark's account of will to power as second-order desire is not an apt characterization of Nietzsche's meaning. The desire for power is not the desire for the capacity to satisfy our other desires. Rather, all goals are instances of controlled transformations of our environment. For example, I might have a desire to eat cherry ice cream or a desire to eat blueberry pie. Each desire can also be characterized at a higher level of abstraction as a desire to eat food. Eating is itself an example of a controlled transformation of my environment. Nietzsche's claim is that at the highest level of abstraction, every desire is a desire for a controlled transformation of my environment.[14] In short, power is not the means to the satisfaction of our preferences. It is an aspect of all preferences.

We are now in a position to grasp in what sense Nietzsche straddles the line between an objective and a subjective conception of value. For Nietzsche, as for Hume and Kant, it makes no sense to say that value is independent of human preferences. In this sense he is a subjectivist. As MacIntyre observed, Nietzsche shares the liberal tradition's rejection of a transcendent normative

---

[13] For Schopenhauer, the possibility of morality is 'explained' by the illusory character of individuation, so that other-regarding attitudes turn out to be a variety of self-regarding attitudes after all.

[14] This is more clearly seen if we keep in mind that 'power' translates *Macht*, a cognate of the English word 'make'. The key connotations are to make someone do something, as a ruler does, or to make an object, as an artist does. This is why it is helpful to speak here of desires as involving control and transformation.

standard (natural or supernatural) to which human action must conform.[15] That said, Nietzsche's view is naturalistic since he sees human preference satisfaction as an instance of a larger tendency to impose control over the environment common to all biological systems. All living things 'want' to have their way with the world. But there is no 'right' (healthy, natural) way to do this; only success sets the standard.

Whether an act leads to success, given the agent's preferences, capacities, and circumstances, is itself a matter which transcends the agent's opinion. Suppose that my goal is to collect fine art which I find personally satisfying, in a world where there are no transcendent standards of value. Some of my choices will be good investments; when these works are sold, I will have more money at my disposal to purchase more art. By contrast, if I play the art investment game badly, in the end I will have no money and no art. I will be unable to satisfy my subjective desires. There a fact of the matter as to whether I am a successful art collector, for having no art and no money is failure. Also, successful art collecting involves certain skills and habits, 'virtues' which art collectors acquire with more or less success. Though a skilful collector may fail by accident, and an inept collector may get lucky, the former but not the latter possesses skills the value of which is fixed by their propensity to promote success.

If we generalize this account, we have Nietzsche's positive ethic. There is no objective pattern to which a human being should conform to achieve objective flourishing. If there is any objective pattern at all, it is the fact that all desires are a desire for 'power'. But this pattern provides no normative force, since it is a pattern we cannot help but follow anyway. That means that whatever normative force there is to be had must come from preference satisfaction itself. And though no preference is intrinsically more worthwhile than any other, the pursuit and satisfaction of a preference will lead to either enhancing or diminishing the agent's control over the environment. It is this enhancing and diminishing that Nietzsche can claim is independent of an agent's opinion, and at least in that sense, objective. Thus he is able to say, 'What is good? Everything that heightens the feeling of power in man, the will to power, power itself' (*A* 2).

In a society where preferences are uniform, the means one must cultivate to satisfy them will also tend to converge, thus conveying the misleading appearance

---

[15] Nietzsche cannot secure values from a supernatural order because for him there isn't one. The clearest piece of evidence for the claim that Nietzsche cannot secure values from a natural order either is Nietzsche's critique of Stoicism. To imitate nature's collective character is impossible. To imitate nature's distributive character is inevitable since agents are parts of nature already. Thus nature provides no normative guidance (*BGE* 9).

that certain virtues are valuable as such. The content constituting flourishing will appear objective while only being contingently intersubjective. In a society where preferences diverge, it will become more and more difficult to say what virtues of character will be beneficial to all; the content of ethical advice useful to all will become thinner and thinner. Nonetheless, Nietzsche meant his ethical recommendations to be 'life enhancing', not by some objective standard of health in a Platonic or Aristotelian sense, but by a standard of success independent of the game one chooses to play or the goals one sets for oneself.

If this is Nietzsche's view, it also helps to make sense of why he cannot wholeheartedly endorse master morality. Given its function and goals (military conquest, social subordination, preservation of a caste successful in these), it not only 'strengthens' its adherents, making them more fit for its characteristic activities. It also binds them to standards of tradition and conformity, making it more difficult to achieve the satisfaction of more exotic preferences. This is what lies behind Nietzsche's disturbing admiration for Julius Caesar: Caesar could not have done what he did if he did not acquire capacities (valour, ambition, cunning) inculcated by the tradition-bound, conformist culture of the Roman Republic. But in the end, these Republican norms stood in his way, and he was free enough of them to be able to act in defiance of them to achieve his own, highly anti-Republican ends. Nietzsche's affection here is not for political tyranny; rather the capacity to achieve it is a sign of the kind of highly capable individual Nietzsche wanted to see more of. The important thing is not that there be some particular project or not, but that there be successful projects at all.

Thus, there is a layer of irony in Nietzsche's account of masters and slaves which many readers have missed. Aristotle was wrong to think that there is a human essence which must be actualized if a human being is to flourish objectively and achieve the condition normative for it. But when people believe that there is such an essence, and identify it with the qualities Aristotle recommends, the result is the production of people more successful at imposing their will on the world, more successful at satisfying their preferences. By contrast, when Kant claims that there is no objectively valuable pattern of conduct (formal constraints aside) because no preference is inherently more worthy of satisfaction than any other, he promotes attitudes and behaviours which make it more and more difficult for agents to achieve their objectives whatever they may be. That is why Nietzsche calls Kant 'decadent'. What is worse, by insisting on the equality of agents independent of their non-moral qualities, Kant levels the playing field between decadent and non-decadent patterns of action, devalorizing the conditions of success and valorizing the conditions of failure.

If success is the only game in town, valorizing the conditions of failure can only be seen as the profoundly anti-human, destructive stance that it is. Ironically, Kant's humanism, grounded in the correct observation that ultimate value is subjective, once widely accepted, proves destructive for human beings as value seekers. Nietzsche's complex stance towards Kant thus shows that he is neither a conservative seeking to restore an ancient virtue ethic, nor a modern, seeking to liberate the individual from all standards. Rather, he seeks to appropriate ancient practices and norms in order to realize better the 'liberal' project of the fulfilment of the individual.

In summary, before the second reading Nietzsche discovered the distinction between master and slave morality (in *HA* I. 45), and had applied it in an earlier genealogical attempt. But he had at that time identified our morality with master morality. After he returned to reading Kant in the 1880s, he attacked Kant's claim to ground the categorical imperative in practical reason (in *GS* 335). As his concern with Kant's ethics grew (in part from reading the second *Critique*) he came to the realization that our morality is significantly indebted to slave morality. The absence of rational ground, coupled with the genealogical debunking of egalitarian intuitions, significantly undermined morality as Kant had characterized it. Despite this, Nietzsche accepted Kant's subjectivism, and the accompanying high value to be assigned to the individual and the individual's success at self-chosen goals. But acting on egalitarian intuitions is likely to lead to the reduction of an agent's capacity to act successfully, and thus to a diminution of realized value.[16]

Second essay: conscience and the analysis of agency

In the first essay, Nietzsche sought to undermine the intuition that all agents should be treated equally as ends in themselves. By calling this intuition into question, Nietzsche undermines Kant's reconstructive methodology which takes intuitions as data for testing moral theory. In the second essay, Nietzsche attacks the idea that the 'voice of conscience' has moral authority, that by

---

[16] Does Nietzsche's project of promoting 'higher humanity' imply that he simply thinks it is agent-neutrally 'better' that there be more successful people? Any move to agent-neutrality here would move Nietzsche perilously close to Kant's (and Mill's) own agent-neutral ethics. Preserving agent-relativity may lie behind Nietzsche's notion of philosophers as 'legislators' (*BGE* 211). Cultivating higher humanity by reorienting the values of Western civilization successfully would be for Nietzsche to effect the most profound controlled transformation of his environment conceivable.

avoiding actions which induce in us a feeling of guilty conscience[17] we thereby avoid those actions which are objectively morally bad.

The second pillar of Kantian ethics was the idea that Glaucon's challenge (that the dictates of morality and the dictates of rational self-interest diverge) can be met by proposing a new model of practical reason. This model identifies the constraints of morality with formal constraints on practical reasoning, thereby justifying morality as rational. The model is further supported by the light it sheds on the phenomenology of temptation and guilt. Finally the model suggests a moral ideal: the moral individual as autonomous and self-legislating. Nietzsche modifies Kant's analysis of agency and practical reasoning, using it to explain away rather than justify the voice of conscience. Finally, in appropriating Kant's notion of autonomy while rejecting its link to the categorical imperative and the 'formal constraints' interpretation of morality, Nietzsche creates his own ideal of the autonomous individual, an individual who in self-legislating transcends moral constraints altogether.

In 'our' morality, and thus in Kant's, those actions which provoke feelings of guilty conscience are defined as 'evil' (in the slave-moral sense).[18] These actions involve the use and abuse of others without regard for their status as agents with preferences of their own. Though Kant is not a straightforward moral intuitionist, he does regard the deliverances of conscience as authoritative.

For Kant, when we violate our duty, we are being irrational in a formal sense. As agents endowed with practical reason, we are aware of this fact. Given this account of morality, why do we not experience our immorality with the same indifference that we experience other errors of reasoning? Kant's identification of the good will (the will which possesses a good conscience) with the will that follows universalizable maxims, that is, the will whose set of

---

[17] Nietzsche believes that what we regard as a simple feeling of a lack of moral worth is in fact a composite, the product of 'the moralization of the concepts guilt (*Schuld*) and duty . . . [that is] their being pushed back into bad conscience' (*GM* II. 21). As we shall see, the moralization involves combining the sense of something owing yet unpaid with the sense of the self as something to be attacked; each concept and associated feeling is possible in isolation from the other.

[18] Largely, but not entirely. There are desires stigmatized by Christianity which can be satisfied without violating others. Kant characterizes these desires as violations of duties to one's self. It is interesting that I must remind myself and the reader of the existence of these at all; this is an indication of the extent to which moral culture has changed. The very idea of a victimless crime has become dubious. Nietzsche's theory of bad conscience claims that the feeling of having a bad conscience derives from introjected aggression, and therefore its intensity is a function of the degree to which social norms and institutions inhibit its more direct satisfaction. It is interesting to speculate that the growing availability of vicarious satisfaction of aggressive desires through films, novels, television, etc. may have eliminated the 'hydraulic' condition for feelings of bad conscience, thus making the idea of victimless or solitary evil increasingly unintelligible to us.

intentions lack the relevant formal flaw, means that experiencing oneself as morally good and experiencing oneself as a consistent practical reasoner are the same thing. 'Respect for the law, which in its subjective aspect is called moral feeling, is identical with consciousness of one's duty' (Kant, vi. 464, emphasis mine). We feel pleasure in reaction to our awareness that our faculty of desire conforms to the moral law; we are directly aware of it in this conformity. I say 'directly' because for Kant 'an *erring* conscience is an absurdity' (Kant, Ak. vi. 401, emphasis Kant's).[19] Conversely, to experience oneself as formally flawed in one's practical reasoning will be identical to experiencing oneself as lacking worth, as having a guilty conscience. Thus when we *feel* morally evil, this should be a reliable sign that we *are* morally evil. For Kant, the voice of conscience should have the same authority that it has for a moral intuitionist. The latter simply lacks any account of *why* it possesses this authority.

Interestingly, Nietzsche does not entirely reject Kant's claim that the worth of an agent is a function of their intentions, if by 'intention' we understand basic evaluative commitments underlying behaviour. The worth of a person, for Nietzsche as well as for Kant, lies not in what they do, but in why they do it: 'Kant is right that because there are different maxims of differing ethical value, the value of an action always leads back in the end to the question of the values which furnish the reason for the maxim' (*KGW* vii.2. 169). Nietzsche uses this normative claim to undermine Kantian morality, by unearthing its 'intentions' and displaying the values that furnish the rationale (or rationalization) of its maxims.

Nietzsche traces the psychological origin of guilty conscience to the primitive experience of debt at a time when enforcement of debt was more cruel than now. The inner mechanism mediating this experience is the product of introjected aggression. This genealogical account replaces the Kantian or intuitionist explanation of guilt as a connection between a psychological mechanism and a moral fact.

Nietzsche does not reject Kant's account of the moral agent. He thinks there is something fundamentally right about Kant's account of agency as an arena of conflict between self-made laws and passions, and of freedom as the capacity to impose these laws on oneself. This power is what makes human action qualitatively different from animal behaviour. Not only does Nietzsche agree with this characterization of the agent autonomously legislating in the face of

---

[19] For Kant's notion of pleasure or pain as the felt reaction to the state of one's other faculties, see the discussion of the *Critique of Judgement* in Ch. 2 above.

recalcitrant impulses and thus achieving freedom. Surprisingly, he also agrees with Kant in the great value such beings possess.[20]

Precisely this necessarily forgetful animal in whom forgetting represents a force, a form of strong health, has now bred in itself an opposite faculty, a memory, with whose help forgetfulness is disconnected for certain cases, namely for those cases where a promise is to be made: it is thus by no means simply a passive no-longer-being-able-to-get-rid-of the impression once it has been inscribed, not simply indigestion from a once-pledged word over which one cannot regain control, but rather an active no-longer-wanting-to-get-rid-of, a willing on and on of something one has once willed, a true memory of the will: so that a world of new strange things, circumstances, even acts of the will may be placed without reservation between the original 'I want', 'I will do', and the actual discharge of the will, its act, without this long chain of the will breaking. But how much this presupposes! In order to have this kind of command over the future in advance, man must first have learned to separate the necessary from the accidental occurrence, to think causally, to see and anticipate what is distant as if it were present, to fix with certainty what is end, what is means thereto, in general to be able to reckon, to calculate,— for this, man himself must first of all have become calculable, regular, necessary, in his own image of himself as well, in order to be able to vouch for himself as future, as one who promises does! . . . With the help of the morality of custom and the social straitjacket man was made truly calculable. If, on the other hand, we place ourselves at the end of the enormous process, where the tree finally produces its fruit, where society with its morality of custom finally brings to light that to which it was only the means: then we find as the ripest fruit on its tree the sovereign individual, the individual resembling only himself, free again from the morality of custom, autonomous and supramoral (for 'autonomous' and 'moral' are mutually exclusive), in short, the human being with his own independent long will, the human being who is permitted to promise—and in him a proud consciousness, twitching in all his muscles, of what has been finally achieved and become flesh in him, a true consciousness of power and freedom, a feeling of the completion of man himself. This being who has become free, who is really permitted to promise, this lord of the free will, this sovereign—how could he not know what superiority he thus has . . . The 'free' human being, the possessor of a long, unbreakable will, has in his possession his standard of value as well: looking from himself toward the others, he honours or holds in contempt . . . (*GM* II. 1–2)

---

[20] There is no indication in the text that Nietzsche sees the emergence of rational agency as peculiar to master or slave morality. As *GM* II. 20 makes clear, there is the following sequence of events. First, there is the emergence of contractual relations that 'are older than even the beginnings of any societal associations and organizational forms' (*GM* II. 8). Second, there is the community itself, which can be a party to contracts, in the first instance, with its own members (*GM* II. 9). Third, the community 'acknowledges a juridical obligation to the earlier generations' from which emerges the concept of gods out of the practice of ancestor worship. Fourth, 'the middle period in which the noble clans take shape' assigns noble qualities to the gods (*GM* II. 19). Presumably we have at this point both masters and rational agency; slaves only appear after masters. Hence agency as the product of punishment is not peculiar to slave morality.

Allowing for differences of style, much of what Nietzsche says in *GM* II. 1–2 could have been said by Kant with two crucial exceptions. First, Nietzsche contrasts rather than identifies autonomy with obedience to moral law, 'for "autonomous" and "moral" are mutually exclusive'. This follows directly from his denial of absolutely obligatory claims deriving from formal constraints alone. All that remains of the concept of self-legislation is the concept of the will positing some end or other, and organizing its behaviour in pursuit of it. Doing something because 'one must' do it cannot be subordinating one's preferences to reason, and Kant has ruled out the possibility that submission to anything else could be autonomous. Hence if Kant were wrong about the status of the categorical imperative as a principle of reason, his rejection of heteronomy and his identification of every other submission of the will with heteronomy would push him to Nietzsche's position.

The second crucial difference from Kant is that Nietzsche does not accept Kant's claim in the second *Critique* that the only way an agent could possibly act on a policy other than a prudential one would be if he could somehow act independently of natural necessity. This forces Kant to choose: either there are no non-prudential maxims, or else agents are non-natural. According to Kant, the authority of conscience shows that there must be non-prudential maxims. Hence we must be non-natural. Kant's attempt to explain how this could be makes use of the phenomenal/noumenal distinction from the first *Critique*.

Nothing compels Nietzsche to follow Kant here. Once we reject the initial claim that acting on the categorical imperative is impossible for a natural being, there is no reason to require that moral agents be non-natural beings. Thus Kant's moral argument for the noumenal self collapses. Consequently, Nietzsche can conceive agency in purely naturalistic terms. It is this which forces upon him the question of the natural origin of agency. Genealogy starts with the rejection of an argument for some non-natural item on independent grounds, and then responds to the question 'how else could it have possibly come about, if not in a non-natural fashion?' with a genealogy.

Nietzsche's account of the genesis of the Kantian agent is complex, but briefly, he claims the following. The agent is able to organize its own behaviour rationally because, set against its present impulses, it has equally present memories of past promises and past punishments. These qualities in the agent are the product of an institution of promising and punishment, which has its origins in primordial contractual relations of exchange, along with the creditor's right to enjoy the compensatory pleasures of inflicting pain in the event of default. For Nietzsche, such exchange relations, even the agreement to offer oneself over for torture as surety, are self-interested and pre-moral, preceding any sense of obligation to the community and its customs and laws, let alone any sense of absolute obligation.

This concept of pre-moral obligation is crucial to Nietzsche's critique of Kant. By tracing the moral intuition of absolute obligation to the conditional obligations of primitive exchange, Nietzsche is suggesting that the intuition of unconditionality is nothing more than the residue of the experience of terror; the claim 'if I am to avoid torture, I must do X' is still a hypothetical imperative for all that. It might be thought that the very idea of exchange involves promising, an intrinsically moral institution, but Nietzsche rightly thought otherwise. Compare Nietzsche's historical speculations and David Gauthier's rational reconstruction of morality.[21] According to Gauthier, when agents face 'prisoner's dilemma' situations, straightforward calculation of rational self-interest, taking the probabilities of the actions of the other as data, can lead to non-optimizing choices. In light of this fact, it is rational to choose to adopt a *disposition* to choose cooperatively. This choice, when reciprocated, leads to optimizing results, even if the cooperative disposition sometimes leads to reduced utility. Gauthier calls this disposition 'constrained maximization'. Since it can be adopted in light of rational self-interest, it does not require appeal to any bedrock moral principles. Gauthier claims that adopting the cooperative disposition is tantamount to being moral; hence being moral is justified by rational self-interest.

Kant, of course, would be horrified by such an argument, for it would make moral imperatives hypothetical imperatives of prudence after all. Gauthier would be the shopkeeper who makes correct change because it is good for business. Nietzsche agrees with Kant that it is essential to moral obligation as we understand it that the obligation be absolute and non-prudential; hence he could not characterize Gauthierian agents as 'moral'. But Gauthier's notion of cooperative disposition shows that it is possible to have exchanges, what we might call 'quasi-promising', without any prior commitment to the idea that one *ought* to keep promises in a moral sense. Of course one ought to perform one's quasi-promises: otherwise, one might get tortured. But this ought is the ought of rational self-interest. Gauthier sees adherence to moral principles as rationally self-interested under the right conditions. This rational self-interest thus justifies the claim of morality to be binding. Nietzsche uses the notion of agreement not to justify cooperation but to show that we need not appeal to an independent notion of moral obligation to explain the emergence of moral practices from the interaction of self-interested agents. It might be thought that

[21] David Gauthier, *Morals by Agreement* (Oxford: Oxford University Press, 1986).

grounding moral practices in promising is circular in so far as promising is itself a moral practice. But Nietzsche and Gauthier evade this difficulty by speaking not of the *obligation* to keep a promise but of the *disposition* to behave a certain way. By making that disposition transparent to the other party, one causes the other to act on the basis of what the partner's dispositions appear to be.[22]

At this point in the development of practical reason, we have not yet arrived at the Kantian subject, because we have not yet seen the 'moralization of the concepts guilt and duty, with their being pushed back into *bad* conscience' (*GM* II. 21). What we have, instead, is what we might call a Gauthierian subject. By 'bad conscience' Nietzsche refers to a distinct faculty or function that generates a feeling of self-hatred and worthlessness. This faculty emerges from the introjection of aggression that accompanies submission to social constraints (*GM* II. 16–18). Thus instead of feeling 'I had best comply with this constraint—if I don't, terrible things will be done to me' we come to feel 'If I do not comply with this constraint, I am a worthless person and terrible things should be done to me'. The experience of bindingness has been cut free from self-interested considerations altogether. The very pursuit of one's own interest inspires feelings of worthlessness and a desire for punishment, whereas 'the selfless, the self-denying, the self-sacrificing feel [a] pleasure [that] belongs to cruelty' (*GM* II. 18). These affects can find expression in both master and slave morality. For example, the Romans were fervent in the value they assigned to giving one's life on the battlefield for the sake of the state. Once the value attached to self-sacrifice links up with the egalitarianism of slave morality, the construction of the Kantian subject is complete.

Nietzsche is by no means entirely hostile to this process, since he believes that the bad conscience can attach itself not only to slave values but also to their negation (*GM* II. 24). Furthermore, practical rationality is a precondition of true (non-Kantian) autonomy as self-legislation. Such an agent would resemble the Stoic in being self-regulating without adhering to slave values. But it would also resemble the Kantian in following only self-made laws rather than subordinating itself to laws of nature (*BGE* 9).

Our resistance to wishing to become such supramoral 'sovereign individuals' rests ultimately on our moral intuition that to become such would render us

---

[22] One might object that Nietzsche's account is wildly implausible as history, given his claim that 'purchase and sale, together with their psychological accessories, are older than even the beginnings of any societal associations and organizational forms' (*GM* II. 8). However, some recent (albeit controversial) anthropological research supports Nietzsche. For several examples of exchange driven by rational self-interest in hunter-gatherer societies, see Matt Ridley, *The Origins of Virtue: Human Instincts and the Evolution of Cooperation* (New York: Viking, 1997), 87–124, 197–210.

worthless and deserving of punishment. But if Nietzsche's account is successful, he will have shown that this intuition lacks any particular authority. It can be explained genealogically without reference to objective worthlessness. The Kantian explanation (we feel worthless because we have violated the canons of practical reason) fails because agency exists prior to this experience of worthlessness. The two are independent. Furthermore, the experience of worthlessness emerges prior to being given specific egalitarian content by slave morality. In short, it is nothing more than irrational self-hatred, which historically has been made use of in various ways, and which might be made use of in other ways.

In summary, Kant presents us with a certain moral phenomenology of guilt and an explanation of this phenomenon as the noumenal self's listening to the constraints of practical reasoning. This explanation establishes the moral authority of conscience. Nietzsche, while accepting Kant's phenomenology, rejects this explanation, arguing instead that the guilty conscience is a natural phenomenon, linked to but separable from the emergence of practical reasoning. Nietzsche's explanation does not require appeal to moral facts; consequently, the voice of conscience has no moral authority. However, Nietzsche agrees with more than Kant's phenomenology. He also agrees with Kant's characterization and high evaluation of the autonomous agent as self-legislatiting, unbound by laws of custom or normative laws of nature. Nonetheless, he rejects Kant's identification of the content of this self-legislation with the formal laws of practical reason or with the values of slave morality. The laws the self gives to itself must be unique and truly self-created; nor need they have egalitarian content. Though the self-rejecting disposition of the bad conscience cannot be eliminated, it can be yoked to the rejection of the slave moral 'temptation' to repudiate the pursuit of autonomy.

Third essay: asceticism and the phenomenal–noumenal contrast

In the third essay, Nietzsche asks why we regard asceticism so highly. He reveals its psychological roots in the sour grapes of the ascetic. Its persistence is due to the pseudo-therapeutic and socially stabilizing functions of the ascetic's ideology of sin and contrition. Modern science is an outgrowth of the ascetic ideal, its self-hating contempt for pleasurable illusion expressing itself in a commitment to truth.

The third pillar of Kant's ethics is the use of the phenomenal–noumenal contrast to explain the possibility of free will, moral accountability, and divine sanctions for moral and immoral conduct. If there were no noumenal domain, moral blame would be impossible and agents would have no assurance that their morally motivated activities in the phenomenal domain would have any point. Nietzsche turns Kant's argument on its head. Nietzsche claims that otherworldly posits like the noumenal domain are motivated by ascetic hatred of the world. Given the use to which Kant puts noumena, this suggests that morality itself is entangled with ascetic hatred. It is not that the character of morality gives us reason to think there is a noumenal domain; rather, the fact that morality leads us to such a life-hating hypothesis sheds light on the hidden character of morality. Again, Nietzsche's use of Kant here presupposes that Kant's analysis of our morality is essentially correct, that Kantian moral theory and our own moral commitments stand or fall together.

The relevance of the third essay to Kant's second *Critique* lies in Nietzsche's association of the practical postulates of God and immortality in the noumenal realm with nihilism. He traces nihilism in turn to the ascetic ideal and its hold over our imagination. Kant had argued that though no 'theoretical' argument for the existence of God could compel rational assent, there was a 'practical' argument for the existence of God. We have an obligation to act morally, but we cannot if we lack confidence that the good can be realized. Realizing the good requires that those who act with good intentions receive the happiness they deserve, and that the bad suffer. In the phenomenal realm, it seems as if good intentions are impotent and the wicked prosper. Yet if we believe this, we cannot act morally. Therefore we have a moral obligation not to believe this. Since the phenomenal realm is not all the world there is, for all we know there may be a noumenal God who intervenes to secure happiness for the good and unhappiness for the bad. Believing this does not interfere with our cognitive obligations in the phenomenal realm, since it does not concern the phenomenal realm at all. Since we have a moral obligation to do that which is necessary to fulfil our other moral obligations, we ought to believe there is a God.

This argument struck Nietzsche as wishful thinking scarcely better than 'I cannot bear to believe that there is no God. Therefore there is a God.' But Nietzsche's reaction to this argument was more than dismissive: he saw it as revelatory of a destructive attitude that Kant shares with almost all Western moralists and metaphysicians, an attitude leading inexorably to nihilism if not checked. The crux of Nietzsche's objection is that Kant takes the tension between empirical knowledge and morality (the unrealizability of moral goodness in the natural world), and concludes that there must be two distinct metaphysical realms, one for nature and one for morality. The latter is genuinely real, the former is mere appearance.

The Second Reading

Nietzsche's repudiation of this complex of ideas derives in part from the Feuerbachian strategy of regarding the content of the posited noumenal realm as a projection of our needs and desires, a strategy Marx also took from Feuerbach. Marx had claimed, in effect, that the way Christianity characterizes heaven is the way this world ought to be. The problem with projecting our needs onto another world is that by producing substitute gratifications, we delay activity that can transform this world into the shape dictated by our desires. Feuerbach claimed that this world already accords with our desires, if we simply stop thinking non-sensuously and attend to the world as it presents itself to our senses.

Nietzsche rejects both of these lines. Though they correctly reject the existence of the other world and trace our imagining of it to our needs and desires, both of them uncritically assume that our desires are the right ones and realizable in this world. Kant's insight, with which Nietzsche concurs, is more profound: 'our' moral desires *cannot* be satisfied in the phenomenal world.

In itself injuring, doing violence, pillaging, destroying naturally cannot be 'unjust', in so far as life acts *essentially*—that is, in its basic functions—in an injuring, violating, pillaging, destroying manner and cannot even be *thought* at all without this character. . . . A legal system conceived of as sovereign and universal, not as a means in the battle of power complexes, but rather as a means *against* all battle generally, say in accordance with Dühring's communist cliché that every will must accept every other will as equal, would be a principle *hostile to life*, a destroyer and dissolver of man, an attempt to kill the future of man, a sign of weariness, a secret pathway to nothingness.   (*GM* II. 11)

What is the significance of Kant's response to this fact? For one might have thought that being moral, if it is so at odds with the character of life, is what should be rejected. Instead, Kant concludes that morality will triumph, but not in this world. Not only is this world to be resisted as the source of immoral impulses; it is not even altogether real. Nietzsche, given his characterization of life and morality, cannot adopt Marx's version of a Feuerbachian projection theory. The fantasy of the other world is not the expression of a hostility toward this-worldly *obstacles* to life's flourishing. It is an expression of a hostility to life itself.

Nietzsche calls this hostility 'the ascetic ideal'. He characterizes it as

a *ressentiment* without equal . . . that of an unsatiated instinct and power-will that would like to become lord not over something living but rather over life itself, over its deepest, strongest, most fundamental preconditions; an attempt is made here to use energy to stop up the source of energy; here the gaze is directed greenly and maliciously against physiological flourishing itself, in particular against its expression, beauty, joy; whereas pleasure is felt and *sought* in deformation, atrophy, in pain, in accident, in the ugly, in voluntary forfeit, in unselfing, self-flagellation, self-sacrifice. This is all paradoxical in the highest degree: we stand here before a conflict that *wants* itself to be conflicted, that *enjoys* itself in this suffering and even becomes ever more self-assured and triumphant to the extent that its own presupposition, physiological viability *decreases.* (*GM* III. 11)

Though Kant is not the only representative of the ascetic ideal, his role is a special one nonetheless. For it is from Kant that Nietzsche inherits the phenomenal/noumenal contrast with which he wrestled from the earliest stage of his philosophizing. He had rejected the possibility of knowing the noumenal world as early as *Birth of Tragedy*. He had rejected the idea of associating anything of human importance with it in *Human, All-too-human*. By the time that he returned to reading and reflecting on Kant in the 1880s, Nietzsche began to argue that the very idea of the noumenon was incoherent. But it was only after reading the second *Critique* that he explicitly made the connection between the noumenal world, the satisfaction of moral interests, and the ascetic ideal understood as an expression of hostility to life. After the *Genealogy*, Nietzsche's respect for Kant drops precipitously and he never tires of making the point that morality is anti-life.

The purpose of the third essay is to undermine our allegiance to the normative intuition that there is something admirable and meaningful about renunciation as such. This intuition is distinct from any consideration of the purpose of the renunciation, whether as an expression of discharging moral obligation, or of respect for the equal value of persons. Nietzsche claims that we have a tendency to revere renunciation itself. When we admire Mother Teresa for her service to the poor, this is not because we value the amelioration of suffering and see her actions as having been reasonable and effective at bringing this about. If we were motivated by such concerns we might wonder why she did not focus her efforts more efficiently on lobbying for political and economic reforms that would make charity unnecessary. When we admire Gandhi for using hunger strikes as a means of achieving independence for India, this is not because we value political freedom and see refusing to eat when one does not get one's way as reasonable and effective at bringing this about. If we were motivated by such concerns we might wonder why he did not focus his efforts more efficiently on armed insurrection.

The awe that we feel for these figures, even in the now predominantly secular West, derives from an intuition that people who voluntarily expose themselves to hunger, filth, disease, and agony are onto something that we who thrive are not. Their pursuit of what one should avoid, calls into question life and our attachment to it in a manner that mystifies and awes us. It is this response, central to the hypnotic power almost all organized religions have had

225

over their followers, that Nietzsche seeks to understand and oppose. Morality's use of this hypnotic power has made it difficult to be objective or critical about it. Consequently, genealogical demystification of asceticism is crucial to Nietzsche's critique of Kantian, and therefore our, morality.

The key to explaining the ascetic impulse without reference to supernatural assumptions lies in something we have already encountered in passing, that the ascetic 'would like to become lord not over something living but rather over life itself'. Since we have already seen that, for Nietzsche, life is essentially the tendency to 'become lord over' things, this quote identifies what the ascetic and the non-ascetic have in common. Though the non-ascetic seeks, for example, to lord it over a steer by eating a steak dinner while the ascetic seeks to lord it over his own desire for a steak dinner, both can be interpreted as seeking a kind of mastery and power over something.

The ascetic's peculiar choice of mastery over his own needs and desires has two sources. First, to have needs and desires makes one a 'slave' to the conditions of their satisfaction. A drug addict is not free even when obtaining the drug, because while he may have some control over the world, in the end, the drug has control over him. For the ascetic, everything people ordinarily pursue can be construed in this fashion.

The other motive for asceticism is less attractive. Suppose that one suffers from some failure to obtain some good central to a satisfying human life. For example, suppose one suffers from a chronic functional illness which causes one great pain. When one is more vital, one suffers more intensely. Naturally, the preferred course of action would be to cure the disease somehow. But if that should prove impossible, one can come to regard vitality as little more than a means enabling the disease to inflict suffering. One possible response would be to come to resent one's own vitality as a kind of enemy, an enemy easy to give in to and become 'enslaved' to, somewhat along the same lines as the drug addiction. In this case, the addiction is to life itself. In response, the ascetic resents the imposition that life is and develops vengeful feelings towards it. Ascetic practices and techniques then become an expression not of one's attachment to a higher goal like knowledge, or of one's desire for absolute freedom from all constraints, but of a vengeful hostility toward life itself.

However, this account is incomplete. Fundamentally, what troubles the ascetic is not the suffering. Suppose that one was struggling with such an illness in the knowledge that one was testing a vaccine which, if successful, would save millions of lives? Then one could take up a stance towards one's pain that incorporated it into one's project, as a means towards the satisfaction of a valued preference. One might even welcome attacks of more intense suffering as signs that one's project is succeeding, that one's commitment to it is strong. On Nietzsche's view, pain that is the inevitable by-product of the pursuit of one's goals is not necessarily distressing (*GM* III. 28). But pain in the absence of some associated meaning or purpose is intolerable. What the ascetic achieves is an interpretation of suffering that turns it into a sign of success in the project of overcoming life itself. To do this, the ascetic must construct an imaginary value or goal which can be regarded as more valuable than life. This leads to the positing of two worlds to facilitate the identification of this world with anti-value and the other world with value. Thus suffering, which on Nietzsche's view is inevitable anyway, can be welcomed as a sign of the ascetic's progress at disentangling oneself from the world.

One may well wonder what the importance of this speculative psychology is, now that we are several centuries removed from the Middle Ages. First, Nietzsche claims that the ascetic priest not only invents an ascetic interpretation of life as something to be transcended, but links this idea to the guilty conscience by teaching others that the guilty conscience troubles us because we have not transcended life. By connecting the guilty conscience with ascetic ideals, the apparent authority of the former then supports the latter, leading moralized, i.e. Kantian, subjects to reject their this-worldly desires and needs in favour of self-destructive practices.[23] Though one could argue that by the late twenty-first century, at least in the West, the last thing we need to worry about is a shortage of self-indulgence, Nietzsche would reply that even if we no longer follow the ideal, we still judge in light of it. We feel that our failure to be ascetic renders our this-worldly pursuits empty and meaningless. This puts modernity on a collision course with nihilism.

That aside, there is a crucial aspect of modern culture which Nietzsche believes does express asceticism: scientific research. The desire for scientific knowledge is not driven by a desire for technological advantages. It is driven by the desire to eschew, not the pleasure of the body, but the psychological

---

[23] Nietzsche thinks ascetic practices also have positive functions besides conferring meaning on suffering. Some have therapeutic effects, and even those that harm the individual may have social uses. Nietzsche divides the ascetic practices into two broad groups, which we might designate as the hypnotic (e.g. meditation) and the hysterical (e.g. penance). The former ameliorate suffering by calming, the latter by distracting. While the former can promote genuine psychological healing, the latter weaken the constitution as they anaesthetize. However, hysterical practices prevent the sufferer from venting frustration on the healthy by 'reversing the direction of *ressentiment*' from other-blame to self-blame, and thus serve, Nietzsche thinks, a desirable stabilizing and segregating function. Those who do not need asceticism are then free to pursue their projects without interference from the resentful.

pleasure of false beliefs that pamper our sense of self-importance. The insistence upon the hard truth at the expense of psychological comforts is ultimately a moral demand, driven by the determination that we not flourish. If flourishing depends upon expedient falsifications, the search for truth is masochistic.

That it is also a moral demand, Nietzsche does not elaborate on, though it is easy to see how he might account for its moralization.[24] First of all, Nietzsche had claimed in the first essay that social superiors tend to speak plainly, and from the self-valorization of master morality, truth speaking becomes valorized. Second, Nietzsche, distinguishing between the 'knightly-aristocratic' and the 'priestly-aristocratic', claims that though the ascetic priest can preach slave morality, he need not do so. Third, the ascetic tends to identify the non-existent other world with the real one, while disparaging the real world as an illusion; thus the pursuit of the valuable other world comes to be construed as the pursuit of the truth. This is especially ironic, since Nietzsche thinks that once the desire for truth becomes moralized, it leads to inquiries which undermine precisely these exotic beliefs of the ascetic. Fourth, one can easily imagine how the practices of exchange and punishment discussed in the second essay could come to be associated with truth-speaking. Deception is usually pursued to escape from obligations. The product of these factors is what we might call Galileo's pathos: there is something sublime about self-sacrifice for the sake of knowledge.

At the climax of essay three (*GM* III. 25), Kant is singled out as the exemplar of modern scientific asceticism. First, natural science has the effect of de-centring our sense of our place in the cosmos. Second, Kant's epistemological critique humiliates our sense of cognitive competence because neither the senses nor reason provide us with access to things-in-themselves. Third, Kant's rejection of rational theology is masochistic. Religious ideas are comforting. When critique deprives us of reassuring proofs, we injure ourselves emotionally. Conversely, when rationality dissuades us from religious belief, and critique places limits on the scope of rationality and makes room for faith, we injure ourselves again by doing violence to our cognitive interests.

In short, Nietzsche sees the Kantian complex of ideas (de-centring cosmology, epistemological critique, phenomenal/noumenal distinction, moral

---

[24] Nietzsche had already provided a preliminary account of the moralization of the will to truth in *Truth and Lie*. In Ch. 3 we discussed this, along with some of the reasons why Nietzsche would have rejected elements of it in his mature phase—in short, the account depends upon the 'utility' of truth-telling and our subsequent 'forgetting' of this fact—precisely those characteristics of 'English' genealogy Nietzsche rejects in the first essay.

absolutism and the unattainability of moral values in the phenomenal world) as expressions of the ascetic devaluation of this world. Though it was the unattainability of moral value in the phenomenal world that served as the clue to Kant's asceticism, this in turn cast doubt on Kant's cognitive interests, which Nietzsche concludes are expressions of a subtler form of asceticism as well. While the phenomenal/noumenal contrast no longer has much purchase on modern minds, Kant's characteristic cognitive attitudes—de-centring cosmology, humility about reason's *a priori* powers, worries about subjective contributions (or distortions) in our cognitive apparatus or practices, confidence in the intrinsic worth of 'research' as the dominant cultural activity—all are representative of modernity and hardly idiosyncratic to Kant.

Kant's characteristic moral and political attitudes—subjectivism about value (subject to reasoned formal constraints) with its accompanying emphasis on the absolute good of personal freedom, egalitarianism, universalism about the preceding moral commitments—are also representative of modernity and not idiosyncratic to Kant. Taken together, this leads to an unexpected conclusion. If Nietzsche is right, Kant expresses the normative commitments of the modern world. Kant justified these normative commitments by reference to his theory of rationality. But even if Kant's critiques are successful as descriptive psychology (and Nietzsche thinks that they are) they fail to show that these psychological operations are rational. What is worse, Nietzsche suggests that our powerful intuitions to the contrary are undercut by deflationary 'genealogical' interpretations that yield the same intuitions, minus their normative authority. Modernity is deluded about its foundations: it has none. Worst of all, Nietzsche thinks that his own theorizing in terms of the 'will to power' reveals that modernity's commitments are positively pernicious to further human development. Nietzsche also retrieves the content of an ancient noble ethos that Christianity and modernity alike have conspired to efface, his own normative theorizing remains indebted to Kant's. For both of them, the self-legislating individual, freed from the constraints of natural law, historical tradition, and transcendent religion, is the height of human aspiration.

Conclusion
The Ruins of Reason?

In Chapter 1, we broached the question of Nietzsche's contemporary relevance. If Nietzsche proves to be as indebted to Kant as we have suggested, does this not make him a footnote in the history of ideas rather than a daring critic of modernity's most cherished dogmas? There are two aspects to Nietzsche's alleged postmodernity. First, modernity shares a commitment to Enlightenment morality, to the empowerment of the individual cut free from the authoritative moorings of tradition and religion. Not only does the Enlightenment seek to champion human freedom lacking such moorings, it sees the moorings as bonds to be broken. The problem of how to structure a community that does not dissolve into anarchy in the face of this individualism leads to Kant's notion of morality as a neutral framework for preventing the clash of wills from destroying each other. Though Kant is not the only figure to articulate these themes, he is arguably the most persuasive, and in his later incarnation as Rawls, among the most popular. Nietzsche's repudiation of Kant in the *Genealogy of Morals* seems to attack this Kantian approach to human freedom and community, reducing it to a slave revolt of power-seekers who attempt to deny or undo the fact of human inequality. In his opposition to liberal humanism, Nietzsche fascinates both neo-conservatives like Alistair MacIntyre, who see liberalism as a degeneration from the medieval, and post-Marxists like Michel Foucault, who see liberalism as a mask for oppression. Though their destinations may differ, they share a sense that liberalism is a dead end.

Yet as we have seen, Nietzsche hardly rejects all of Kant's ethical project. Underneath his rejection of morality as a neutral framework embodying egalitarian values lies a commitment to the unfettered subjectivity of human ends and a valorization of human freedom. Even his attempt to reanimate a kind of ancient virtue ethic has to be seen in the context of what such virtue serves: the empowerment of the individual. This explains, in part, the attractiveness of Alexander Nehamas's interpretation of Nietzsche, with its emphasis on an ethic of self-creation. This is what is left of Kantian morality once the restraint of the categorical imperative is taken away. For those who remain committed to the Enlightenment's championing of individual autonomy, but who have become sceptical of the prospects for imposing rational constraints upon it, Nietzsche articulates both our deepest value and our greatest anxiety. Yet it seems disingenuous to see this as postmodern. To commit to the Enlightenment's valorization of human freedom and autonomy while abandoning its egalitarianism is to move eccentrically within the orbit of the Enlightenment rather than to shear away from it. That Nietzsche uses Kant to such good effect in making his critique of egalitarianism suggests that they are closer to one another than they seem. That Nietzsche's central complaint against Kant is that Kantian morality is heteronomous shows this decisively.

Nietzsche's other postmodern theme is his perspectivism, his seeming repudiation of univocal truth. Nietzsche's debt to Kant's metaphysics parallels his debt to Kant's ethics. Kant had sought to replace mind-independent reality as the constraint on our thought with a common, necessary structure imposed on mind-dependent experience. Nietzsche's epistemological anthropocentrism also traces back to Kant. Without a common, necessary structure to constrain us, the world seems to dissolve into a plurality of perspectives. Nietzsche's attempt to recreate a univocal world picture in such a setting leads to a return to empiricism. If Hume and Hegel are still moderns, then Nietzsche is also.

Tracing these themes to their source has an inevitably disintoxicating effect. If the preceding interpretation has done anything, it has restored to Nietzsche his original context in a way that explains and in part demystifies him. Kant emerged from a tradition that attempts to solve epistemological problems by constructing a model of the individual human mind. But Kant did not just produce a more elaborate theory of the mind. He produced a metaphysics significantly at variance with common sense: nature proves to be mind-dependent. The next generation, excited by this development, created metaphysical systems rivalling Plotinus' in their grandiosity. After half a century of floundering about in the wake of this development, German philosophy decided to go 'back to Kant'. This was the milieu Nietzsche found himself in. History repeated itself, though not in the same form. *Birth of Tragedy* is another grandiose metaphysical system spun from the strands of Kantianism. And though Nietzsche tried, for several years, to be 'French', in the end, the temptation to spin with the threads of Kantianism again became irresistible.

If we are to read Nietzsche, not as the legislator of a new post-theistic religion or as the bellelettrist of acute psychological and cultural observation, that is, if we are to read him as a philosopher, we will be led inexorably to the context of Neo-Kantianism, and to the highly peculiar things Nietzsche did with Kant. We have seen repeatedly how questionable Nietzsche's further development of his Kantian materials often is, how very far he is from the Nietzsche of alleged contemporary relevance often invoked. Nietzsche fits badly the notion of a postmodern rupture with the past, despite his emergence from Kant, the quintessential modern. The debts to Kant are too great. Nietzsche, like Hegel, was still operating within a universe of discourse whose terms are defined by the late eighteenth century and their repetition in the late nineteenth. This is no shame. But it is ironic in a figure who so thoroughly cultivated a 'pathos of distance' from modernity. Those who wish to cultivate such a pathos themselves would do well to consider to what extent they too are indebted.

Bibliography

Primary literature

FISCHER, KUNO, *Immanuel Kant und seine Lehre* (*Geschichte der neuern Philosophie, iv–v*), 4. neu bearb. Aufl. (Heidelberg: C. Winter, 1898).

KANT, IMMANUEL, *Werke*, ed. Königlich Preussische Akademie der Wissenschaften, et al. Academy text edition (Berlin: de Gruyter, 1968).

LANGE, FRIEDRICH ALBERT, *Geschichte des Materialismus und Kritik seiner Bedeutung in der Gegenwart*, reprint 2nd edn. (Frankfurt am Main: Suhrkamp Verlag, 1974).

NIETZSCHE, FRIEDRICH WILHELM, *Kritische Gesamtausgabe (Werke)*, ed. Giorgio Colli and Mazzino Montinari c.40 vols. (Berlin and Munich: Walter de Gruyter, 1967–).

——*Kritische Gesamtausgabe (Briefe)*, ed. Giorgio Colli und Mazzino Montinari c.20 vols. (Berlin and Munich: Walter de Gruyter, 1975–93).

SCHOPENHAUER, ARTHUR, *Sämtliche Werke*, 7 vols., ed. Arthur Hübscher (Wiesbaden: Brockhaus, 1946–50).

Translations

FISCHER, KUNO, *A Commentary on Kant's Critick* [*sic*] *of Pure Reason*, a translation of *Geschichte der neuern Philosophie*, vol. 4, trans. John Mahaffy (repr. New York: Garland Publishing, 1976).

KANT, IMMANUEL, *Critique of Judgment*, trans. Werner Pluhar (Indianapolis: Hackett Publishing Co., 1987).

——*Critique of Practical Reason*, trans. Lewis White Beck (New York: Liberal Arts Press, 1956).

——*Critique of Pure Reason*, trans. Werner Pluhar (Indianapolis: Hackett Publishing Co., 1996).

LANGE, FRIEDRICH, *The History of Materialism and Criticism of its Present Importance*, 3rd. edn., trans. Ernest Chester Thomas (London: Kegan Paul, Trench, Trubner & Co., 1925).

NIETZSCHE, FRIEDRICH, *The Basic Writings of Nietzsche*, trans. Walter Kaufmann (New York: Random House, 1968). (Contains *Birth of Tragedy, Beyond Good and Evil, Genealogy of Morals, Case of Wagner*, and *Ecce Homo*.)

Bibliography

NIETZSCHE, FRIEDRICH, *Daybreak: Thoughts on the Prejudices of Morality*, trans. R. J. Hollingdale (Cambridge: Cambridge University Press, 1982).

——*The Gay Science: With a Prelude in Rhymes and an Appendix of Songs,* trans. Walter Kaufmann (New York: Random House, 1974).

——*Human, All-too-human: A Book for Free Spirits*, trans. R. J. Hollingdale (Cambridge: Cambridge University Press, 1986).

——*Philosophy and Truth: selections from Nietzsche's Notebooks of the Early 1870's*, ed. and trans. Daniel Breazeale (Atlantic Highlands: Humanities Press, 1979). (Includes *Truth and Lie*.)

——*Philosophy in the Tragic Age of the Greeks*, trans. Marianne Cowan (Chicago: Regnery Gateway, 1962).

——*The Portable Nietzsche*, trans. Walter Kaufmann (New York: Viking, 1954). (Includes *Twilight of the Idols, Antichrist*, and *Nietzsche contra Wagner*.)

——*Thus Spoke Zarathustra: a book for everyone and no one*, trans. R. J. Hollingdale (Harmondsworth: Penguin Books, 1961).

——*Untimely Meditations*, trans. R. J. Hollingdale (Cambridge: Cambridge University Press, 1983).

——*The Will to Power*, trans. R. J. Hollingdale and Walter Kaufmann, ed. Walter Kaufmann (New York: Random House, 1967).

SCHOPENHAUER, ARTHUR, *Parerga and Paralipomena*, 2 vols., trans. E. F. J. Payne (Oxford: Oxford University Press, 1985).

——*The World as Will and Representation*, 2 vols., trans. E. F. J. Payne (New York: Dover Publications, 1966).

Secondary literature: general

GAULTIER, JULES DE, *From Kant to Nietzsche*, trans. Gerald M. Spring (New York: Philosophical Library, 1961).

HAMACHER, WERNER, *Entferntes Verstehen. Studien zu Philosophie und Literatur von Kant bis Celan* (Frankfurt am Main: Suhrkamp, 1998).

KÖHNKE, KLAUS CHRISTIAN, *The Rise of Neo-Kantianism: German Academic Philosophy between Idealism and Positivism*, trans. R. J. Hollingdale (Cambridge: Cambridge University Press, 1991).

LÖWITH, KARL, *From Hegel to Nietzsche: The Revolution in Nineteenth Century Thought*, trans. David Green (New York: Holt, Rinehart and Winston, 1964).

PIPPIN, ROBERT B., *Modernism as a Philosophical Problem: On the Dissatisfactions of European High Culture* (Cambridge, MA: Blackwell, 1991).

——*Idealism and Modernism: Hegelian Variations* (Cambridge: Cambridge University Press, 1997).

234

SCHNÄDELBACH, HANS, *Philosophy in Germany: 1831–1933* (Cambridge: Cambridge University Press, 1984).

Secondary literature: Kant

ALLISON, HENRY, *Kant's Transcendental Idealism* (New Haven: Yale University Press, 1983).

BENNETT, JONATHAN, *Kant's Dialectic* (Cambridge: Cambridge University Press, 1974).

CAYGILL, HOWARD, *Art of Judgement* (Oxford: Blackwell, 1989).

GINSBORG, HANNAH, 'Reflective Judgment and Taste', *Nôus*, 24 (1990), 63–78.

GUYER, PAUL, *Kant and the Claims of Taste*, 2nd edn. (Cambridge, MA: Harvard University Press, 1997).

——*Kant and the Claims of Knowledge* (Cambridge: Cambridge University Press, 1987).

KITCHER, PATRICIA, *Kant's Transcendental Psychology* (Oxford: Oxford University Press, 1990).

LONGUENESSE, BEATRICE, *Kant and the Power of Judgment: Sensibility and Discursivity in the Transcendental Analytic of the Critique of Pure Reason*, trans. Charles T. Wolfe (Princeton: Princeton University Press, 2001).

LYOTARD, JEAN-FRANÇOIS, *Lessons on the Analytic of the Sublime*, trans. Elizabeth Rottenberg (Palo Alto: Stanford University Press, 1994).

STRAWSON, PETER, *The Bounds of Sense* (London: Routledge, 1966).

SULLIVAN, ROGER J., *Immanuel Kant's Moral Theory* (Cambridge: Cambridge University Press, 1989).

WALKER, RALPH, *Kant* (London: Routledge & Kegan Paul, 1978).

WAXMAN, WAYNE, *Kant's Model of the Mind: A New Interpretation of Transcendental Idealism* (Oxford: Oxford University Press, 1991).

ZAMMITO, JOHN H., *The Genesis of Kant's Critique of Judgment* (Chicago: University of Chicago Press, 1992).

Secondary literature: Nietzsche

BABICH, BABETTE E., *Nietzsche's Philosophy of Science: Reflecting Science on the Ground of Art and Life* (Albany: State University of New York Press, 1994).

BERKOWITZ, PETER, *Nietzsche: The Ethics of an Immoralist* (Cambridge, MA: Harvard University Press, 1995).

BROBJER, THOMAS, *Nietzsche's Ethic of Character* (Cambridge: Cambridge University Press, forthcoming).

Bibliography

CLARK, MAUDEMARIE, *Nietzsche on Truth and Philosophy* (Cambridge: Cambridge University Press, 1991).

DANTO, ARTHUR, *Nietzsche as Philosopher* (New York: Macmillan, 1965).

DE GAULTIER, JULES, *From Kant to Nietzsche*, trans. Gerald M. Spring (New York: Philosophical Library, 1961).

DELEUZE, GILLES, *Nietzsche and Philosophy*, trans. Hugh Tomlinson (New York: Columbia University Press, 1983).

DE MAN, PAUL, *Allegories of Reading* (New Haven: Yale University Press, 1980).

DERRIDA, JACQUES, *Spurs: Nietzsche's Styles*, trans. Barbara Harlow (Chicago: University of Chicago Press, 1979).

HAYMAN, RONALD, *Nietzsche: A Critical Life* (London: Weidenfeld & Nicolson, 1980).

HEIDEGGER, MARTIN, *Nietzsche*, trans. David Farrell Krell (New York: Harper and Row, 1979).

HILL, R. KEVIN, 'MacIntyre's Nietzsche: A Critique', *International Studies in Philosophy*, 24/2 (1992), 135–44.

HUNT, LESTER H., *Nietzsche and the Origin of Virtue* (London and New York: Routledge, 1991).

JASPERS, KARL, *Nietzsche: An Introduction to the Understanding of his Philosophical Activity*, trans. Charles F. Wallraff and Frederick J. Schmitz (Chicago: Regnery, 1965).

KAUFMANN, WALTER, *Nietzsche: Philosopher, Psychologist, Antichrist* (Princeton: Princeton University Press, 1950).

MAGNUS, BERND, 'The Use and Abuse of the *Will to Power*', in Robert Solomon and Kathleen M. Higgins (eds.), *Reading Nietzsche* (Oxford: Oxford University Press, 1988), 218–35.

MOLES, ALASTAIR, *Nietzsche's Philosophy of Nature and Cosmology* (New York: P. Lang, 1990).

NEHAMAS, ALEXANDER, *Nietzsche: Life as Literature* (Cambridge, MA: Harvard University Press, 1985).

POELLNER, PETER, *Nietzsche and Metaphysics* (Oxford: Oxford University Press, 1995).

REBOUL, OLIVIER, *Nietzsche, critique de Kant* (Paris: Presses universitaires de France, 1974).

RICHARDSON, JOHN, *Nietzsche's System* (Oxford: Oxford University Press, 1996).

SALAQUARDA, JÖRG, 'Der Standpunkt des Ideals bei Lange und Nietzsche', *Studi Tedeschi*, 22/1 (1979), 133–60.

SCHACHT, RICHARD, *Nietzsche* (London: Routledge & Kegan Paul, 1983).

236

SILK, M. S. and STERN, J. P., *Nietzsche and Tragedy* (Cambridge: Cambridge University Press, 1981).

STACK, GEORGE, *Lange and Nietzsche* (Berlin: de Gruyter, 1983).

WILCOX, JOHN, *Truth and Value in Nietzsche* (Ann Arbor: University of Michigan Press, 1974).

YOUNG, JULIAN, *Nietzsche's Philosophy of Art* (Cambridge and New York: Cambridge University Press, 1992).

Secondary literature: miscellaneous

HAMLYN, D. W., *Schopenhauer* (London: Routledge and Kegan Paul, 1980).

ROSEN, MICHAEL, *Hegel's Dialectic and its Criticism* (Cambridge: Cambridge University Press, 1982).

Other

ARISTOTLE, *The Complete Works of Aristotle*, trans. J. L. Ackrill and ed. Jonathan Barnes (Princeton: Princeton University Press, 1984).

BERKELEY, GEORGE, *Three Dialogues between Hylas and Philonous*, in *Berkeley's Philosophical Writings*, ed. David M. Armstrong (New York: Macmillan, 1965), 130–225.

BOSCOVICH, RUGGERO GIUSEPPE, *A Theory of Natural Philosophy*, trans. of *Philosophiae Naturalis Theoria Redacta ad Unicam Legem Virium in Natura Existentium*, 2nd edn. (1763) (Chicago, London: Open Court Publishing Company, 1922).

GAUTHIER, DAVID, *Morals by Agreement* (Oxford: Oxford University Press, 1986).

GOETHE, JOHANN WOLFGANG VON, *Goethe's Collected Works*, ed. and trans. Douglas Miller (Princeton: Princeton University Press, 1995).

HELVÉTIUS, CLAUDE ADRIEN, *A Treatise on Man: His Intellectual Faculties and his Education*, trans. W. Hooper (New York: B. Franklin, 1969).

KIRKHAM, RICHARD L., *Theories of Truth: A Critical Introduction* (Cambridge, MA: MIT Press, 1992).

MILLIKAN, RUTH, *Language, Thought and Other Biological Categories* (Cambridge, MA: MIT Press, 1984).

QUINE, W. V. O., 'Two Dogmas of Empiricism', in *From a Logical Point of View* (Cambridge, MA: Harvard University Press, 1953), 20–46.

—— *Word and Object* (Cambridge, MA: MIT Press, 1960).

RIDLEY, MATT, *The Origins of Virtue: Human Instincts and the Evolution of Cooperation* (New York: Viking, 1997).

Index

Index

Index

DATE DUE

NOV 0 9 2001			

#47-0108 Peel Off Pressure Sensitive